The Chartered Institute of Marketing

Professional Diploma in Marketing

STUDY TEXT

Delivering Customer Value Through Marketing

2010 edition

First edition 2009
Second edition August 2010

ISBN 9780 7517 8940 9
(Previous ISBN 9780 7517 6813 8)

e-ISBN 9780 7517 9148 8

British Library Cataloguing-in-Publication Data
A catalogue record for this book
is available from the British Library

Published by

BPP Learning Media Ltd
Aldine House, Aldine Place
London W12 8AA

www.bpp.com/learningmedia

Printed in the United Kingdom

We are grateful to the Chartered Institute of Marketing for
permission to reproduce in this text the syllabus, tutor's
guidance notes and past examination questions.

Author: Kate Machattie
Template design: Yolanda Moore
Photography: Terence O'Loughlin

Your learning materials, published by BPP Learning Media Ltd,
are printed on paper sourced from sustainable, managed
forests.

Contents

Introduction

• Aim of the Study Text • Studying for CIM qualifications • The Professional Diploma Syllabus • Assessment materials • The CIM's Magic Formula • A guide to the features of the Study Text • A note on pronouns • Additional resources • Your personal study plan v

Chapters

Review form & free prize draw

1 Aim of the Study Text

This book has been deliberately referred to as a 'Study Text' rather than *text book,* because it is designed to help you though your specific CIM Professional Diploma in Marketing studies. It covers Unit 2 *Delivering Customer Value Through Marketing*.

So why is it similar to, but not actually, a text book? Well, the CIM has identified key texts that you should become familiar with. The purpose of this book is not to replace these texts but to pick out the important parts that you will definitely need to know in order to pass, simplify these elements, and to suggest a few areas within the texts that will provide good additional reading but that are not absolutely essential. We will also suggest a few other sources and useful press and CIM publications which are worth reading.

We know some of you will prefer to read text books from cover to cover whilst others amongst you will prefer to pick out relevant parts or dip in and out of the various topics. This text will help you to ensure that if you are a 'cover to cover' type, then you will not miss the emphasis of the syllabus. If you are a 'dip in and out' type, then we will make sure that you find the parts which are essential for you to know. Unlike a standard *text book* which will have been written to be used across a range of alternative qualifications, this *study text* has been specifically written for your CIM course, and so if a topic appears in this book then it is part of the syllabus and will be a subject on which the examiners could potentially test you.

Throughout the study text you will find real examples of marketing in practice as well as key concepts highlighted. You will be encouraged not only to lean the theory but how to apply it.

2 Studying for CIM qualifications

There are a few key points to remember as you study for your CIM qualification:

(a)   You are studying for a **professional** qualification. This means that you are required to use professional language and adopt a business approach in your work.

(b)   You are expected to show that you have 'read widely'. Make sure that you read the quality press (and don't skip the business pages), read *Marketing*, *The Marketer*, *Research* and *Marketing Week* avidly.

(c)   Become aware of the marketing initiatives you come across on a daily basis, for example when you go shopping look around and think about why the store layout is as it is, consider the messages, channel choice and timings of ads when you are watching TV. It is surprising how much you will learn just by taking an interest in the marketing world around you.

(d)   Get to know the way the CIM writes the exam papers and assignments. They use a specific approach which is referred to as The Magic Formula to ensure a consistent approach when designing assessment materials. Make sure you are fully aware of this as it will help you interpret what the examiner is looking for. (A full description of the Magic Formula appears later and is heavily featured within the chapters).

(e)   Learn how to use Harvard referencing. This is explained in detail in our CIM Professional Diploma Assessment Workbook.

(f)   Ensure that you read very carefully all assessment details sent to you from the CIM. The CIM is very strict with regard to deadlines, eg completing the correct paperwork to accompany any assignment or project and making sure you have your CIM membership card with you at the exam. Failing to meet any assessment entry deadlines or complete written work on time will mean that you will have to wait for the next round of assessment dates and will need to pay the relevant assessment fees again.

3 The Professional Diploma Syllabus

The Professional Diploma in Marketing is aimed at anyone who is employed in a marketing management role such as Brand Manager, Account Manager or Marketing Executive. If you are a graduate, you will be expected to have covered a minimum of a third of your credits in marketing subjects. You are therefore expected at this level of the qualification to be aware of the key marketing theories and be able to apply them to different organisational contexts.

The aim of the qualification is to provide the knowledge and skills for you to develop an 'ability to do' in relation to marketing planning. CIM qualifications concentrate on applied marketing within real workplaces.

The complete qualification is made from four units:

- Unit 1 Marketing Planning Process
- Unit 2 Delivering Customer Value Through Marketing
- Unit 3 Managing Marketing
- Unit 4 Project Management in Marketing

The CIM stipulates that each module should take 50 guided learning hours to complete. Guided learning hours refer to time in class, using distance learning materials and completing any work set by your tutor. Guided learning hours do not include the time it will take you to complete the necessary reading for your studies.

The syllabus as provided by the CIM can be found below with reference to our coverage within this study text.

Unit characteristics

This unit's primary focus is the development and execution of marketing activities that have been designed to achieve customer satisfaction and meet organisational objectives, through effective marketing mix strategies which deliver stakeholder value.

The unit includes the development of the product portfolio, managing marketing channels, managing the communications mix and managing the service expectations of customers.

The unit examines the use of the marketing mix to achieve an organisation's corporate and marketing objectives, and to deliver marketing activities which reflect the desired positioning of the organisation's products and services in addition to its brand values.

By the end of the unit, you should be able to apply the marketing mix and determine strategies that deliver highly effective and competitive marketing activities that meet customer needs and organisational objectives, in different organisational contexts and sectors. Students should be aware that the unit addresses marketing in the context of both domestic and international activities.

Overarching learning outcomes

By the end of this unit students should be able to:

- Develop and manage a brand and product portfolio in the context of the organisation's marketing strategies and objectives

- Develop and implement an effective and efficient channel management strategy which reflects the needs of stakeholders and considers the impact of the external environment

- Develop an effective and innovative communications strategy and plan which clearly delivers the organisation's proposition to the market, through effective segmentation and targeting of internal and external markets

- Utilise an innovative and effective integrated marketing mix to reinforce the organisation's brand values and overall marketing proposition and competitive advantage

- Determine customer requirements for product and service delivery to ensure the marketing proposition is customer-focused, efficient and effective

SECTION 1 – Product proposition and brand management (weighting 25%)

		Covered in chapter(s)
1.1	Critically evaluate the process for managing and developing an organisation's product portfolio to deliver best value products for customers in different market segments and achieve organisational and marketing objectives	1
	• Definitions of 'product' in the context of different sectors	
	• Product management's contribution to delivering customer value. Competitive advantage and achieving organisational/marketing objectives	
	• The rationale for managing and planning product portfolios for different market segments	
	• Managing product profitability	
	• Product life cycle	
	• BCG Matrix	
	• General Electric Model	
1.2	Critically evaluate the role of branding in the context of the product portfolio, recommending different branding strategies which are appropriate to a range of organisational contexts and sectors	1
	• Role and importance of brand	
	• Developing and building brand value	
	• Rebranding	
	• International and global brands	
	• Brand strategies	
1.3	Critically evaluate the role and process of innovation and new product development including consideration of innovative, replacement, re-launched and imitative products and explain the strategic benefit in achieving best value	1
	• Developing a culture of innovation across the organisation	
	• The role of innovation in product management and new product development	
	• Rejuvenating existing products	
	• Generating new and enhanced product ideas	
	• Developing new products	
	• Standardisation versus adaption	
	• Adoption	
1.4	Assess the links between product development, product positioning and pricing in terms of fit and alignment with an organisation's corporate and marketing strategies and customer requirements	2
	• Positioning new products	
	• Positioning strategies	
	• Repositioning existing products	
	• Positioning of products against competitors	

1.5	Critically evaluate the importance of linking the product portfolio to price perception to ensure perceived value for money as part of the overall customer proposition	2

- The role of pricing in product management
- Pricing in the context of value for money
- Price sensitivity
- The role of pricing in influencing customers
- The impact of changes in pricing on customer perception

1.6	Assess pricing frameworks that could be utilised by organisations to aid decision making about product lifecycles, product development and innovation	2

- Understanding price versus cost
- Determining pricing levels
- Pricing in relation to customer satisfaction
- Pricing in relation to competition
- Pricing in relation to value
- Pricing for international markets
- The role of pricing in building market share
- Pricing approaches and strategies

SECTION 2 – Channel management (weighting 25%)

		Covered in chapter(s)
2.1	Determine and prioritise the key principles and purposes of innovative and effective distribution strategies in order to deliver the organisation's business and marketing objectives in a range of different contexts and different sectors to maximise customer requirements	3

- Different types of distribution channels
- Establishing channel strategies
- Establishing channel needs (appropriate to different customers, organisations, sectors and countries)
- Developing distribution objectives
- Approaches to international distribution; agent; strategic alliance; joint venture; in-country operation, virtual/digital channels
- Different marketing tools required to give a co-ordinated marketing approach

2.2	Critically analyse the implications, challenges and constraints arising from the internal and external environment in the context of the development of channel strategies	3

- Internal and external environment in the context of the development of developing channel strategies
- Internal factors which influence channel strategy
- International and global factors influencing channel strategies
- Ethical considerations
- Intermediaries' engagement with competitors
- Environmental considerations
- Economic/financial considerations
- Understanding and determining customer channel requirements
- Analysing competitor channel strategies

2.3	Assess the nature and scope of intermediaries and determine criteria for selecting intermediary partners and the likely Return on Investment (ROI) they can achieve	4

- Different types of intermediaries in distribution and the strengths and weaknesses of each
- Level of innovation and development demonstrated
- The roles and responsibilities of intermediaries in distribution
- Criteria for selecting intermediaries
- How intermediaries can influence profitability
- Impact of new and emerging channels

2.4	Determine the level and scope of controls required for effectively monitoring and managing distribution channels	4

- Setting objectives
- Monitoring performance of distribution channels
- Benchmarking of other sectors/organisations/countries
- Managing third party relationships in channel management, locally and internationally

2.5	Assess the requirements for managing the various stakeholders' needs within the distribution channel, in particular reviews, reporting, communications and conflict management	5

- Identification of the key stakeholders in channel management
- Determining stakeholders' needs in channel management
- The role of information in channel management
- The importance of communications in channel management, locally, internationally and globally
- Potential sources of conflict in local and international markets
- Reducing time to market
- Competitor conflicts
- Identifying, managing and resolving conflict

2.6	Determine the contractual requirements and service level agreements for engaging intermediary partners within the distribution channel	4

- Types of contracts and typical terms
- Implications of contracting with overseas
- Role of service level agreements
- Determining service levels based upon efficiency expectations
- Establishing and monitoring key performance indicators
- On-going management and review of service level agreements

SECTION 3 – Managing marketing communications (weighting 30%)

		Covered in chapter(s)
3.1	Determine marketing communications strategy and objectives to align with and deliver the organisation's marketing strategy and plans	6
	• The role of marketing communications	
	• Legal aspects of marketing communications	
	• Global/international aspects of marketing communications	
	• Aligning communications strategy to corporate and marketing strategy	
	• Utilising communications strategies to achieve competitive advantage	
	• Strategic aims of marketing communications	
	• The role of communications in achieving competitive advantage	
	• The contribution of marketing communications in relationship marketing for all stakeholders	
3.2	Prioritise the internal and external marketing segments to be targeted for marketing communications in different organisational contexts and sectors	6
	• Role of internal communications	
	• Identifying key internal audiences	
	• Internal communications methods, Intranet; notice boards; seminars; briefings, newsletters; portals; SMS	
	• Identifying key external audiences	
	• Role of marketing communications in different organisational contexts and sectors	
	• Internal marketing as a key tool to aid and deliver service excellence	
3.3	Critically evaluate a range of communications mixes and recommend appropriate creative, innovative, sustainable and co-ordinated approaches to communications activities and creating the optimal mix for internal and external marketing activities	7
	• Advertising, including writing and checking copy	
	• Personal selling	
	• Direct marketing	
	• Online media	
	• Media tools and media message	
	• Sales promotions	
	• PR, exhibitions and sponsorships	
	• Online forums; blogs; social networks	
3.4	Develop and manage a co-ordinated marketing communications plan, in the context of the strategic marketing plan, in order to establish and build relationships appropriate to the needs of customers, stakeholders and prospects in different organisational contexts and sectors	7
	• Developing a communications plan	
	• Communications planning frameworks	
	• The role of communications in building customer relationships and value	
	• Role of communications in gaining new prospects	
	• Communications planning and execution in different organisational contexts and sectors,(B2B, B2C, Third Tier, Not-for-Profit, International/global)	

3.5	Critically evaluate and select the most appropriate marketing communications agency for the utilisation of marketing communications capability against agreed criteria	8
	• The role and value of agencies in marketing communications	
	• The inclusion of innovative and effective means of communication	
	• How agencies are structured	
	• Criteria and process for selecting an agency	
	• Fees and fee structures	
3.6	Recommend and justify an approach to managing agency relationships including reporting, monitoring and measuring performance	8
	• Managing agencies locally and internationally	
	• Conducting regular reviews against clearly defined service level agreements	
	• Key information in managing agency relationships	
	• Establishing objectives and measuring agency performance	
3.7	Recommend appropriate methods for measuring marketing communications activities and successful delivery of the marketing communications strategy	6
	• Setting marketing communications objectives	
	• Measuring the effectiveness of marketing communications activities	
	• Benchmarking communication effectiveness against other organisations, sectors, countries and competitors	
	• The role of market research, locally and internationally	

SECTION 4 – Managing and achieving customers' service expectations through the marketing mix (weighting 20%)

		Covered in chapter(s)
4.1	Develop clear objectives relating to the provision of service to key customer accounts	9
	• Identifying the needs and behaviours of customers	
	• What constitutes 'service' to customers?	
	• The role of service in building customer loyalty and competitive advantage	
	• Organisational and financial benefits of customer acquisition and retention	
	• Determining customer service requirements	
	• The role of key account management in developing customer service excellence	
4.2	Develop a customer service plan and customer care programme, designed to support customer service requirements, including innovative communications; relationship management and development; support; and operations/process management	9
	• Identifying and evaluating key components of the plan/programme	
	• Identifying, analysing and managing key issues	
	• Use of resources	
	• Effective implementation	
	• Measuring and monitoring performance	
	• Role of communications in delivering customer service	
	• Importance of operations and processes in delivering customer service	

4.3	Assess the value, importance and financial implications of providing service level agreements to customers	9

- Role of service level agreements with customers
- Typical service level agreements
- The costs of delivering against service level agreements
- Benefits to the organisation of establishing service level agreements with customers

4.4	Determine the most feasible and viable approaches for managing key account customers for different organisational contexts	10

- Criteria for and identification of key account customers
- Different approaches for managing key account customers
- Role of communications
- The role of people in key account management and service provision
- Key accounts in different organisational contexts and sectors

4.5	Assess the role and value to the organisation of sales/product information, including storage, retrieval and communication of information and its role in ensuring that revenue is increased or maintained for key account customers	10

- Use and value of information and how it will be used
- Managing information
- Storing and accessing information
- Using information to develop marketing activities
- Role of information in revenue generation

4.6	Critically evaluate and assess the customer relationship for possible risks, problems and issues and prepare contingencies for dealing with those risks as they emerge	10

- Likely risks, problems and issues in managing customer relationships
- Contingency planning
- Role of communications in dealing with problems

4 Assessment of the Unit

The unit covered by this Study Text is assessed in a three-hour formal examination, with compulsory set tasks which are based upon pre-seen material. The pre-seen material takes the form of a company case study, which will be sent to you prior to the exam. As part of your exam preparation will need to carry out a detailed analysis of the information contained in the case study, and condense this into PESTEL and SWOT analysis. As an illustration of the nature of the pre-seen material that you can expect, the CIM has published a specimen case study for this unit entitled 'The Fruit Juice Revolution'. It comprises a study of the business and marketing issues facing the UK smoothie company Innocent Drinks, and is included as an appendix at the back of this text.

In order to help you revise and prepare for the exam we have also written a Professional Diploma in Marketing Assessment Workbook which is available either through your usual book retailer or our website www.bpp.com/learningmedia.

5 The CIM's Magic Formula

The Magic Formula is a tool used by the CIM to help both examiners write exam and assignment questions and you to interpret more easily what you are being asked to write about. It is useful for helping you to check that you are using an appropriate balance between theory and practice for your particular level of qualification.

Contrary to the title, there is nothing mystical about the Magic Formula and simply knowing it (or even mentioning it in an assessment) will not automatically secure a pass. What it does do, however, is to help you to check that you are presenting your answers in an appropriate format, including enough marketing theory and that you are applying it to a real marketing context or issue. Students working through the range of CIM qualifications are expected to evaluate to a greater extent and to apply a more demanding range of marketing decisions as they progress from the lower to the higher levels. At the Chartered Postgraduate Diploma level, there will be an emphasis on evaluation, whilst at the Introductory Certificate level the emphasis is on developing concepts.

Graphically, the Magic Formula for the Professional Diploma in Marketing is shown below:

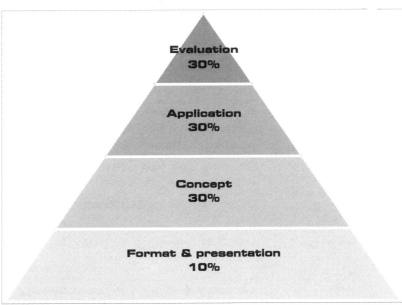

The Magic Formula for the Professional Diploma in Marketing

You can see from the pyramid that for the Professional Diploma marks are awarded in the following proportions:

- ## Format of presentation – 10%

   Remember that you are expected to present your work professionally which means that it should ALWAYS be typed and attention should be paid to making it look as visually appealing as possible, even in an exam situation. It also means that the CIM will stipulate the format that you should present your work in. The assessment formats you will be given will be varied and can include things like reports to write, slides to prepare, emails, memos, formal letters, press releases, discussion documents, briefing papers, agendas and newsletters.

- ## Concept – 30%

   'Concept' refers to your ability to state, recall and describe marketing theory. The definition of marketing is a core CIM syllabus topic. If we take this as an example, you would be expected to recognise, recall and write this definition to a word perfect standard to gain the full marks for concept. Understanding marketing concepts is clearly the main area where marks will be given within your assessment.

- ## Application – 30%

   Application-based marks are given for your ability to apply marketing theories to real-life marketing situations. For example, you may be asked to discuss the definition of marketing, and how it is applied within your own organisation. Within this sort of question, 30% of the marks would have been awarded within the 'concept' aspect of the Magic Formula. You will gain the rest of the marks through your ability to evaluate the extent to which the concept is applied within your own organisation. Here you are not only using the definition, but are applying it in order to consider the market orientation of the company.

- ## Evaluation – 30%

   'Evaluation' is the ability to asses the value or worth of something, sometimes through careful consideration of related advantages and disadvantages, or through weighing up of alternatives. Results from your evaluation should enable you to discuss the importance of an issue, using evidence to support your opinions.

If you were being asked to evaluate whether or not your organisation adopts a marketing approach, it would be expected that you would both provide reasons and specific examples why you thought they might take this approach, but also that you would consider issues such as why they may not be marketing orientated, before coming to a final conclusion.

You should have noticed that for the Professional Diploma, you are expected to consider the equal weightings of concept, application and evaluation in order to gain maximum marks in assessments.

6 A guide to the features of the Study Text

Each of the chapter features (see below) will help you to break down the content into manageable chunks and ensure that you are developing the skills required for a professional qualification.

Chapter feature	Relevance and how you should use it	Corresponding icon
Chapter topic list	Study the list. Each numbered topic denotes a numbered section in the chapter. Identified as a key concept within the syllabus	–
Introduction	Shows why topics need to be studied and is a route guide through the chapter.	–
Syllabus linked Learning Objectives	Outlines what you should learn within the chapter based on what is required within the syllabus	–
Format & Presentation	Outlines a key marketing presentation format with reference to the Magic Formula	
Concept	Key concept to learn with reference to the Magic Formula	
Application	An example of applied marketing with reference to the Magic Formula	
Evaluation	An example of evaluation with reference to the Magic Formula	
Activity	An application-based activity for you to complete	
Key text links	Emphasises key parts to read in a range of other texts and learning resources	
Marketing at work	A short case study to illustrate marketing practice	
Exam/ Assessment tip	Key advice based on the assessment	
Quick quiz	Use this to check your learning	
Objective check	Review what you have learnt	

7 A note on pronouns

On occasions in this Study Text, 'he' is used for 'he or she', 'him' for 'him or her' and so forth. Whilst we try to avoid this practice it is sometimes necessary for reasons of style. No prejudice or stereotyping according to sex is intended or assumed.

8 Additional resources

8.1 The CIM's supplementary reading list

We have already mentioned that the CIM requires you to demonstrate your ability to 'read widely'. The CIM issues an extensive reading list for each unit. For this unit they recommend supplementary reading. Within the Study Text we have highlighted within the wider reading links specific topics where these resources would help. The CIM's supplementary reading list for this unit is:

Jobber, D. (2007) Principles and practice of marketing. 5th edition. Maidenhead, McGraw-Hill, London.

McDonald, M. and Woodburn, D. (2007) Key account management. 2nd edition. Oxford, Butterworth Heinemann, Oxford.

Cook, S. (2008) Customer care excellence: how to create and effective customer service focus. 5th rev edition. London, Kogan Page.

Kapferer, J. (2008) The new strategic brand management. 4th rev edition. London, Kogan Page.

8.2 Assessment preparation materials from BPP Learning Media

To help you pass the entire Professional Diploma in Marketing we have created a complete study package. **The Professional Diploma Assessment Workbook** covers all four units for the Professional Diploma level. Practice questions and answers, tips on tackling assignments and work-based projects are written to help you succeed in your assessments.

This unit is assessed by a pre-seen case exam.

Our A6 set of spiral bound **Passcards** are handy revision cards which are ideal to reinforce key topics for the *Delivering Customer Value Through Marketing* pre-seen case study exam.

9 Your personal study plan

Preparing a study plan (and sticking to it) is one of the key elements to learning success.

The CIM has stipulated that there should be a minimum of 50 guided learning hours spent on each unit. Guided learning hours will include time spent in lessons, working on distance learning materials, formal workshops and work set by your tutor. We also know that to be successful, students should spend *at least* an additional 50 hours conducting self study. This means that for the entire qualification with four units you should spend 200 hours working in a tutor-guided manner and at least an additional 200 hours completing recommended reading, working on assignments, and revising for exams. This Study Text will help you to organise this 50-hour portion of self study time.

Now think about the exact amount of time you have (don't forget you will still need some leisure time!) and complete the following tables to help you keep to a schedule.

	Date	Duration in weeks
Course start		
Course finish		Total weeks of course:

Examination date	Revision to commence	Total weeks to complete revision:

Content chapter coverage plan

Chapter	To be completed by	Revised ?
1 Developing the product portfolio		
2 Pricing and value		
3 Effective distribution strategies		
4 Managing channel partners		
5 Managing stakeholder needs		
6 Approaches to effective marketing communications		
7 Planning the communications mix		
8 Managing communications agencies		
9 Customer service and customer care		
10 Managing key customer relationships		

Chapter 1

Developing the product portfolio

Topic list

Introduction

This syllabus is all about 'delivering value', and that value is effectively 'in the eye of the customer'. Organisations need to understand exactly what aspects of their offering customers will place value on. Dell Computers, for example, promise to configure computer equipment to an individual customer's specifications and to have it delivered and up and running within days: the 'value' here is mainly based on customisation and service – rather than technology, image or price.

Customer loyalty is built on the creation and delivery of superior customer value – that is, greater than that offered by competitors, and on a sustained basis.

In line with this, Michael Porter (1980) argued that competitive advantage comes from the **value** a company creates for its customers. Value is the 'worth' of the product or service: what it costs the organisation to produce and what the customer is willing to pay for it. In other words:

- A firm **creates value** – by performing its activities and satisfying customers better, differently or more efficiently than its competitors. (The term '**added value**' refers to a product or service being given greater value as a result of the processes that support it: customer service, product customisation and home delivery are some obvious examples.)

- Customers **purchase value** – basing purchasing decisions on the perceived value they will receive, relative to the perceived costs, over the lifetime of the purchase. Jobber (2007, p.15) defines value using an equation: 'Customer value equals perceived benefits minus perceived sacrifice.'

From an accountant's perspective, added value is measured by the amount customers are willing to pay for a product or service **above** the cost to the firm of carrying out all its value-creating activities: in other words, profitability. From this point of view, the organisation gains value **either** by inducing its customers to pay more **or** by reducing its costs.

From a marketing point of view, added value resides in augmenting the product: the total bundle of benefits that offer customers value, confer competitive advantage and help the organisation to meet its marketing and corporate objectives.

A study of products forms the subject of this first chapter. The **augmented product** (Kotler & Armstrong, 2003) may include a range of tangible and intangible elements which add value (and differentiate competing products): enhanced features and optional extras, warranties, delivery and credit facilities, after-sales service, installation, brand image and fashionability, customisation, the esteem/prestige value of ownership, value for money – and the total 'customer experience' of purchasing and using the product/service.

In this chapter we'll start off in section 1 by thinking about the essential characteristics and definitions of products, and the main types of product. The management of product portfolios (through tools such as the BCG matrix and the General Electric Business Screen) and analysis of product profitability enable the organisation to see where most value is being created.

We also need to think about the 'life' of a product. As you can probably appreciate, the marketing implications for a product that has just been introduced to the market are different to the implications for a product that consumers already know and love – or one that has 'had its day' and been supplanted by the 'Next Big Thing'. The importance and role of branding strategy is covered in section 2.

We'll think about innovation and new product development in section 3: where do ideas for new products come from, and how do they get onto the market? Finally we examine the process of product and service adoption.

Syllabus linked learning objectives

By the end of the chapter you will be able to:

Learning objectives	Syllabus link
1 Critically evaluate the process for managing and developing an organisation's product portfolio to deliver best value products for customers in different market segments and achieve organisational and marketing objectives	1.1
2 Critically evaluate the role of branding in the context of the product portfolio, recommending different branding strategies which are appropriate to a range of organisational contexts and sectors	1.2
3 Critically evaluate the role and process of innovation and new product development including consideration of innovative, replacement, re-launched and imitative products and explain the strategic benefit in achieving best value	1.3

1 The product portfolio

1.1 Definitions of 'product'

Jobber (2009) defines product as:

"The core element in the marketing mix is the company's product because this provides the functional requirements sought by customers" Jobber, D. (2009)

KEY CONCEPT

concept

A product is a bundle of benefits which satisfy a set of wants that customers have. It can be anything that can be offered to a market for attention, acquisition, use or consumption. It is a 'thing' with 'features', which offer a total package of benefits. Products have:

- A **physical aspect**, which relates to the components, materials and specifications (colour, size etc) of the product: for example, a size 12 pullover made of 100% pure wool in a natural colour.

- A **functional aspect**, which describes how a product performs and for what purpose it is likely to be bought: for example, a pullover which gives warmth and comfort and lasts well through washing.

- A **symbolic aspect**, which represents the qualities the product suggests to, or offers, the buyer: the '100% pure wool' label may represent quality, status or eco-friendliness.

1.1.1 Product attributes

For the marketer, the total benefit package will include:

(a) **Tangible attributes**

- Availability and delivery
- Performance (usefulness, effectiveness, efficiency)
- Price
- Design (appearance, feel etc)
- Packaging (durability, convenient size, information given)
- The range of complementary products in a 'line'
- The availability of accessories and suppliers for product use or maintenance

(b) **Intangible attributes**

- Image
- Perceived value

These features are interlinked. A product has a tangible **price**, but customers obtain the **value** that they perceive the product to have. The suitability of the product for its purposes (ease of use, convenient storage, low maintenance) may be important to a customer. So may its aesthetic qualities (looks good, favourite colour, says 'modern'). So may its 'esteem' value (rare, high quality, trendy, impressive to friends, sentimental value).

Whether or not the customer perceives the product as offering 'value for money' depends not only on how much they pay for it – but what value they get from it.

1.1.2 Product levels

It is useful for marketers to think of a product, and its attributes, at different levels.

Figure 1.1 Levels of product

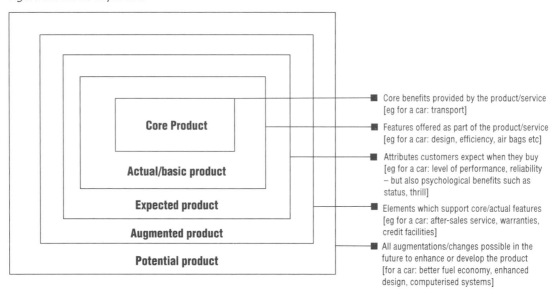

The **core/generic product** is those benefits that all the products in the category would have – all cars, for example, provide transport.

The **augmented product** is the core product plus extra benefits that differentiate it from other products in the category. These might include warranty, delivery, installation, after-sales support.

Many products are marketed at the **augmented product** level – the total package of the customer's experience of purchasing and consuming the product/service is relevant.

The **expected product** level is also important, because of the potential for customers to be dissatisfied (by disappointed expectations) or delighted (by exceeding expectations).

The **potential product** is important in providing the marketing organisation with future avenues to develop the product (and marketing message) in order to stay competitive and 'fresh' in the market.

1.1.3 Product classification

Products can be classified as **consumer goods** or **industrial goods**. Consumer goods are sold directly to the person who will ultimately use them. Industrial goods are used in the production of other products.

FMCG stands for **f**ast **m**oving **c**onsumer **g**oods – items such as packaged food, beverages, toiletries, and tobacco.

Consumer goods can be classified as follows.

Convenience goods	The weekly groceries are a typical example. There is a further distinction between **staple goods** (eg bread and potatoes) and **impulse buys**, like the bar of chocolate that you find at the supermarket checkout. **Brand awareness** is extremely important in this sector.
Shopping goods	These are the more durable items that you buy, like furniture or washing machines. This sort of purchase is usually only made after a good deal of advance planning and shopping around.
Speciality goods	These are items like jewellery or more expensive items of clothing.
Unsought goods	These are goods that you did not realise you needed! Typical examples are new and sometimes 'gimmicky' products, such as 'wardrobe organisers', or fire resistant car polish!

 ACTIVITY 1 | application

Think of three products that you have bought recently, one low-priced, one medium-priced, and one expensive item. Identify the product attributes that made you value, and therefore buy, each of these items. Categorise them according to the classifications shown above.

Industrial goods can be classified as follows.

- **Installations**, eg major items of plant and machinery like a factory assembly line
- **Accessories**, such as PCs
- **Raw materials**, for example plastic, metal, wood, foodstuffs and chemicals
- **Components**, eg the Lucas headlights on Ford cars, the Intel microchip in most PCs
- **Supplies**, such as office stationery and cleaning materials

 MARKETING AT WORK | application

Faced with the most brutal economic downturn in recent memory, famous manufacturer brands such as Nescafe coffee or Pampers nappies are under even greater threat from store brands owned by the retail giants. These 'home brands' today control more than 40% of the UK FMCG market, being bought in increasing quantities by consumers faced with the pressing need to save money. These consumers may never return to manufacturer brands, even if the economy improves.

1.2 Product management, customer value and competitive advantage

The immediate task of a marketing manager with respect to the products of the organisation may be any of the following:

- To **create** demand where none exists
- To **develop** a latent demand
- To **revitalise** a sagging demand
- To attempt to **smooth out** uneven demand
- To **sustain** a buoyant demand
- To **reduce** excess demand

Customer value is the customer's estimate of how far a product or service goes towards satisfying needs. Every product has a cost, and so the customer makes a trade-off between the expenditure and the value offered.

According to Kotler and Armstrong (2003), a customer must feel that he or she gets a better deal from buying an item than by buying any of the alternatives (such as those offered by competitors).

Marketing has a role in the organisation's value chain. The end result of a value chain is a product or service whose price must in some way equate with the customer's perception of value, but whose cost allows the producer a margin or profit.

1.3 Managing and planning product portfolios

 KEY CONCEPT

concept

A company's **product portfolio** (or product range, assortment or mix) is all the product lines and items that the company offers for sale.

A company's product range can be described in the following terms.

Characteristic	Defined by:
Width/Breadth	Number of product lines: eg cosmetics, haircare, toiletries and health products.
Depth	Average number of items per product line: eg cosmetics including moisturiser, cleanser, toner, lipstick, eyeshadow etc.
Consistency	Closeness of relationships in product range for the benefit of users and production/distribution processes

1.3.1 Managing the product range

There are benefits to be gained from using a systematic approach to the management of the product range. It can be **reduced** (eg by discontinuing a product) or **extended** by:

- Introducing variations in models or style (eg a paint manufacturer introducing different colours, types and pot sizes)

- Differentiating the quality of products offered at different price levels (eg 'premium' paints and 'value' paints)

- Developing associated items (eg a paint roller and brushes, paint trays, colour charts)

- Developing new products with little technical or marketing relationship to the existing range (eg wallpaper and DIY accessories)

Managing the product range also raises broad issues such as:

- What role a product should play in the range. ('Flagship' brand? Profit provider? Niche filler? New market tester/developer? Old faithful, retaining customer loyalty?) The roles of products in the mix should create a balanced range, with sufficient **cash-generating** products to support **cash-using** (declining or new/market-developing) products

- How resources should be allocated between products

- What should be expected from each product

- How far products should be integrated within the brand image and be recognisable as part of the brand family

Marketing is not an exact science and there is no definitive approach or technique which can determine how resources should be shared across the product range. There are, however, techniques which can aid decision making. Ultimately the burden of the decision is a management responsibility and requires judgement, but tools such as the **BCG matrix** and the **product life cycle** can help the portfolio planning process.

1.4 Product profitability

A firm should want to know what profits or losses are being made by each of its products, and why. One technique is known as **direct product profitability**, which analyses the profit on each individual product line to arrive at relative profitabilities of different products.

Direct product profitability (DPP) is used primarily within the retail sector and involves the attribution of both the purchase price and other indirect costs (such as distribution, warehousing and retailing) to each product line. Thus a profit can be identified for each product.

It has grown primarily from the need for manufacturers to encourage retailers to place new products on their shelves. Supermarkets analyse the direct profitability of every branded and non-branded product that they sell. In an ever more crowded market, this helps them to decide what ranges to present in store and also provides a focus for individual marketing initiatives. The profitability of entire groups of products is presented after taking account of factors in addition to cost, such as supplier discounts and wastage levels.

1.5 The product life cycle

Jobber (2009) notes:

"No matter how wide the product mix, both product lines and individual brands need to be managed over time. A useful tool for conceptualising the changes that may take place during the time that a product is on the market is called the product life cycle

1.5.1 What is the product life cycle?

The **product life cycle** (PLC) uses a 'biological' analogy to suggest that products are born (or introduced), grow to reach maturity and then enter old age and decline.

The profitability and sales position of a product can be expected to change over time. The 'product life cycle' is an attempt to recognise distinct stages in a product's sales history. Here is the classic representation of the life cycle.

Figure 1.2 The product life cycle

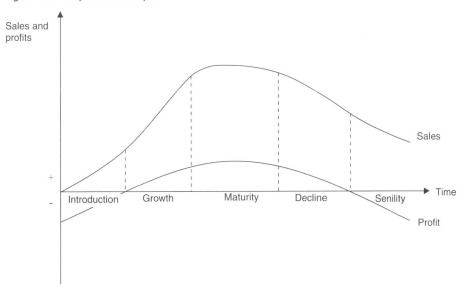

(a) **Introduction**. A new product, following development, takes time to find acceptance by consumers and there is slow growth in sales. Only a few firms sell the product, unit costs are high due to low output and there may be early teething troubles with production technology. Prices may be high to cover production costs and sales promotion expenditure. For example, pocket calculators, video cassette recorders and mobile telephones were all very expensive when launched. The product is, initially, a loss maker.

(b) **Growth**. If the new product gains market acceptance, sales will rise more sharply and the product will start to make profits. New customers buy the product and, as production rises, unit costs fall. Since demand is strong, prices tend to remain fairly static for a time. However, the prospect of cheap mass production and a strong market will attract competitors, so that the number of producers increases. With increased competition, manufacturers must spend a lot of money on product improvement, sales promotion and distribution to obtain a dominant or strong market position.

(c) **Maturity**. The rate of sales growth slows down and the product reaches a period of maturity, which is probably the longest period of a successful product's life. Most products on the market are at the mature stage of their life. Eventually sales will begin to decline so that there is overcapacity of production. Severe competition occurs, profits fall and some producers leave the market. The remaining producers seek means of prolonging the product life by modifying the product and searching for new market segments.

(d) **Decline**. Most products reach a stage of decline, which may be slow or fast. Many producers are reluctant to leave the market, although some inevitably do because of falling profits. If a product remains on the market too long, it will become unprofitable and the decline stage in its life cycle then gives way to a 'senility' or **'obsolescence'** stage.

1.5.2 Non-classic PLC

Figure 1.3 shows a non-classic product life cycle. This is a good starting point when thinking about any product, even though very few products will follow the cycle exactly. For example, the life cycle of new products such as the 'cyber pet', or fast changing information technology products, would look like this.

Figure 1.3 Short PLC

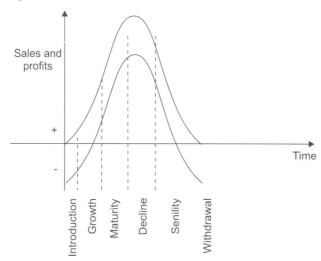

The product goes through all stages at a rapid rate. A short introduction phase leads to extreme sales growth, but maturity is short-lived, and decline is just as rapid as growth was. Often products are withdrawn completely as they have become unprofitable.

Blythe (2006), who has a good coverage of the PLC so it would be worth looking at this text. Blythe notes:

"Some products, for example computer games, may go through the entire life cycle in a matter of months. Others, like pitta bread, have a life cycle measured in thousands of years, and may never become obsolete."

MARKETING AT WORK

3G stands for third-generation mobile communication and is best understood as wireless broadband for mobile phones. Hutchison Whampoa, the company that owns 3, has led the growth of the global 3G market. It has invested heavily in new technology and provides the most comprehensive network for 3G communications. 3G technology has significantly more bandwidth than 2G technology. More bandwidth means more space for transmitting large amounts of data eg videos rather than text.

Innovative production and marketing go hand in hand in successful businesses in the communications technology sector. 3 can only convince customers that it can meet their needs (for quick music downloads, pictures, videos, messaging, internet access, email and even the standard phone call) if it has the products to do so. Having invested seriously in the 3G market, it has hoped to acquire 'first mover advantage' by being the first one to develop a specific market. The first mover becomes associated by customers with that expansion. It is then able to be at the leading edge of new developments so its rivals are continually trying to catch up.

3 is always seeking to improve its products and services to maintain its market leading position. In 2006 these included:

- Signing an exclusive deal to stream ITV1 – ITV's flagship channel – to its 3.75 million customers in the UK

- Signing deals with leading handset producers such as Nokia, Motorola and Sony Ericsson to provide handsets to complement the network

- Screening the 2006 World Cup directly on customer mobile phones. This created an all-time high in mobile television usage

- Launch of the X Series from 3, which is supported by a commercial link with key Internet service and software providers such as Microsoft, Yahoo, Google, eBay and Skype

A major strength of 3 is an emphasis on anticipating and meeting customers' needs. The company recognises that it can continue to be the market leader only if its product is superior to that of its rivals and continues to evolve. In a fast-moving industry, it is important to find out not only what clients prefer today, but perhaps more importantly to research their future requirements. It must also frequently research new technologies – in this way it will stay at the forefront of the field, ahead of its rivals on the product life cycle curve, and thereby retain market leadership. Adapted from www.thetimes100.co.uk – accessed 14 May 2008

 Make sure that you take a look at the 'Times 100' website. It is a rich source of examples of current business and marketing practice. ∎

 ACTIVITY 2

At what point do you consider the following products or services to be in their product life cycle?

(a)   Digital cameras
(b)   Baked beans
(c)   MP3 players
(d)   Cigarettes
(e)   Carbon paper
(f)   Mortgages
(g)   Writing implements
(h)   Car alarms
(i)   Organically grown fruit and vegetables

1.5.3 Criticisms of the product life cycle

Criticisms of the practical value of the PLC include the following.

(a)   The stages cannot easily be defined.

(b)   The traditional bell-shaped curve of a product life cycle does not always occur in practice. Some products have no maturity phase and go straight from growth to decline. Others have a second growth period after an initial decline. Some have virtually no introductory period and go straight into a rapid growth phase, while others (the vast majority of new products in fact) do not succeed at all.

(c)   Strategic decisions can change a product's life cycle: for example, by repositioning a product in the market, its life can be extended. If strategic planners 'decide' what a product's life is going to be, opportunities to extend the life cycle might be ignored.

(d)   Competition varies in different industries and the strategic implications of the product life cycle will vary according to the nature of the competition. The 'traditional' life cycle presupposes increasing competition and falling prices during the growth phase of the market and also the gradual elimination of competitors in the decline phase. This pattern of events is not always true.

1.6 The Boston Consulting Group (BCG) matrix and the General Electric Business Screen (GEBS)

1.6.1 The BCG matrix

 KEY CONCEPT

 concept

The **BCG matrix** classifies products or brands on the basis of their market share and according to the rate of growth in the market as a whole, as a way of assessing their role in the product range.

Figure 1.4: The BCG matrix

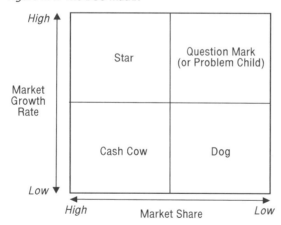

On the basis of this classification, each product may fall into one of four broad categories.

(a)   **Problem Child** (or question mark): A small market share in a high growth industry. The generic product is clearly popular, but customer support for the particular brand is limited. A small market share implies that competitors are in a strong position and that if the product is to be successful it will require substantial funds, and a new marketing mix. If the market looks good and the product is viable, then the company should consider a 'build' strategy to increase market share: increasing the resources available for that product to permit more active marketing. If the future looks less promising, then the company should consider withdrawing the product. What strategy is decided will depend on the strength of competitors, availability of funding and other relevant factors.

(b)   **Star**: A high market share in a high growth industry. The star has potential for generating significant earnings, currently and in the future. At this stage it may still require substantial marketing expenditure as part of a 'maintain' strategy, but this is probably regarded as a good investment for the future.

(c)   **Cash Cow**: A high market share in a mature slow-growth market. Typically, a well established product with a high degree of consumer loyalty. Product development costs are typically low and the marketing campaign is well established. The cash cow will normally make a substantial contribution to overall profitability. The appropriate strategy will vary according to the precise position of the cash cow. If market growth is reasonably strong then a 'holding' strategy will be appropriate, but if growth and/or share are weakening, then a 'harvesting' strategy may be more sensible: cut back on marketing expenditure and maximise short-term profit.

(d)   **Dog**: A low market share in a low-growth market. Again, typically a well established product, but one which is apparently losing consumer support and may have cost disadvantages. The usual strategy would be to consider divestment, unless the cash flow position is strong, in which case the product would be harvested in the short term, prior to deletion from the product range.

Jobber (2009 gives a thorough analysis of the weaknesses of the BCG model

1.6.2 BCG and PLC

You may have spotted a relationship between the BCG matrix and the classic product life cycle. The typical new product is likely to appear in the 'problem child' category to begin with (introduction). If it looks promising, and with effective marketing, it might be expected to become a 'star' (growth). Then, as markets mature, a 'cash cow' (maturity) and finally a 'dog' (decline). The suggestion that most products will move through these stages does not weaken the role played by marketing. Poor marketing may mean that a product moves from being a problem child to a dog without making any substantial contribution to profitability. Good marketing may enable the firm to prolong the 'star' and 'cash cow' phases, maximising cash flow from the product.

1.6.3 GEBS

The approach of the GE Business Screen (GEBS) is similar to that of the BCG matrix. The GEBS includes a broader range of company and market factors. A typical example is provided below. This matrix classifies products according to industry attractiveness and company strengths. The approach aims to consider a variety of factors which contribute to both of these variables.

Figure 1.5 General Electric Business Screen

		Strong	Invest for growth	Invest selectively for growth	Develop for income
Business strength		Average	Invest selectively and build	Develop selectively for income	Harvest or divest
		Weak	Develop selectively and build on strengths	Harvest	Divest
			Attractive	*Average*	*Unattractive*

Market attractiveness

The broader approach of the GE matrix emphasises the attempt to match **competences** within the company to **conditions** within the market place.

Company competences	Conditions defining market attractiveness
Strength of assets	Market size
Relative marketing and brand strength	Market growth rate
Market share	Market profitability
Customer loyalty	Pricing trends
Cost structure versus the competition	Competitive intensity

Company competences	Conditions defining market attractiveness
Relative profit margins versus the competition	Overall risk
Distribution strength	Entry barriers
Productive capacity	Opportunity to differentiate
Record of innovation	Demand variability
Quality	Segmentation
Access to financial and other investment resources	Distribution structure
Management strength	Technology

EXAM TIP

concept

One of the most important things to remember about the BCG matrix or GEBS is that they emphasise the important strategic point that different products should have different strategic roles in the product portfolio. In the sample case study, Innocent Drinks introduces orange juice as a way of establishing a new lower price point with the aim of expanding the demographic for the brand.

2 The role of branding

2.1 The importance of 'the brand'

Blythe comments as follows on branding

"Branding is the culmination of a range of activities across the whole marketing mix, leading to a brand image that conveys a whole set of messages to the consumer... about quality, price, expected performance and status."

KEY CONCEPT

concept

A **brand** is a name, term, sign, symbol or design intended to identify the product of a seller and to differentiate it from those of competitors.

Branding is a very general term covering brand names, designs, trademarks, symbols, jingles and the like. A brand name refers strictly to letters, words or groups of words which can be spoken. A brand image distinguishes a company's product from competing products in the eyes of the user.

Branding might be discussed under any of the four Ps. For instance, part of the branding of a Rolls Royce is the unmistakeable design of the product; or you might buy a 'cheaper brand' of washing-up liquid if you are concerned about price. However, as the definition above suggests, most brands are created and maintained by **marketing communications** such as advertising and promotions.

Branding is now apparent in just about all markets. Not long ago – and this is still the case in many less developed countries – most products were sold unbranded. Today even salt, oranges, nuts and screws are often branded. There has been a return recently in some developed countries to 'generics': cheap products packaged plainly and not heavily advertised. This apparent lack of branding is in fact establishing a brand identity itself.

For customers, the benefits of brands are as follows:

- Branding makes it easier to choose between competing products, if brands offer different benefits. Brands help consumers cope with information overload;

- Brands can support aspirations and self image;

- Branding can confer membership of reference groups.

Branding and a firm's reputation are linked. The important thing to remember is that a **brand is something that customers value**: it exists in the customer's mind. A brand is the link between a company's marketing activities and the customer's perception.

The added satisfactions conferred by brands are largely subjective. In blind testing many consumers cannot tell the difference between different products; however, they will exhibit a preference for a strong brand name when shown it.

Most consumer buying decisions do not depend therefore on the functionality of the product. Products are often bought for emotional reasons. For example, most sports trainers are fashion products.

 MARKETING AT WORK

application

Tesco has been named the most valuable brand on the high street, worth £8.6bn, almost £4bn more than rival Sainsbury's. A report has said that Tesco's top ranking was 'almost inevitable' following sales of £32bn and its market leading share in the supermarket and convenience store markets. Brands in the study were valued after looking at public sales figures for the last five years and attributing a score to measures such as future growth, price positioning, customer service and brand heritage.

Tesco's strong brand is likely to give it a better chance to weather tougher times on the UK high street, because consumers need more reasons to buy. [With 2009 showing real signs of a major economic slowdown, strong brands are more important than ever.]

(www.brandrepublic.com accessed 12 May 2008)

A brand identity may begin with a name, such as 'Kleenex' or 'Ariel', but extends to a range of visual features which should assist in stimulating demand for the particular product, such as the Nike 'swoosh' or the Ferrari horse (Jobber, 2007). The additional features include typography, colour, package design and slogans.

In addition, of course, a brand shares the attributes of a product: it is a bundle of tangible and intangible benefits which deliver customer value.

 ACTIVITY 3

application

What characteristics do the following brand names suggest to you?

- Brillo (scouring pads)
- Pampers (baby nappies)
- Cussons Imperial Leather (soap)
- Kerrygold (butter)
- Hush Puppies (shoes)

2.1.1 Objectives of branding

The key benefit of branding is product differentiation and recognition. Products may be branded for a number of reasons.

(a) It aids **product differentiation**, conveying a lot of information very quickly and concisely. This helps customers readily to identify the goods or services and thereby helps to create a customer loyalty to the brand. It is therefore a means of increasing or maintaining sales.

(b) It maximises the impact of **advertising** for product identification and recognition. The more similar a product (whether an industrial good or consumer good) is to competing goods, the more branding is necessary to create a separate product identity.

(c) Branding leads to a **readier acceptance** of a manufacturer's goods by wholesalers and retailers.

(d) It reduces the importance of **price differentials** between goods.

(e) It supports **market segmentation**, since different brands of similar products may be developed to meet specific needs of categories of uses. (Think of all the cereal brands produced by Kellogg's, for example.)

(f) It supports **brand extension** or **stretching**. Other products can be introduced into the brand range to 'piggy back' on the articles already known to the customer (but ill-will as well as goodwill for one product in a branded range will be transferred to all other products in the range).

(g) It **eases the task of personal selling**, by enhancing product recognition.

The relevance of branding does not apply equally to all products. The cost of intensive brand advertising to project a brand image nationally may be prohibitively high. Goods which are sold in large numbers, on the other hand, promote a brand name by their existence and circulation.

The decision as to whether a brand name should be given to a **range of products** or whether products should be branded **individually** depends on quality factors.

(a) If the brand name is associated with quality, all goods in the range must be of that standard.

(b) If a company produces different quality (and price) goods for different market segments, it would be unwise to give the same brand name to the higher and the lower quality goods because this would deter buyers in the high quality/price market segment.

2.2 Developing and building brand value

The effort put into building a brand can create a valuable asset that can be valued, though the value of such an intangible asset may only be shown on the balance sheet if it has been purchased.

A brand can be an important business asset. Customers learn to trust the brand to deliver greater satisfaction than the generic product. This satisfaction can be realised by the supplier in the form of increased revenue. Investment in building a brand thus has the potential to increase the value created by the supplier. However, success is not guaranteed and even when achieved it may not last long. Successful brands must be defended and maintained if their value is not to be eroded by competition, neglect and even mismanagement.

 MARKETING AT WORK   application

Tommy Hilfiger

It has been quite a decade for Tommy Hilfiger. During the 90s, it seems his brand could do no wrong. The business experienced meteoric growth and, by 2000, was generating $2bn in worldwide sales. But then came the new century, and Hilfiger struggled to maintain the momentum. (Eventually) the brand was brought by Apax Partners, a global private equity firm, for $1.6bn (£850m). Perhaps the first step under the new regime will be to look back on some of the major errors that the brand made in the 90s, because Tommy Hilfiger learned some of the key lessons of brand management the hard way.

First, growth and success are the two biggest enemies of all the strong brands. Hilfiger's global sales grew tenfold during the 90s. It is a classic conundrum for most niche brands that experience market success. Their scale increases, they lose focus and, eventually, all the elements that made the brand successful are lost.

Second, watch out for retail 'partners'. Hilfiger, like most fashion brands, relies both on its own outlets and selling through major department stores. The latter are not necessarily motivated to protect and care for brand equity over the long haul. Hilfiger experienced first-hand the classic one-two-three of retail sales. 'The problem was the department stores in the US', he said. 'First of all they copy you, then they underprice you and then they discount the brand. They don't take care of your shop areas in stores'.

Third, the financial markets are run by brand morons with unreasonably short-term profit goals. Hilfiger himself accepts the pressure of the market made his life a very difficult and had a negative impact on the brand. Everything you do is looked at under a microscope, so you make decisions based on Wall Street agendas, and maybe those aren't always the right decisions to make'.

Fourth, pressure from Wall Street often leads to a focus on short-term sales at the expense of long-term marketing focus. There is a big difference between marketing and sales. When you are sales-orientated, all customers are equally valuable additions to your quarterly sales figures. Marketers, however, know that all customers are not created equally.

To succeed over the long term, a fashion brand must aim high and deliberately avoid appealing to customers lower down the fashion hierarchy. According to the company's new chief executive Fred Gehring, this is something that he will attempt to redress. 'Over the part couple of years, everything was top-lined focused', he said. 'In a (non-publicly listed) situation, we don't have to have an obsession with the top line anymore and can focus on quality, not quantity'.

Fifth, beware sales promotions. The single fastest way to kill any brand is to over-produce and then discount heavily through sales promotions. Price-based promotions kill brand equity and, when the former is more prominent then the latter, disaster is rarely far away.

Creating a successful brand can be very expensive in money and effort. When a company makes a significant investment in creating and enhancing a brand, it is appropriate to measure the degree of success that it achieves. This is the process of **brand valuation**.

You must be careful to distinguish between brand value and brand values. Brand values are the intangible factors that make up the identity or image of the brand. They are usually quoted as a list of adjectives, such as young, active, exclusive, fun, reliable, secure, safe and so on. Brand value, on the other hand, is value in an economic sense: the monetary worth of the brand, or the cash value it represents.

Shareholders rightly expect to see a return on their investment. The greater the value achieved from a given cash investment, the better the performance of the company and its management is assessed to be. This applies as much to investment in intangible assets, such as brands, as to investment in tangible ones such as machinery or premises. The problem is that intangible assets are much more difficult to value than tangible ones.

 MARKETING AT WORK application

In a recession, shoppers have a tendency to switch to 'home brands' in order to save money. The logical thing for manufacturer brands to do is to lower their own prices, or offer sufficient 'non-price' reasons to consumers to buy their brand (such as enhanced image, or improved performance).

Most brands appear to do exactly the opposite. Promotional pricing activity tends to decrease in recessionary times, as does innovation and advertising activity. Market research is likely to disappear, too.

It could be argued that cutting back on such expenditure, which it saves money in the short term, undermines long-term brand value. Marketing expense should be a strategic investment, and not just a short-run cost that can be cut when the going gets tough.

(Adapted from: Jan-Benedict E M Steenkamp and Marnik G Dekimpe; 2009)

2.3 Rebranding

At times, the performance of a brand will falter and managers will attempt to rectify the situation, either by enhancing sales volume or improving profits in other ways.

Revitalisation means increasing the sales volume through:

- New markets (eg overseas)
- New segments (eg personal computers are being sold for family, as opposed to business, use)
- Increased usage (encouraging people to eat breakfast cereals as a snack during the day)

Many brands in the US attempted to piggyback on the enthusiasm for Barack Obama. Pepsi, for example, launched a new logo and ushered in 2009 with a celebration of 'Optimismmm' under the umbrella slogan 'Refresh everything'.

Repositioning is more fundamental as a competitive strategy, aimed at changing position in order to increase market share.

Type of position	Comment
Real	Relates to actual product features and design
Psychological	Change the buyer's beliefs about the brand
Competitive	Alter beliefs about competing brands
Change emphasis	The emphasis in the advertising can change over time

'Premiumisation'

Sometimes big brands surprise you. Take Burger King, for example – its sudden aspiration for luxury led it to declare plans to launch the world's most expensive burger, featuring Kobe beef and an £85 price tag…It is part of the ongoing trend known as premiumisation… (which) originated in the drinks business about five years ago. It refers to the practice of introducing a brand or repositioning an existing one as premium or luxury in a mature category. Diageo, for example, has a series of brands such as Tanqueray Ten and Don Julio Tequila designed to premiumise their offering in some of their biggest categories…

On the manufacturer side, we are finally entering an era of mass maturity. Most categories, especially in food and beverages, are now established. With no apparent direction left or right into new product areas, many marketers are attempting to move up instead. Higher prices reduces significantly the need to sell in huge numbers.

Then there are private-labels. As British private-labels have grown in quality and popularity, they have forced brands to premiumise to find a high watermark where the rising tide of store brands won't affect them. But retailers are no dummies, they, too, have discovered the potential of premiumisation; Tesco Finest is possibly the best example of premiumisation in the UK…

Like it or not, £85 burgers, luxury doggy puddings and £75 glasses of vodka are here to stay. Consumers are quickly growing accustomed to super-premium products – the age of premiumisation is upon us.

Mark Ritson, Marketing, 29 April 2008

ACTIVITY 4

application

Times have changed in the short time since this article was written! Do you think that there is still a place for premiumisation in the economic order prevailing in 2010/2011?

2.4 International and global brands

 concept

Global branding is 'the achievement of brand penetration worldwide (Jobber, D; 2009).

 MARKETING AT WORK application

- The Rolex watch is the same all over the world. Its positioning as the watch for the high achiever is the same across the globe. It is an upmarket product and will be found in upmarket outlets.

- Unilever's Lifebuoy soap is positioned identically in India and East Africa, despite having different ingredients. It is promoted as an inexpensive soap that protects health.

Ideally, a firm would prefer to offer the same product, with the same pricing policy using the same promotional methods and through the same distribution channels in all its markets. But in practice, this is never possible. '...the fact that the French eat four times more yogurt than the British, and the British buy eight times more chocolate than the Italians reflects the kinds of national differences that will affect the marketing strategies of manufacturers.' Jobber, D. (2009)

Complete global standardisation would greatly increase the profitability of a company's products and simplify the task of the international marketing manager. The extent to which standardisation is possible is controversial in marketing. Levitt (1983) wrote:

'The global corporation operates with resolute constancy, at low relative cost, as if the entire world (or major regions of it) were a single entity; it sells the same things in the same way everywhere.'

At the other end of the spectrum, it has been argued that adaptability is the key ingredient for global success. Much of the decision making in an international marketing manager's role is concerned with taking a view on the necessity, or lack of it, of adapting the product, price and communications to individual markets.

A firm's approach to this decision depends to a large extent on its attitude towards internationalisation and its level of involvement in international marketing. There are broadly three types of approach in this context.

(a) **Ethnocentrism**. Overseas operations are viewed as being secondary to domestic operations and are often simply a means of disposing of surpluses. Any plans for overseas markets are developed at home with very little systematic market research overseas. There is little or no modification of any aspects of the mix with no real attention to customer needs. This is the first step into international marketing and involves a centralised strategy.

(b) **Polycentrism**. Subsidiaries are established, each operating independently with its own plans, objectives and marketing policies on a country by country basis. Adaptation will be at its most extreme with this approach. Polycentrism can be viewed as an evolutionary step and involves a decentralised strategy. It is easy to fall into a **multidomestic** pattern of operations that does not take advantage of co-ordinating actions across differential markets.

(c) **Geocentrism**. The organisation views the entire world as a market with standardisation where possible and adaptation where necessary. It is the final evolutionary stage for the multinational organisation and involves an integrated marketing strategy.

In general terms, the extent to which the mix has to be adapted depends on the type of product. Some products are extremely sensitive to the environmental differences, which bring about the need for adaptation; others are not at all sensitive to these differences, in which case standardisation is possible.

A useful way of analysing products internationally is to place them on a continuum of environmental sensitivity as shown below in Figure 1.6. (We are referring to the social, legal, economic, political and cultural environments here.) The greater the environmental sensitivity of a product, the greater the necessity for the company to adapt the marketing mix.

Figure 1.6 Continuum of environmental sensitivity

Environmentally sensitive	Environmentally insensitive
Adaptation necessary	Standardisation possible

- Fashion clothes
- Convenience foods

- Industrial and agricultural products
- World market product, eg denim jeans

A more sophisticated approach is a two-dimensional matrix. The vertical dimension measures the advantages of standardised marketing and the horizontal dimension takes the need for localised marketing into account. This is illustrated below in Figure 1.7.

There are strong forces in the business environment drawing companies towards global marketing strategies and global branding, the most important of which are as follows.

(a) **Demographic, cultural** and **economic convergence** among consumer markets and increasing homogeneity in the needs of industrial customers worldwide.

(b) Increased need for **investment and research** to ensure long term competitiveness, longer lead times involved in bringing products to market and the growing return needed for this process.

(c) The growing importance of **economies of scale** (purchasing, manufacturing, distribution).

(d) Changes in **regional economic cooperation** resulting in freer movement of goods and capital.

(e) The impact of technology on manufacturing, transportation and distribution.

(f) The **deregulation** of national markets, in areas such as air transport, financial services, telecommunications and power generation.

Figure 1.7 Standardised v localised marketing

Sector 1 GLOBAL • Aircraft manufacturing • Computers • Industrial machinery • Automobiles	Sector 3 BLOCKED GLOBAL • Telecommunications • Generators • Pharmaceuticals	High *Advantages of standardised marketing*
Sector 2 MULTINATIONAL/ MULTIMARKET • Medical equipment • Synthetic fibres • Cash dispensers • Electrical equipment	Sector 4 NATIONAL/LOCAL • Breweries • Cement • Retail trade • Processed food	Low
Low	High	

Need for localised marketing

However, despite these strong worldwide forces, there are still many situations where the advantages of, or need for, local adaptation is high.

(a) **Sector 1** contains true global marketing companies with a geocentric orientation. Local adaptation is inappropriate and globalising forces can be exploited to great advantage to the company. Examples include aircraft, computers and industrial machinery.

(b) **Sector 2**. Multinational or multimarket companies with a polycentric orientation adopt this approach. Products require only a low degree of local adaptation. The world market for such multinational organisations is divided into regions or countries with different characteristics, such as W Europe, S America or the Far East. Products in this sector include electrical equipment.

(c) **Sector 3**. Blocked global businesses are those in which both the need for local adaptation and the globalising factors discussed above are strong. This sector includes businesses that are dominated by economies of scale and would be global but for the influence of legal or political constraints (eg government purchasing policies) creating the need to adapt their products. Regional telephone networks offer a typical example.

(d) **Sector 4** contains true local businesses. Strong local adaptation is necessary for success and there are no strong arguments in favour of globalisation (eg brewing and retail trade).

Kenichi Ohmae (1999) writes (in The Borderless World) that 'the lure of a universal product is a false allure', simply because local tastes are so different (eg American cars are generally too large and bulky for Europe's narrow streets). It is a similar story with brands. Some brands are global while many others are present in only one country.

2.5 Brand strategies

Brand extension is the introduction of new flavours, sizes etc to a brand, to capitalise on existing brand loyalty. Examples include the introduction of Persil washing up liquid and Mars ice cream. New additions to the product range are beneficial for two main reasons.

(a) They require a lower level of marketing investment (part of the 'image' already being known).

(b) The extension of the brand presents less risk to consumers who might be worried about trying something new. (This is particularly important in consumer durables that require relatively large 'investment', such as a car, stereo system or the like.)

Multi-branding is the introduction of a number of brands that all satisfy very similar product characteristics. This can be used where there is little or no brand loyalty, in order to pick up buyers who are constantly changing brands.

The best example is washing detergents. The two majors, Lever Brothers and Procter & Gamble, have created a barrier to fresh competition as a new company would have to launch several brands at once in order to compete.

Family branding uses the power of the brand name to assist all products in a range. This strategy is being used more and more by large companies, such as Heinz. In part it is a response to retailers' own-label (family branded) goods. It is also an attempt to consolidate expensive television advertising behind one message rather than fragmenting it across the promotion of individual items.

3 Innovation and new product development (NPD)

Blythe (2006) comments:

"There is a strong positive relationship between a firm's innovative activities and its ability to survive and prosper, so many companies place a strong emphasis on developing new products to replace those which become obsolete, or which are superseded by competitors' offerings."

Jobber (2009) believes:

"The lifeblood of corporate success is bringing new products to the marketplace".

 KEY CONCEPT

concept

New product development (NPD) is the process of developing new products from idea stage through to launch on the market. The NPD sequence typically includes: conception; screening of ideas; business analysis; product development and marketing mix planning; test marketing; and commercialisation and launch.

'The best antidote to margin degradation, in good times or bad, is innovation'. While it may not be a good idea to launch a new product in a recession if it is merely a superficial line extension that adds little value, an exciting and genuinely new product should not be held back, for the following reasons.

- New product releases are likely to be less frequent than normal, so there will be less 'clutter'.
- Delaying until recovery comes means that you will be caught up in the rush.
- Additional products that you have in the pipeline will be delayed.

3.1 Developing a culture of innovation

Creative ideas can come from anywhere and at any time, but if management wish to foster innovation they should try to provide an organisation structure in which innovative ideas are encouraged to emerge.

(a) **Innovation requires creativity**. Creativity may be encouraged in an individual or group by establishing a climate in which free expression of abilities is allowed.

(b) Creative ideas must then be **analysed rationally** to decide whether they provide a viable proposition.

(c) A system of organisation must exist whereby a viable creative idea is converted into action through **effective control** procedures.

There is increasing evidence of time-based competition. In other words many firms are reducing the time spent to get new products researched, designed and launched.

- It wrongfoots competitors (eg early mover advantages)
- It enables the firm to get the maximum return from patents
- It might enable the firm to set industry standards for new products
- It enables a premium or skimming pricing strategy

Speed in NPD can be facilitated by co-ordination between marketing and R&D throughout the design process. There are many good reasons why R&D should be more closely co-ordinated with marketing.

(a) If the firm operates the marketing concept, then the 'identification of customer needs' should be a vital input to new product developments.

(b) The R & D department might identify possible changes to product specifications so that a variety of marketing mixes can be tried out and screened.

Other measures might be used to speed the pace of new product development.

(a) **Parallel engineering** (ie different aspects of the design are carried out simultaneously, rather than being shuffled to and fro in a sequence)

(b) **Design for manufacture** (ie product design specification should, as far as possible minimise new equipment or machine modification, which can be time consuming)

(c) Setting up relationships with **distributors** early on to encourage rapid takeup

3.2 The role of innovation in product management

New product development is important for maintaining customer satisfaction through change; refreshing or extending the product range; and adapting to environmental opportunities and threats. These will all contribute towards the success of a company's long-term business strategy.

There are a number of reasons why a company may consider extending its product mix with the introduction of new products.

(a) To meet the **changing needs/wants of customers**: a new product may meet a new need (eg for environmentally friendly alternatives) or meet an existing need more effectively (eg digital cameras).

(b) To **match competitors**: responding to innovations and market trends before or shortly after competitors, so as not to miss marketing opportunities.

(c) To **respond to environmental threats and opportunities**: capitalising on opportunities presented by new technology, say (digital cameras), or other products (accessories and supplies for digital cameras); minimising the effects of threats such as environmental impacts (developing 'green' alternatives) or safety concerns (developing new safety features).

(d) To **extend the product/brand range** as part of a product development or diversification growth strategy. New products can bring new customers to the brand and enable cross-selling of products in the mix.

(e) To **extend the 'maturity' stage of the PLC** for a product, by modifying it to maintain interest, simulate re-purchase (because it is 'new and improved') and/or target as yet unreached market segments.

(f) To **refresh the product range**, as products go into the decline stage of their life cycle. Some products may become obsolete and need updating. Others will simply be deleted, and the company will need to replace them in the product mix in order to maintain brand presence and profitability.

  EXAM TIP application

The sample case study points to Innocent Drinks' record of innovation – developing new recipes and continually revitalising its range. Its introduction of orange juice to its range is also perceived as innovative!

3.3 Rejuvenating existing products

 MARKETING AT WORK application

Companies are opening up to ideas from external sources. Procter & Gamble operates what it calls its 'Connect and Develop' innovation model, which reduces the time and cost of product development by inviting ideas from outside. When the company wanted to print text and pictures on Pringles crisps, it partnered with an Italian professor who had developed the necessary food technology.

3.3.1 What is 'new'?

New products may be genuinely innovative, but 'newness' may also mean 'adapted', 'repackaged' or 'introduced' in a new market.

What is a new product?

- One that opens up an entirely new market
- One that replaces an existing product
- One that broadens significantly the market for an existing product

An old product can be new if:

- It is introduced to a new market
- It is packaged in a different way
- A different marketing approach is used
- A mix variable is changed – for example, a new price is set, or a new distribution channel is used

Jobber (2009) quotes the following percentages applicable to 'new' products:

- 45% of them are replacements of existing products
- 25% are additions to existing lines
- 20% are new product lines
- 10% are 'new to the world', creating entirely new markets

Can you think of an example of each of the above?

3.3.2 Degrees of 'newness'

(a) **The unquestionably new product**, such as new medicines for the treatment of AIDS and cancer. Marks of such a new product are technical innovation, high price, possible initial performance problems and limited availability.

(b) **The partially new product**, such as the DVD player. The main mark of such a product is that it performs better than the equivalent old product.

(c) **Major product change**, such as the digital camera. Marks of such a product are radical technological change altering the accepted concept of the order of things (eg no need to get your films developed: print them out at home or share them via e-mail!).

(d) **Minor product change**, such as styling changes. The motor industry does this all the time.

3.4 Generating ideas and developing new products

New products should only be taken to advanced development if there is evidence of:

- **Adequate demand**
- Compatibility with existing **marketing ability**
- Compatibility with existing **production ability**

 MARKETING AT WORK

application

Jobber (2009) cites a study of 60 innovations and the key success factors behind them. The key findings were:

1   There must be delivery of added consumer value.

2   'Speed to market' counts – generally this means that a company must launch its idea within a year of its inception, in order to beat others and get into the market before tastes change.

3   Inferiority in the value offered cannot be masked by high communications spending. In fact, that will make it worse: 'advertising makes bad products fail quicker'.

The stages of new product (or service) development are as follows.

Figure 1.8 NPD

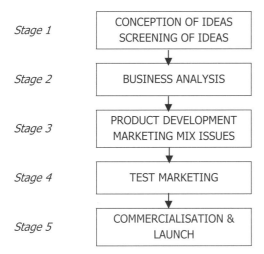

The mortality rate of new products is very high. To reduce the risk of failure new product ideas must be screened. Only the best will make it to the next development stage.

3.4.1 Conception and screening of ideas

The **concept** for the new product could be **tested on potential customers** to obtain their reactions. Some caution does need to be exercised when interpreting the results however.

(a)   When innovative new designs are tested on potential customers it is often found that they are conditioned by traditional designs and are dismissive of new design ideas.

(b)   However, testers may say they like the new concept at the testing stage, but when the new product is launched it is not successful because people continue to buy old favourites.

3.4.2 Business analysis

A thorough business analysis is required for each product idea, projecting future sales and revenues, giving a description of the product so as to provide costs of production, providing estimates of sales promotion and advertising costs, the resources required, profits and return on investment. Other factors such as the product life cycle, legal restrictions, competitors' reactions etc must also be evaluated. Products which pass the business evaluation will be developed. A timetable and a budget of both resources required and cost must be prepared, so that management control can be applied to the development project.

3.4.3 Product development

Money is invested to produce a working **prototype** of the product, which can be tried by customers. This stage ensures that the product can be produced in sufficient quantities at the right price. The form which the product **test** takes will depend very much on the type of product concerned. The test should replicate reality as closely as possible.

(a)   If the product is used in the home, a sample of respondents should be given the product to use at home.

(b)   If the product is chosen from amongst competitors in a retail outlet (as with chocolate bars), then the product test needs to rate response against competitive products.

(c)   If inherent product quality is an important attribute of the product, then a 'blind' test could be used.

(d)   An industrial product could be used for a trial period by a customer in a realistic setting.

The marketing mix for the product will need to be planned at this stage.

3.4.4 Test marketing

The purpose of **test marketing** is to obtain information about how consumers react to the product. Will they buy it, and if so, will they buy it again? With this information an estimate of total market demand for the product can be made.

A market test involves implementing marketing plans in selected areas which are thought to be 'representative' of the total market. In the selected areas, the firm will attempt to distribute the product through the same types of sales outlets it plans to use in the full market launch, and also to use the intended advertising and promotion plans.

3.4.5 Commercialisation and launch

Finally the product is developed for **full launch**. This involves ensuring that the product is in the right place at the right time, and that customers know about it.

3.5 Standardisation versus adaptation

3.5.1 Factors encouraging product standardisation

(a)   **Economies of scale**

-     Production
-     Marketing/communications
-     Research and development
-     Stock holding

(b)   Easier management and **control**

(c)   **Homogeneity** of markets, in other words world markets available without adaptation (eg denim jeans).

(d)   **Cultural insensitivity**, eg industrial components and agricultural products.

(e)   **Consumer mobility** means that standardisation is expected in certain products.

-     Camera film
-     Hotel chains

(f)   Where **'made in'** image is important to a product's perceived value (eg France for perfume, Sheffield for stainless steel).

(g)   For a firm selling a **small proportion** of its output overseas, the incremental adaptation costs may exceed the incremental sales value.

(h)   Products that are positioned at the **high end of the spectrum** in terms of price, prestige and scarcity are more likely to have a standardised mix.

3.5.2 Factors encouraging adaptation/modification

Mandatory product modification normally involves either adaptation to comply with government requirements or unavoidable technical changes. Using car manufacture as an example it may concern:

(a)   **Legal requirements**

-     Health and safety law
-     Economic law

(b)   **Technical requirements** such as:

-     Modification of heating/cooling systems for different climates
-     Engine modification to use locally available fuels

Discretionary modification is called for only to make the product more appealing in different markets. It results from differing customer needs, preferences and tastes. These differences become apparent from market research and analysis, intermediary and customer feedback etc.

(a)   Levels of customer **purchasing power**. Low incomes may make a cheap version of the product more attractive in some less developed economies.

(b)   **Levels of education** and technical sophistication. Ease of use may be a crucial factor in decision making.

(c)   Standards of **maintenance/repair** facilities. Simpler, more robust versions may be needed.

(d)   **'Culture-bound' products** such as clothing, food and home decoration are more likely to have an adapted marketing mix.

These strategies can be exercised at global and national level, depending on the type of product.

Not all products are suitable for standardisation.

 MARKETING AT WORK application

Take the example of Cadbury-Schweppes which deals with chocolate and soft drinks.

(a)   The UK consumer's taste in chocolate is not shared by most European consumers, who prefer a higher proportion of cocoa-butter in the final product. Marketing Cadbury's UK brands of chocolate on a Europe-wide basis would not seem to be appropriate: instead the acquisition of a European company would be the best way to expand into this market. The UK is thus a segment of a global market with its unique needs.

(b)   The market for soft drinks on the other hand is different, with Schweppes tonic water well established as a brand across Europe.

3.6 Patterns of adoption

 Commenting on adoption, Blythe (2006) notes:

"New products are not immediately adopted by all consumers. Some consumers are driven to buy new products almost as soon as they become available, whereas others prefer to wait until the product has been around for a while before risking their hard-earned money on it".

 KEY CONCEPT concept

The **diffusion** of a new product refers to the spread of information about the product in the market place. **Adoption** is the process by which consumers incorporate the product into their buying patterns.

The classification of adopters is shown below.

Figure 1.9 Adoption of new products

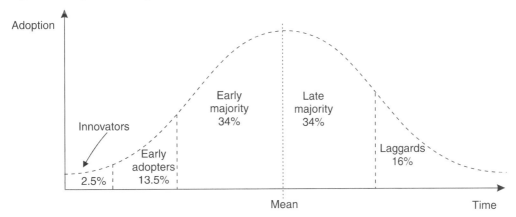

The types of adopters are described below.

Innovators – these are people who like to own the latest products, and value being the 'first' to have them amongst their group of friends and family members.

Early adopters – these people are open to new ideas, but they prefer to wait and see how the product goes after its initial launch, and to observe the experience of the innovators

Early majority – these will buy the product when they are sure that there is no risk with the product

Late majority – of similar numbers to early majority, the late majority will only buy the new product when most other people already have one

Laggards – these people adopt products only when they have no choice but to do so

Innovators and **early adopters** are thought to operate as 'opinion leaders' and are therefore targeted by companies in order to influence the adoption of a product by their friends.

The main problem with this model is that the categories appear to add up to 100% of the target market. This does not reflect marketers' experience. Some potential consumers do not adopt/purchase at all. It has consequently been suggested that an additional category is needed: **non-adopters**, or **non-consumers**.

Learning objectives	Covered
1 Critically evaluate the process for managing and developing an organisation's product portfolio to deliver best value products for customers in different market segments and achieve organisational and marketing objectives	☑ Definitions of 'product' (1.1)
	☑ Product management, customer value and competitive advantage (1.2)
	☑ Product portfolios (1.3)
	☑ Product profitability (1.4)
	☑ Product life cycle (1.5)
	☑ BCG & General Electric model (1.6)
2 Critically evaluate the role of branding in the context of the product portfolio, recommending different branding strategies which are appropriate to a range of organisational contexts and sectors	☑ Importance of 'the brand' (2.1)
	☑ Developing and building brand value (2.2)
	☑ Rebranding (2.3)
	☑ International and global brands (2.4)
	☑ Brand strategies (2.5)
3 Critically evaluate the role and process of innovation and new product development including consideration of innovative, replacement, re-launched and imitative products and explain the strategic benefit in achieving best value	☑ Developing a culture of innovation (3.1)
	☑ The role of innovation (3.2)
	☑ Rejuvenating existing products (3.3)
	☑ Generating ideas and developing new products (3.4)
	☑ Standardisation versus adaptation (3.5)
	☑ Patterns of adoption (3.6)

1   What is the 'symbolic' aspect of a product?

2   How would you define 'value'?

3   What is an 'augmented' product?

4   What is 'brand extension'?

5   Fill in the blanks:

'In the context of the BCG matrix, a 'problem child' has _____ market share in a _____ industry. A 'cash cow' has _____ market share in a _____ industry.'

6   What might happen if a declining product stays on the market for too long?

7   'The traditional bell-shaped curve of a product life cycle does not always occur in practice'. What does this mean?

8   What do you understand by the term 'brand repositioning'?

9   What is the sequence for new product development?

10   What is 'ethnocentrism'?

11   What is the difference between 'testing a concept' on consumers, and 'test marketing'?

12   What buying behaviour characterises the 'late majority'?

1   This depends upon the products you have chosen. The table in paragraph 1.1.3 should have helped if you were stuck for inspiration.

2   You could perhaps pin down some of these items, but most are open to discussion, especially if you take an international perspective. For many you may consider that the PLC is not valid, and you will not be alone, as the discussion within the chapter has shown.

3   Here are some suggestions.

- Brillo (scouring pads) – 'brilliant', shining, clean
- Pampers (baby nappies) – comforting, caring, soft
- Cussons Imperial Leather (soap) – quality, tradition, masculinity
- Kerrygold (butter) – Ireland, farmland, high quality, sunshine, yellow
- Hush Puppies (shoes) – comfort, softness, friendliness

4   In a recession, there are likely to be fewer customers for premium goods. Sales of luxury brands may decline, but it is sometimes the case that the very high end customers who purchase such items are less susceptible to the effects of recession (with its job losses, mortgage stress etc) and have a higher net wealth that enables them to continue spending. It all depends upon individual circumstances. Those consumers who aspire to the luxury brands, but can only afford them once in a while, are more likely to be deterred.

5   Here are some suggestions.

- Product replacements – the Nintendo Wii replacing the Gamecube; one car model replacing another

- Additions to existing lines – Sony introducing a cheap video camera to challenge the 'Flip'; cereal brand extensions

- New product lines – a car maker introducing a brand new model to its range; Mars launching ice cream products

- 'New to the market' – the development of online data backup services as an alternative to using disks or other storage media; hand held games consoles

---

1   The symbolic aspect of a product represents the qualities that the product suggests to buyers – for example, a label stating 'low in fat' will suggest health benefits.

2   Value is the worth of the product or service – what is costs to produce and what a customer is willing to pay for it.

3   An augmented product is the core product plus those extra benefits such as guarantees or after-sales support, that can differentiate it from other products in the category.

4   Brand extension is the introduction of new flavours, sizes etc to a brand, to build upon existing brand loyalty.

5   A 'problem child' has small market share in a high growth industry. A 'cash cow' has high market share in a low growth industry.

6   It may decline to such an extent that it becomes obsolete, taken over by innovative new products. This is possibly what is happening to older style 'cathode ray tube' (CRT) televisions, with the market being taken over by LCD and plasma models.

7   The classic pattern is not always followed. Some products have no maturity phase and go straight from growth to decline. Others have a second growth period after an initial decline. Some have virtually no introductory period and go straight into a rapid growth phase, while others do not succeed at all.

8   'Repositioning' is a strategy aimed at changing market position in order to increase market share.

9   The NPD sequence typically includes: conception; screening of ideas; business analysis; product development and marketing mix planning; test marketing; and commercialisation and launch.

10   'Ethnocentrism' is one kind of approach to international marketing and the desired degree of adaptation to local tastes and markets. An ethnocentrist approach views overseas operations as being of secondary consideration to domestic operations, with little or no modification of the product to suit local needs. There is little market research and the overseas market is often merely a dumping ground for unwanted surplus.

BPP LEARNING MEDIA

11 'Testing a concept' involves gauging initial reactions to the product before committing resources to further development. 'Test marketing' follows that development, and involves implementing marketing plans in selected areas which are thought to be representative of the total market.

12 The late majority will only buy a new product when most other people already have one.

Blythe, J (2009) <u>Principles and Practice of Marketing</u>, 2nd edition, South-Western/Cengage Learning.

Blythe, J (2008) <u>Essentials of Marketing</u>,4th edition, FT Prentice Hall.

Brassington, F and Pettitt, S (2006) <u>Principles of Marketing</u>, 4th edition, FT Prentice Hall.

Jobber (2009) <u>Principles and Practice of Marketing</u>.6th edition, McGraw Hill Higher Education

Kotler, P. & Armstrong, G. (2003) <u>Principles of Marketing</u> (10th edition). New Jersey: Prentice Hall, New Jersey.

Levitt, T. (1983) *'The Globalization of Markets'* Harvard Business Review, May/June 1983.

Ohmae, K. (1999) <u>The Borderless World: Power and Strategy in the Interlinked Economy</u>, Rev. Ed, Harper Business, New York.

Porter, M.E. (1980) <u>Competitive Strategy</u>, Free Press, New York.

Sodhi, M.S. & Tang, C.S. *'Rethinking links in the global supply chain'*, FT.com Special Reports, 29 January 2009.

Steenkamp, Jan-Benedict E. M. & Dekimpe, Marnik G. *'Marketing strategies for fast moving consumer goods'*, FT.com Special Reports 5 February 2009.

Chapter 2
Pricing and value

Topic list

1   Product positioning
2   Price perception
3   Pricing frameworks

Introduction

This chapter explores the importance of pricing in the achievement of 'value' for the organisation and the customer. There are various factors at work.

Product positioning (section 1) is an important aspect of understanding customer value, and this positioning is upheld (or undermined) by customer perceptions of the product (section 2). Perceptual maps enable organisations to identify their product positioning options. Companies competing in several segments normally adopt a differentiated marketing mix. They 'position' themselves on price-quality spectrums and other marketing mix variables relative to competitors.

Pricing decisions (section 3) are important to the firm. This may be stating the obvious, but it is worth making it clear that pricing is very important as it is the only element of the marketing mix which generates income, revenue and profits, rather than creating costs. All profit organisations, and many non-profit ones, face the task of pricing their products or services. Price can go by many names: fares, fees, rent, assessments etc.

Price was once the single most important decision made by the sales department. Today, though, marketing managers view price as just one of the factors involved in customer value and satisfaction. In fact it is sometimes suggested that marketing aims to make price relatively unimportant to the consumer's decision-making process. There is certainly some truth in this view. The other elements of the marketing mix are concerned with adding value to the product and tailoring it to the consumers' needs, to ensure that the choice between two products is not simply based on their different prices.

Syllabus linked learning objectives

By the end of the chapter you will be able to:

Learning objectives	Syllabus link
1 Assess the links between product development, product positioning and pricing in terms of fit and alignment with an organisation's corporate and marketing strategies and customer requirements	1.4
2 Critically evaluate the importance of linking the product portfolio to price perception to ensure perceived value for money as part of the overall customer proposition	1.5
3 Assess pricing frameworks that could be utilised by organisations to aid decision making about product lifecycles, product development and innovation	1.6

1 Product positioning

According to Jobber (2009)

"Positioning is the choice of:

- *Target market – where we want to compete*
- *Differential advantage – how we wish to compete"*

1.1 Positioning new products

KEY CONCEPT

concept

Positioning is how a product appears (how it is perceived by the market) in relation to other products in the market. It is the act of designing the company's offer and image so that it offers a distinct and valued place in the target customer's mind.

The 'positioning' of a product or brand is defined in terms of how consumers/customers perceive key characteristics of the product. Possible positioning characteristics include:

- Specific product features, eg price, speed, ease of use

- Benefits, problems, solutions, or needs

- Specific usage occasions

- User category, such as age or gender

- How it compares against another product, eg comparison with a market leader

- Product class disassociation ('stand-out' features from the general mass of products), eg organic food, lead-free petrol, hypo-allergenic cosmetics

- Hybrid basis: a combination of any of the above

Market perceptions can be plotted on product maps, to suggest marketing opportunities, brand perception and competitive position. The following basic **perceptual map** is used to plot brands in perceived price and perceived quality terms.

Figure 2.1 Price/quality matrix

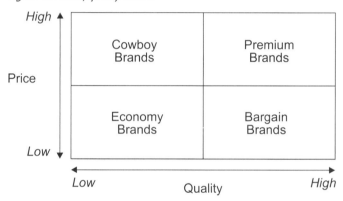

Most consumers will not see price and quality as independent variables. A 'high' price will usually be associated with high quality, and low price with low quality.

Market research can determine where customers perceive competitive brands in relation to each other, and in relation to target characteristics, and any perceived gaps in the market can be identified on a perceptual map.

Figure 2.2 Perceptual map for restaurant brand

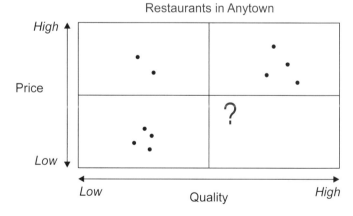

 ACTIVITY 1   application

What is indicated by the perceptual map above?

Competitive positioning concerns implementing a general idea of what kind of offer a company should make to the target market in relation to competitors' offers.

Kotler identified a 3 × 3 matrix of nine different competitive positioning strategies.

	Product price		
Product quality	*High*	*Medium*	*Low*
High	Premium strategy	Penetration strategy	Superbargain strategy
Medium	Overpricing strategy	Average quality strategy	Bargain strategy
Low	Hit-and-run strategy	Shoddy goods strategy	Cheap goods strategy

Once selected, the needs of the targeted segment can be identified and the marketing mix strategy developed to provide the benefits package needed to satisfy them. Positioning the product offering then becomes a matter of matching and communicating appropriate benefits.

The perceptual map below shows how the shoe market might be depicted.

Figure 2.3 Perceptual map

1.1.2 Steps in positioning

Step 1   Identify differentiating factors in products or services in relation to competitors

Step 2   Select the most important differences

Step 3   Communicate the position to the target market

1.2 Positioning strategies

The foundation of a positioning strategy is to align what the company can do with **what customers want**.

1.2.1 How much do people remember about a product or brand?

(a)   Many products are, in fact, very similar, and the key issue is to make them **distinct in the customer's mind**.

(b) People remember 'number 1', so the product should be positioned as 'number 1' in relation to a valued attribute.

(c) Cosmetic changes can have the effect of **repositioning** the product in the customer's mind. To be effective, however, this **psychological positioning** has to be **reinforced by real positioning**. If it is not, then errors in positioning can occur.

Mistake	Consequence
Underpositioning	The brand does not have a clear identity in the eyes of the customer
Overpositioning	Buyers may have too narrow an image of a brand
Confused positioning	Too many claims might be made for a brand
Doubtful positioning	The positioning may not be credible in the eyes of the buyer

1.2.2 Repositioning

This will often be required because of changing customer tastes, or poor sales. Jobber (2009) identifies four generic repositioning strategies.

(a) **Image repositioning**. The product and the target market is the same, but the image is revamped, such as when the supermodel Kate Moss began advertising Burberry.

(b) **Product repositioning**. The product is changed, but the target market remains the same, such as McDonalds 'Happy Meals' for children now including healthier options.

(c) **Intangible repositioning**. Targeting a different market segment with the same product, such as aiming games consoles at a wider audience with the Nintendo Wii/DS.

(d) **Tangible repositioning**. When both product and target market are changed, such as Sony selling cheaper hand held camcorders to compete with the 'Flip'.

2 Price perception

According to Jobber (2009)

"It is ... essential that managers understand how to set prices, because both undercharging (lost margin) and overcharging (lost sales) can have dramatic effects on profitability."

2.1 The role of pricing in product management

KEY CONCEPT

concept

Price can be defined as a measure of the value exchanged by the buyer for the value offered by the seller.

Although it has been suggested that marketing aims to make price relatively unimportant to the consumer's decision-making process, the role of price in the marketing mix should not be underestimated. It contributes towards the organisation's business and financial objectives in the following ways.

• Pricing is the only element of the mix which generates **revenue** rather than creating costs.

• It also has an important role as a **competitive tool** to differentiate a product and organisation, and thereby exploit market opportunities.

• Pricing must be consistent with other elements of the marketing mix, since it contributes to the **overall image** created for the product.

ACTIVITY 2

application

In what circumstances would you expect price to be the main factor influencing a consumer's choice?

2.2 'Value for money' and price sensitivity

Subjective perception is important in the way customers react to price and price changes.

There is a close relationship between 'value' and 'price'. The creation of 'value for money' in the mind of the customer is a goal of marketing-orientated companies, in order to attract and retain customers. The complete 'delivery system' achieves this, and price is just one part. Value for money can come from many aspects (such as food quality, service levels and cleanliness in a restaurant).

Customer value = the perceived benefits from the purchase (eg taste, service, image) <u>minus</u> the perceived sacrifice in making it (cost, time energy risk)

The more value a product gives in comparison to the competition, the higher the price that can be charged.

KEY CONCEPT

application

Price sensitivity refers to the effect a change in price will have on customers.

Price sensitivity will vary amongst purchasers. Those who can pass on the cost of purchases will be least sensitive, and will respond more to other elements of the marketing mix.

(a)   Provided that the price fits the corporate budget, the business traveller will be more concerned about an hotel's level of service and quality of food. In contrast, a family on holiday are likely to be very price sensitive when choosing an overnight stay.

(b)   In industrial marketing, the purchasing manager is likely to be more price sensitive than the engineer who might be the actual user of new equipment. The engineer places product characteristics as first priority, the purchasing manager is more price oriented.

Research on price sensitivity of customers has shown that in general the following apply.

*   Customers have a good concept of a **'just price'** – a feel for what is fair for the benefits offered.

*   For **special purchases**, customers search for price information before buying, become price aware when wanting to buy, but forget soon afterwards.

*   Customers will buy at what they consider to be a **bargain price**, without full regard for their present needs and the level of the price itself.

*   **Down payment and instalment price** are more important than total price.

*   In times of rising prices, the **price image** tends to lag behind the current price.

*   If there are **substitute goods**, especially close substitutes, customers will be more sensitive to price. For example, in a greengrocer's shop, a rise in the price of one fruit such as apples or pears is likely to result in a switch of customer demand to other fruits, many fruits being fairly close substitutes for each other.

*   Over **time**, consumers' demand patterns are likely to change. If the price of something is increased, the initial response might be a small change in demand. But as consumers adjust their buying habits in response to the price increase, demand might fall substantially.

With the general economic downturn, consumers are becoming even more price sensitive. Companies such as Ryanair, Zara, Aldi and Wal-Mart, with their avowed commitment to low prices and their large buying power, are amongst the firms most likely to benefit.

2.3 Price changes

In a highly competitive world, pricing is dynamic – managers need to know when and how to raise or lower prices, and whether or not to react to competitor price moves." (Jobber)

Price increases and cuts can be implemented in many ways – a direct jump or fall does it all in one go, but customers notice! Staged approaches might try customer patience. In the Internet age, people are increasingly price sensitive and more easily able to make price comparisons. More and more are questioning both the wisdom and necessity of paying top dollar.

3 Pricing frameworks

Jobber (2009) notes:

"Since price is a major determinant of profitability, developing a coherent pricing strategy assumes major significance."

3.1 Price versus cost

In practice, cost is the most important influence on price. In **cost-based pricing**, costs are estimated and then a profit margin is added to set the price. There are a number of reasons for the predominance of cost-based pricing.

- Easier assessment of performance
- Emulation of successful large companies
- Belief by management in a 'fair return' policy
- Fear of government action against 'excessive' profits
- Tradition of production orientation rather than marketing orientation
- Tacit collusion in industry to avoid competition
- Easier planning and administration of cost-based pricing strategies based on internal data

There are two types of cost-based pricing: **full cost pricing** and **cost-plus pricing**. We return to cost-based pricing later in the chapter.

Look at the following wording used in an advertisement for SWATCH (watches).

> ### *FROM PLASTIC TO PLATINUM*
>
> ### *WORLDWIDE*
>
> ### *INDIVIDUALLY NUMBERED LIMITED*
>
> ### *EDITION OF 12,999*
>
> ### *£1,000 INC VAT*
>
> - *Most exclusive Swatch ever produced.*
> - *950 Platinum case and crown.*
> - *Stainless steel presentation case with acrylic glass inlay.*
> - *Interchangeable royal blue leather and padded plastic straps.*
> - *Limited availability in the UK.*

Suggest how Swatch might have chosen the price of £1,000.

If you are not familiar with the brand you may find it helpful to refer to www.swatch.com.

3.2 Factors determining pricing levels

Pricing decisions are affected by a range of factors, both internal (to the organisation) and external (in the competitive environment).

Internal factors	External factors
• **Marketing objectives**: profit maximisation; market share leadership; brand targeting and positioning	• **Competition:** the extent of competition in the market; whether there is non-price competition; competitor pricing and promotions
• **Marketing mix strategy**: factoring in the cost/price implications of quality, distribution, brand differentiation	• **Demand**: the sensitivity of customer demand for the product to change in price (elasticity of demand) in the given market
• **Costs**: setting the lowest viable price at which the company can afford to sell the product.	• **Customer perceptions** of price and what it means for quality and value
• **Price-setting methodologies**: negotiated by sales force; set by management	• **Suppliers and intermediaries**: impact on costs; their reaction to price decisions to protect their own margins
• **Product portfolio strategies**: launch/new-product incentive pricing; 'loss leaders' to support the product range	• **PEST factors**: economic factors determining affordability; government price watchdogs; social responsibility dictating affordability; changing perceptions of 'value'; technology lowering production costs.

Pricing decisions are guided by one or other of two business objectives.

Maximise profits	Maintain or increase market share
Charge as **high** a price as possible. This depends on how good the product is and how much demand is affected by higher prices.	Charge a **lower** price than competitors, or the **same** price. This would be appropriate if an organisation wants to hold on to existing customers and/or attract new ones.

Either approach may be used in specifying pricing objectives, and they may appear in combination. It is important that pricing objectives are consistent with overall **corporate objectives**: you might not want to raise prices, for example, if the corporate objective is to be an accessible, ethical low-cost provider of essential services.

3.2.1 Other factors influencing pricing decisions

Several factors influence the pricing decisions of an organisation.

(a) **Intermediaries' objectives**

If an organisation distributes products or services to the market through independent intermediaries, the objectives of these intermediaries have an effect on the pricing decision. Intermediaries aim to maximise their own profits rather than those of suppliers. Conflict over price can arise between suppliers and intermediaries which may be difficult to resolve.

Many industries have traditional margins for intermediaries. To deviate from these might well cause problems for suppliers. In some industries, notably grocery retailing, the power of intermediaries allows them to dictate terms to suppliers.

(b) **Competitors' actions and reactions**

An organisation, in setting prices, sends out signals to competitors and they are likely to react in some way. In some industries (such as petrol retailing) pricing moves in unison. In others, price changes by one provider may initiate a **price war**, with each provider attempting to undercut the others.

(c) **Suppliers**

An organisation's suppliers may attempt to increase prices on the basis that the buying organisation is able to pay a higher price. (This argument is sometimes used by trade unions negotiating the price for the supply of labour.)

(d) **Quality, customer satisfaction and value**

In the absence of other information, customers tend to judge quality by price. A price change may send signals to customers concerning the quality of the product. A rise may be taken to indicate improvements, a reduction may signal reduced quality. Any change in price needs to take such factors into account.

(e) **New product pricing**

Most pricing decisions for existing products concern price changes, which have a **reference point** from which to move (the existing price). A new product has no reference points. It may be possible to seek alternative reference points, such as the price in another market where the new product has already been launched, or the price set by a competitor.

(f) **The economy**

In times of **rising incomes**, price may become a less important marketing variable. When income levels are falling and/or unemployment levels rising, price will become more important. In periods of **inflation** the organisation's prices may need to change in order to pass on increases in the prices of supplies, labour, rent and other overheads.

(g) **Product range**

Most organisations market not just one product but a range of products. The management of the pricing function is likely to focus on the profit from the whole range, using low-cost products to attract customers, who can then be encouraged to buy related products with higher profit margins.

(h) **Social responsibility**

Ethical considerations are involved, such as whether to exploit short-term shortages (or life-and-death products such as some pharmaceuticals) through higher prices.

(i) **Government**

Some organisations are compelled by government to charge certain prices. For instance, in the UK Ofgas regulates prices charged by gas suppliers.

MARKETING AT WORK

application

Customers and competitors now have greater access to price information. Firms could view the many online price comparison sites as a threat, especially if their products or retail outlets comes out as the most expensive!

One of many examples of a price comparison site is DealTime (www.dealtime.co.uk) where you can check the prices of dozens of products. Categories include Appliances (Fridges, Vacuum Cleaners, Washing Machines, etc), Books, Cars (Motor Insurance, Car Loans), Used Cars, Computers, Electronics (Digital Cameras, DVD Players, Televisions, etc), Finance (Loans, Life Insurance, Insurance, etc), Flowers & Wine, Health & Beauty (Women's Fragrance, Face Makeup, Skin Care, etc), Home & Garden, Jewellery, Lingerie , Mobile Phones, Software, Toys & Games, Travel Insurance, Hotels, Car Hire, Video Games.

Several online catalogues use price in a way that has not been so easily available before. For instance, if you need to buy a gift for someone and have no bright ideas you can visit the website of, say, Argos, click on Gifts, and specify the price you want to pay and the sort of person you're buying for (toddler, teenager, 'for him', for her', etc) and be presented with lots of ideas.

Also relevant here is the growth of online auctions. Effectively this means that the customer decides the price (s)he is willing to pay.

The use of ICT may also enable suppliers to reduce prices (especially for products/services sold online), because of the reduction in sales and administration costs enabled by 'self-service' marketing, e-commerce, m-commerce (using mobile phones) and telephone ordering. There are often special discounts available if customers order online, for example.

3.3 Pricing and satisfaction of customer demand

KEY CONCEPT

concept

Demand is defined as a want which can be paid for.

Prices may be based on the intensity of demand: strong demand may lead to a high price, and weak demand to a low price. The concept of **price elasticity** illustrates how demand can be affected by price changes.

3.3.1 Price elasticity of demand

In classical economic theory, price is the major determinant of demand. More recently, emphasis has been placed on other factors. The significance of other elements of the marketing mix (product quality, promotion, personal selling, distribution and brands) has grown.

KEY CONCEPT

concept

Price elasticity of demand is measured as:

$$\frac{\% \text{ change in sales demand}}{\% \text{ chage in sales price}}$$

As you might expect, 'elasticity' indicates how much demand will 'stretch' or how far a change in price will affect demand. The more elastic demand is, the more demand will *increase* if you *lower* the price slightly – and the more demand will *decrease* if you *raise* the price slightly. In other words, if demand is elastic, buyers are very sensitive to price and price changes: if it is inelastic, price is not a key factor in demand.

British Gas announced its first price cut for six years in February 2007. The group apparently signed up 678,000 customers since those original cuts were announced – having lost a million in 2006 after record-breaking price rises, which saw its share of the gas market fall below 50% for the first time ever.

The new round of cuts came just days after it emerged that complaints about British Gas had more than trebled in the past year, due to teething troubles with a new billing system.

Three competitors immediately followed with cuts of their own. The two competitors who kept their rates unchanged were 'slammed' by energy regulator Ofgem, which urged customers to switch to a cheaper supplier!

3.3.2 Price discrimination

A firm might successfully charge higher prices for the same product to people who are willing to pay more. This is called **price discrimination**, or **differential pricing**.

By market segment	By product version	By time
A cross-channel ferry company would market its services at different prices in England, Belgium and France. Services such as cinemas and hairdressers are often available at lower prices to senior citizens and/or students.	Software is written top-down and the full version is sold at a premium price. For less advanced users all the software company has to do is take features out: there is little extra cost.	Travel companies are successful price discriminators, charging more to rush-hour commuters whose demand is inelastic at certain times of the day. Other examples are off-peak travel bargains or telephone charges.

Price discrimination will only be effective under certain conditions.

(a) The market must be **segmentable** in price terms, and different sectors must show **different intensities of demand**. Each of the sectors must be identifiable, distinct and separate from the others, and be accessible to the firm's marketing communications.

(b) There must be little or no chance of a **black market** developing, so that those in the lower priced segment can resell to those in the higher priced segment.

(c) There must be little chance that competitors can/will **undercut** the firm's prices in the higher priced (and/or most profitable) market segments.

(d) The **cost** of segmenting and administering the arrangements should not exceed the extra revenue derived from the price discrimination strategy.

3.4 Pricing and competition

Prices may be set on the basis of what competitors are charging, rather than on the basis of cost or demand. This sometimes results in '**going rate**' pricing. Some form of average level of price becomes the norm, including standard price differentials between brands.

3.4.1 Price as a competitive tool

In established industries dominated by a few major firms, it is generally accepted that a price initiative by one firm will be countered by a price reaction by competitors. Consequently, in industries such as breakfast cereals (dominated in Britain by Kellogg's, Nabisco and Quaker) or canned soups (Heinz, Crosse & Blackwell and Campbell's) a certain **price stability** might be expected without too many competitive price initiatives.

A firm may respond to **competitor price cuts** in a number of ways.

(a) **Maintain existing prices**, if the expectation is that only a small market share would be lost, so that it is more profitable to keep prices at their existing level. Eventually, the rival firm may drop out of the market or be forced to raise its prices.

(b) **Maintain prices but respond with a non-price counter-attack**. This is a more positive response, because the firm will be securing or justifying its price differential with product quality, improved back-up services etc.

(c) **Reduce prices**, to protect the firm's market share. The main beneficiary from the price reduction will be the consumer.

(d) **Raise prices and respond with a non-price counter-attack**. The extra revenue from the higher prices might be used to finance the promotion of product improvements, which in turn would justify the price rise to customers.

3.4.2 Price leadership

KEY CONCEPT

concept

Price leaders are firms whose market share and share of the capacity in the industry are great enough for them to be able to set the prices in the market.

A **price leader** will dominate price levels for a class of products: increases or decreases by the price leader provide a direction to market price patterns. The price-dominant firm may lead without moving at all. (This would be the case if other firms sought to raise prices and the leader did not follow: then the upward move in prices would be halted.)

The role of price leader is based on a track record of having initiated price moves that have been accepted by both competitors and customers. Often, this is associated with a mature, well established management group, efficient production and a reputation for technical competence. A price leader generally has a large, if not necessarily the largest, market share.

3.4.3 Non-price competition

In some market structures, price competition may be avoided by tacit agreement, leading to concentration on **non-price competition**: the markets for cigarettes and petrol are examples of this. Price-setting here is influenced by the need to avoid retaliatory responses by competitors, which could result in a breakdown of the tacit agreement and profit-reducing price competition. Price changes based on real cost changes are led in many instances by a 'representative' firm in the industry, followed by other firms.

Whether agreements exist at all is hard to prove: competitors are exposed to the same market forces and so might be expected to set similar prices. This is a problem for government agencies, such as the Office of Fair Trading, when attempting to establish if unethical pricing agreements exist.

3.4.4 Competitive bidding

Competitive bidding is a special case of competition-based pricing. Many supply contracts, especially concerning local and national government purchases (where it is compulsory) involve would-be suppliers submitting a sealed bid or **tender**.

The firm's submitted price needs to take account of expected competitor bid prices. Often the firms involved will not even know the identity of their rivals but successful past bids are often published by purchasers and it is possible to use this data to calculate a realistic bid. Many use the concept of expected profit:

Expected profit = Profit × Probability of winning the tender

3.5 Pricing and value

Although price is the only element of the marketing mix that generates revenue, it has, in addition to its economic function, a symbolic function. A price conveys information about something.

Price is used as a surrogate for quality. In other words some people assume that something of a high price must be of a high quality.

Furthermore, it can be argued that the price of something does not necessarily reflect the actual cost to the user of 'consuming' the product.

(a) DIY equipment is popular as people prefer to spend the time on home improvements rather than, for example, working overtime to earn the money to hire somebody to do the job professionally. In the user's eyes, the price of DIY equipment is very favourable compared with getting a building firm to do the job.

(b) Is there a national preference for disposable items? For example, in a country where people move home every five years, there are disadvantages in getting a high price high quality cooker, say, with a long life span, as it is inconvenient to transport it to a new house where it might not fit in.

High prices often have a 'snob' value (the Veblen effect: snobbish consumers prefer high prices).

To counter this, customers have recently begun demanding high quality and high levels of service at low prices. This is a relatively new phenomenon and is demonstrated clearly with new cars and mobile phones. In the mobile phone market high levels of competition between many dealers have allowed the customer to become more demanding of features such as free calls and the abolition of peak/off-peak tariff systems.

3.6 Pricing for international markets

Firms can adopt three approaches to pricing goods exported from the home market. These are explained below.

 KEY CONCEPT concept

(a) **Standardised, ethnocentric pricing**. A single price is charged to recover costs and earn the return. As this is translated at local exchange rates, this can lead to price volatility in local terms and a lower volume of sales than would be possible. The demand curve in the overseas market may differ, and using a fixed standard price may not result in a maximised marginal revenue in the overseas market.

(b) **Adaptation or polycentric pricing**. Each local subsidiary sets its own prices. There is no co-ordination. Headquarters has no control, and 'grey markets' develop.

(c) **Geocentric pricing** aims for a global pricing strategy, but in the short term at least (eg introducing a new product) local subsidiaries have some autonomy.

International pricing is affected both by a company's own objectives and a variety of external factors.

(a) The **company's marketing pricing objectives**.

(i)	**Financial**	– cash generation, profit, return on investment
(ii)	**Marketing**	– maintain/improve market share – skim/penetrate depending on stage in product life cycle
(iii)	**Competitive**	– prevent new entry – follow competition – market stabilisation (tacit agreements)
(iv)	**Product differentiation**	– high price aids perception of product differences

A company may have **different objectives in different markets** and may thus need to adopt different pricing policies. For example, in one market early cash recovery may be the objective leading to premium pricing. In another larger market, the objective might be longer-term market share, suggesting a more penetrative pricing strategy.

(b)   **Level of demand**. This is influenced by the market's state of economic development, stage in the product life cycle and cultural attitudes. Relatively low prices would be suitable in the following circumstances.

- In markets of low economic development
- In the maturity/saturation stages of the product life cycle
- Where the product is perceived as a basic one

(c)   The **intensity of competition**, both domestic and international.

(d)   **Cost**.

(e)   **Government restrictions** and controls. Many governments have both maximum and minimum permitted prices for certain products.

(f)   The number and type of **intermediaries** in the distribution channel.

(g)   **Pricing in foreign currency.** A sales value in a company's home currency is uncertain due to exchange rate fluctuations.

The price of a good is something definite, but this should not blind us to some of the cultural implications which can affect its use in the marketing mix in different countries. This does not mean that the economic factors in pricing are unimportant - quite the opposite - but culture does enable a firm to 'tinker at the margins'.

We are used to fixed prices in the West for many goods largely because the relationship between the customer and supplier is often impersonal.

(a)   **Bargaining** still exists for certain purchases.

(i)   On the one hand, the end **consumer** does not bargain over the price of a Mars bar, a packet of aspirin tablets or a newspaper.

(ii)   On the other hand, buying or selling a used car through a newspaper advert, say, often involves bargaining to arrive at a mutually acceptable figure.

(b)   Bargaining still exists in industrial marketing, under the name of volume discounts etc. After all, Michael Porter refers to the **bargaining** powers of customers and suppliers.

In developing countries, bargaining is often still the rule. Time is not a scarce resource, but money is. There are many rituals involved in bargaining. The key lesson for international marketers is that in a society where bargaining is the norm, price may end up being determined by local short-term considerations.

The cost structure of any firm is a major factor in determining price. This is true of exporters, but they must also take other costs into account which will impact the final price at which the product can be sold for a profit.

- Additional **transport** costs
- **Insurance and storage**
- **Taxes**
- Additional overseas **advertising**
- **Product enhancements** if these are needed
- Costs associated with **agents or distributors**

All these additional costs mean that the **international** price of the product is very much higher than the domestic price.

3.7 Building market share

It has been suggested that there are three elements in the pricing decision for a new product.

- Getting the product **accepted**
- **Maintaining a market share** in the face of competition
- **Making a profit** from the product

When a firm launches a new product on to the market, it must decide on a pricing policy which lies between the two extremes of market penetration and market skimming.

3.7.1 Penetration

KEY CONCEPT

concept

Market penetration pricing is a policy of low prices when the product is first launched in order to gain sufficient penetration into the market. It is therefore a policy of sacrificing short-run profits in the interests of long-term profits.

The circumstances which favour a penetration policy are as follows.

(a)   The firm wishes to **discourage rivals** from entering the market.

(b)   The firm wishes to **shorten the initial period** of the product's life cycle, in order to enter the growth and maturity stages as quickly as possible.

(c)   There are significant **economies of scale** to be achieved from a large output. A firm might therefore deliberately build excess production capacity and set its prices very low; as demand builds up, the spare capacity will be used up gradually, and unit costs will fall; the firm might even reduce prices further as unit costs fall. In this way, early year losses will enable the firm to dominate the market and have the lowest costs.

3.7.2 Skimming

KEY CONCEPT

concept

Market skimming pricing is the setting of a high initial price to achieve high unit profits, with the knowledge that a certain number of customers will buy at the high price. This is possible where rival firms are not expected to undercut these high prices, where the fixed costs of output are fairly low so that economies of scale are relatively insignificant and where the customer believes that high prices signify a quality product.

Market skimming involves the following.

(a)   Charging high prices when a product is **first launched**.

(b)   **Spending heavily on advertising** and sales promotion to win customers.

(c)   As the product moves into the later stages of its life cycle charging **progressively lower prices**. The profitable 'cream' is thus 'skimmed' off in progressive stages until sales can only be sustained at lower prices.

The aim of market skimming is to gain high unit profits very early on in the product's life. Conditions which are suitable for such a policy are as follows.

(a)   Where the product is **new and different**, so that customers are prepared to pay high prices so as to be 'one up' on other people who do not own one. Many new technology items come into this category.

(b)   Where **demand elasticity is unknown**. It is better to start by charging high prices and then reducing them if the demand for the product turns out to be price elastic than to start by charging low prices and then attempting to raise them substantially when demand turns out to be price inelastic.

(c)   High initial prices might not be profit maximising in the long run, but they generate **high initial cash flows**.

(d)   Skimming may also enable the firm to identify **different market segments** for the product, each prepared to pay progressively lower prices. If product **differentiation** can be introduced, it may be possible to continue to sell at higher prices to some market segments.

3.8 Pricing approaches and strategies

Companies may undertake any of a variety of pricing strategies, depending on their objectives and the industry they operate in. Pricing strategies can be used to pursue a number of marketing objectives. As noted earlier, however, in practice, cost is the most important influence on price.

3.8.1 Techniques of cost analysis

Whilst you will not need an in-depth knowledge of cost analysis, it is worth being aware of the key techniques and concepts.

- **Fixed costs** are costs which do not vary according to how many units are being produced or sold (eg salaries, advertising costs).

- **Variable costs** are costs which vary directly according to how many units are being produced or sold (eg materials costs, sales force commissions).

- **Contribution** is the amount that a product or project contributes to covering fixed costs. It is calculated as:

  Selling price/revenue *minus* variable cost

  If a product or marketing plan generates sufficient contribution to cover fixed costs, it may be worth pursuing in the short term.

- **Breakeven analysis** is used to calculate how much of a product/service must be output at a given price, in order for sales revenue to equal the total costs of producing/marketing it. The breakeven quantity (BEQ) equals:

  $$\frac{\text{Fixed costs}}{\text{Contribution}}$$

  This calculation enables marketers to calculate the effect of different prices on the breakeven point/quantity.

3.8.2 Full cost pricing

Full cost pricing is a form of cost-based pricing which takes account of the full average cost of production of a product, including an allocation for overheads. A profit margin is then added to determine the selling price. This method is often used for non-routine jobs which are difficult to cost in advance, such as the work of solicitors and accountants where the price is often determined after the work has been performed.

3.8.3 Cost-plus pricing

 KEY CONCEPT

concept

Cost-plus pricing means basing the price calculation on the firm's production costs, plus a predetermined allowance for profit.

Under cost-plus pricing, only the more easily measurable direct cost components such as labour and raw material inputs are calculated in the unit cost, whilst an additional margin incorporates an overhead charge and a residual profit element. This method is used where overhead allocation to individual unit costs is too complex or too time consuming to be worthwhile.

A common example occurs with the use of **mark-up pricing**.

 KEY CONCEPT

concept

Mark-up is the amount of profit calculated as a proportion of the bought-in price.

This is used by retailers and involves a fixed margin being added to the buying-in price. In the UK, for example, fast-moving items such as cigarettes carry a low 5-8% margin (also because of tax factors). Fast-moving but perishable items such as newspapers carry a 25% margin. Slow moving items which involve retailers in high stockholding costs, such as furniture or books, carry 33%, 50% or even higher mark-up margins.

Since the cost-plus approach leads to **price stability**, with price changing only to reflect cost changes, it can lead to a marketing strategy which is reactive rather then proactive.

3.8.4 Limitations of cost-based pricing

There is very limited consideration of **demand** in cost-based pricing strategies.

(a) From a marketing perspective, cost-based pricing may reflect **missed opportunities**, as no account is taken of customer perceptions of value and of the price that they are *willing* to pay, which may be higher than the cost-based price.

(b) Particular problems may be caused for a **new brand**, as initial low production levels in the introduction stage may lead to a very high average unit cost and consequently a high price. A longer-term perspective may be necessary, accepting short-term losses until full production levels are attained.

3.8.5 Product line pricing

 KEY CONCEPT  concept

Product line pricing is the application of differential pricing policies to products that are co-dependent in terms of demand.

When a firm sells a **range of related products**, or a product line, its pricing policy should aim to maximise the profitability of the line as a whole. The pricing must be consistent with its brand image.

(a) There may be a **brand name** which the manufacturer wishes to associate with high quality and high price, or reasonable quality and low price. All items in the line will be priced accordingly. For example, all major supermarket chains have an 'own brand' label which is used to sell goods at a slightly lower price than the major named brands.

(b) If two or more products in the line are complementary, one may be priced as a **loss leader** (a low profit-margin item) in order to attract customers and demand for the related products.

(c) If two or more products in the line share **joint production costs** (joint products), prices of the products will be considered as a single decision. For example, if a common production process makes one unit of joint product A for each unit of joint product B, a price for A which achieves a demand of, say, 17,000 units, will be inappropriate if associated with a price for product B which would only sell, say, 10,000 units. 7,000 units of B would be unsold and wasted.

 ACTIVITY 4  application

An organisation has declared that its primary pricing objective for its new product is 'early cash recovery'. It wants to recover its investment in the product as quickly as possible. What are some possible reasons for having such an objective?

KEY CONCEPT

concept

Promotional pricing is pricing that is related to the promotion of a product, generally over the short term only.

Pricing and promotion are often co-ordinated. According to Dibb, Simkin, Pride and Ferrell (2001) there are four main types of promotional pricing.

(a) **Price leaders** – products that are sold at or below cost to attract customers in the hope that they will buy other, full priced items. This tactic is often used in department stores and supermarkets.

(b) **Special event pricing** – pricing that is linked to an event or a holiday to increase sales volume. An example is the 'Buy 2, get the 3rd free' often seen at Christmas.

(c) **Everyday low pricing** – this involves the reduction of prices for a prolonged period, supported by cutting costs elsewhere in the operation (such as distribution costs, or cutting down on other promotions).

(d) **Experience curve pricing** – the fixing of a low price that competitors cannot hope to match, in order to increase market share. A company can do this when it has been able to reduce manufacturing costs through improvements in processes that have been accumulated through experience.

EXAM TIP

application

To find an appropriate pricing strategy, you have to consider the nature of the product: is it exposed to competition or could a premium price strategy be justified by the niche nature of the product or the prospect of enthusiastic early adopters?

You may like to remember the key factors in pricing strategy as the 4Cs = Costs, Customer (demands), Competition and Company (objectives).

In the sample case study, Innocent Drinks charges £1.79 – £1.99 for 250ml, while PJ Smoothies (owned by Pepsico) only charges £0.99. Quite a difference, explained by the management of Innocent as a reflection of their ideals: it sources fruit from ethically aware farms, uses 100% recyclable bottles and donates 10% of its profits to charity. They promise 'taste, quality and ethics, while Pepsi is about cheaper prices'. With the introduction of orange juice, there is an opportunity for cheaper price points (£1.89 for a litre) and thereby a wider demographic for the brand.

Jobber (2009) Chapter 11 on pricing strategies provides detailed additional coverage on pricing for your further reading. ■

Learning objectives		Covered
1	Assess the links between product development, product positioning and pricing in terms of fit and alignment with an organisation's corporate and marketing strategies and customer requirements	☑ Positioning new products (1.1) ☑ Positioning strategies (1.2)
2	Critically evaluate the importance of linking the product portfolio to price perception to ensure perceived value for money as part of the overall customer proposition	☑ Role of pricing (2.1) ☑ Value for money and price sensitivity (2.2 and 2.3)
3	Assess pricing frameworks that could be utilised by organisations to aid decision making about product lifecycles, product development and innovation	☑ Price versus cost (3.1) ☑ Factors determining pricing levels (3.2) ☑ Pricing and satisfaction of customer demand (3.3) ☑ Pricing and competition (3.4) ☑ Pricing and value (3.5) ☑ Pricing for international markets (3.6) ☑ Building market share (3.7) ☑ Pricing approaches and strategies (3.8)

1 Pricing decisions are guided by one or other of two business objectives. What are they?

1 .... 2 ....

2 Why might a cost-based approach to price setting be problematic from a marketing point of view?

3 List three factors that might influence a farmer's pricing policy.

4 List four ways of responding to a price cut by a competitor.

5 What is price elasticity?

6 In practice, what is the biggest influence on setting prices?

7 Give an example of product line pricing.

8 What is the opposite of penetration pricing?

9 Why are price and quality not necessarily regarded as independent variables?

10 What is the name of the strategy applied to goods of a low quality but a mid-range price?

11 What is 'intangible positioning?'

12 What is the main disadvantage of cost-based pricing?

1   There appears to be a gap in the market for a moderately priced, reasonable quality eating place.

2   You might have identified a number of different factors here. Perhaps the most important general point to make is that price is particularly important if the other elements in the marketing mix are relatively similar across a range of competing products. For example, there is a very wide variety of toothpastes on the market, most of them not much differentiated from the others. The price of a particular toothpaste may be a crucial factor in its sales success.

3   One possibility is that the cost of the product was established (to make sure of breaking even), VAT added since it makes a significant difference for the customer, and comparisons were made with items of similar quality and rarity on the market. A range of possible prices, based on this data, might then have been presented to potential customers to see how they reacted to them. Data may also have been collected about the results of similar exercises by other watchmakers (or the like) in the past.

4   The objective of 'early cash recovery' would tend to be used in the following conditions:

   •   The business is high risk
   •   Rapid changes are expected (maybe in fashion or technology)
   •   The innovator is short of cash!

1   Maximise profits; Maintain or increase market share.

2   Because it does not take proper account of the price consumers may be willing to pay and because in the case of a new product it does not take account of the typical pattern of the product life cycle or the diffusion of innovation.

3   The main one will be intermediaries' objectives. Many farmers have gone out of business in recent years because, they claim, supermarkets drive down the prices they can obtain for their goods. Other factors may play a part: for instance competition from cheap imported goods, the quality of their goods (eg organic vegetables), government subsidies or quotas.

4   Maintain existing prices; maintain prices but respond with extra advertising; reduce prices; raise prices and respond with extra features or higher quality.

5   A measure of how much demand will 'stretch', or how far a change in price will affect demand

6   Cost.

7   If two or more products in the line are complementary, one may be priced as a loss leader (a low profit-margin item) in order to attract customers and demand for the related products.

8   Price skimming. Instead of setting a price low to get into the market, a company deliberately sets prices high in order to take advantage of those buyers prepared to pay a high price for innovation, and then gradually reduces the price to attract more price sensitive segments.

9   Consumers will usually associate a high price with high quality, and a low price with low quality.

10   A 'shoddy goods' strategy.

11   Targeting a different market segment with the same product.

12   There is very little consideration of the actual demand for a product, and therefore what customers may be actually willing to pay.

Blythe, J (2009) <u>Principles and Practice of Marketing</u>, 2nd edition, South-Western/Cengage Learning.

Blythe, J (2008) <u>Essentials of Marketing</u>,4th edition, FT Prentice Hall.

Brassington, F and Pettitt, S (2006) <u>Principles of Marketing</u>, 4th edition, FT Prentice Hall.

Dibb S, Simkin L, Pride WM, Ferrell OC (2005) <u>Marketing: Concepts and Strategies</u>, 5th edition, Houghton Mifflin.

Jobber (2009) <u>Principles and Practice of Marketing</u>.6th edition, McGraw Hill Higher Education

Kotler, P (2001) <u>Principles of Marketing</u>, FT Prentice Hall, London.

Delivering Customer Value Through Marketing

Chapter 3
Effective distribution strategies

Topic list

1   Principles of distribution strategy
2   The internal and external environment

Introduction

Distribution involves certain basic processes.

- Bringing customers and sellers into contact
- Offering a sufficient choice of goods to meet the needs of customers
- Persuading customers to develop a favourable opinion of a particular product
- Distributing goods from the manufacturing point to retail outlets
- Maintaining an adequate level of sales
- Providing appropriate level of service (eg credit, after-sales service)
- Maintaining an acceptable price

The benefits of effective distribution management include the following.

(a) **Customer value** through more choice and customisation; better quality control; faster delivery; less likelihood of stockouts; service-driven supply planning; convenient, safe and undamaged handling, storage, transport and display of goods.

(b) **Cost savings** that can be made when a properly planned approach is undertaken, allowing long, steady production runs and minimising inefficient stock holding.

(c) **Closer links between suppliers and manufacturers**, for example using EDI (Electronic Data Interchange), e-commerce and relationship marketing (particularly in B2B markets, where direct supply from manufacturer to buyer is far more likely than the use of intermediaries).

This chapter examines the major principles behind an effective distribution strategy, and the environmental influences upon it.

Syllabus linked learning objectives

By the end of the chapter you will be able to:

Learning objectives	Syllabus link
1 Determine and prioritise the key principles and purposes of innovative and effective distribution strategies in order to deliver the organisation's business and marketing objectives in a range of different contexts and different sectors to maximise customer requirements	2.1
2 Critically analyse the implications, challenges and constraints arising from the internal and external environment in the context of the development of channel strategies	2.2

1 Principles of distribution strategy

According to Jobber (2009):

"Producing products that customers want, pricing them correctly and developing well designed promotional plans are necessary but not sufficient conditions for customer satisfaction. The final part of the jigsaw is distribution" ■

Distribution accounts for a large percentage of the cost of a product. There are two main elements to it.

- The **tangible** and physical movement of goods to the customer as easily as possible

- The **intangible** aspects such as ownership, control and communication flows (otherwise known as 'supply chain management')

A variety of functions are involved in distribution.

- **Transport**

  This function may be provided by the supplier, the distributor or may be sub-contracted to a specialist. For some products, such as perishable goods, transport planning is vital.

- **Stock holding and storage**

  For production planning purposes, an uninterrupted flow of production is often essential. A good stock or inventory control system is designed to avoid stockouts whilst keeping stockholding costs low.

- **Local knowledge**

  As production has tended to become centralised in pursuit of economies of scale, the need to understand and be 'close to' local markets has grown.

- **Promotion**

  Whilst major promotional campaigns for national products are likely to be carried out by the supplier, the translation of the campaign to local level is usually the responsibility of a distributor or retail outlet.

- **Sales displays**

  Presentation of the product at the local level is often the responsibility of the distributor. Specialist help from merchandisers can be bought in if required.

1.1 Types of organisational relationship

Relationships require at least two parties who are in contact with each other. If we focus on only two parties (for example, a supplier and its customer), the relationship will be a 'one to one' or 'dyad' (two-party) relationship.

However, basic supplier-customer exchanges usually happen within the wider context of a distribution/supply process: a producer of raw materials supplies a processing plant or producer of components, which supplies a manufacturing organisation, which supplies a distributor or retail outlet, which supplies the consumer. This configuration is often called a chain or channel.

But even this picture is simplified. The fact is that each organisation in the supply chain has multiple other relationships with customers, suppliers, industry partners and so on. Many writers (eg Cox & Lamming, 1997; Christopher, 2005) have therefore argued that a more appropriate metaphor is a network or web.

We will look briefly at each of these types of relationship in turn.

1.1.1 One to one (dyadic) relationships

The relationship between a supplier and a customer is the classic two-sided relationship (dyad) of marketing (Gummesson, 2002). Marketing and supply management often focus on this dyad: focusing on how the firm could secure and exploit the contribution of its immediate upstream suppliers – and what it could offer to its immediate downstream customers.

Figure 3.1 Classic dyadic (one-to-one) relationship

(based on Gummesson, 2002)

Despite the trend towards looking at networks, the management of a firm's immediate upstream and downstream relationships is still crucial, as reflected in approaches such as customer relationship management (CRM) and supplier relationship management (SRM). In marketing, in particular, each supplier focuses upon the customer relationship through approaches such as customer research, customer relationship management, personal selling, direct marketing, and customer loyalty/retention programmes.

Note that 'one-to-one' relationships may or may not imply interactions between individual people. The marketing organisation may be represented by a salesperson, customer service team member, negotiator or some another individual 'touch point' with an individual customer. The term 'one to one' marketing has been coined for techniques which use (or simulate) direct person-to-person interactions with customers: personalised communications, for example, or offers tailored to the individual customers' past buying patterns and preferences. (If you have ever registered with an online store such as Amazon.co.uk, you will be aware of the extent to which a total offering can be personalised to you as an individual.)

In other words, one-to-one marketing means establishing relationships not just with 'customers' (mass marketing), nor even with 'this group of customers' (target marketing) but with 'this particular customer'. It has been made possible in recent years by developments in information and communication technology (ICT).

Christopher *et al* (2002, p 27) argue that: 'A prime objective of relationship marketing is to create superior customer value at the one-to-one level. The premise is that while it is impossible to have a relationship with a market or even a segment, it may be possible to establish a relationship with an individual customer or consumer'.

1.1.2 Chains and channels

The supply chain is the classic example of chain or channel relationships in marketing (see Figure 3.2).

 KEY CONCEPT  concept

The **supply chain** is 'that network of organisations that are involved, through upstream and downstream linkages, in the different processes and activities that produce value in the form of products and services in the hands of the ultimate customer' (Christopher, 2005).

Figure 3.2 A simple supply chain

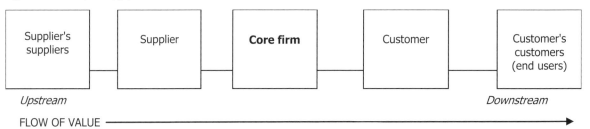

Of course, this is a simplified picture, because material and information flows in both directions up and down the supply chain: customers send specifications and orders upstream to suppliers; suppliers send goods and services downstream; and customers send payments upstream, for example. (Increasingly, they may also send goods back up the supply chain for recycling and re-use, a process called 'reverse logistics' – which effectively turns the supply chain into a loop.)

The chain concept highlights several useful aspects of marketing relationships.

- It emphasises 'serial co-operation': each player needs to add value through its contribution to the sequence or process.

- It emphasises the linkages and interfaces between members, and co-operation between them, because each link in the chain is essential to the completeness and strength of the whole. Weak links and breakages (ie poor supply chain relationships) may disrupt the flow of supply and value to the ultimate customer.

Supply chains are also sometimes referred to as channels, emphasising that they provide a structure for flows of materials, goods, information and so on. This metaphor also helpfully raises 'push' and 'pull' issues: whether flows are driven by supply-side (push) or demand-side (pull) factors. Push marketing strategies, for example, are aimed at getting goods into the front end of the pipeline by selling to distributors and retailers, while pull marketing strategies are aimed at stimulating consumer demand and drawing goods out of the pipeline at the other end.

It is worth noting that there are internal supply chains, as well as inter-business or external ones. The internal value chain describes the processes which integrate all the business functions and units responsible for the flow of materials and information into and through the organisation. This is why we can talk about internal marketing (covered later in this text).

1.1.3 Networks

The concept of the supply chain is helpfully sequential and linear – but doesn't really do justice to the complexity of the real picture! Any given firm in a supply chain in fact has its own relationships and connections with multiple other players: multiple suppliers and customers, industry contacts, partners/collaborators and advisers – any or all of whom may themselves be connected with each other.

The network metaphor is arguably a more realistic model for mapping and analysing business relationships.

- It raises the possibility of a wider range of connections and collaborations (eg knowledge sharing, alliances and co-promotions) which may offer mutual advantages – and help to add value for the end customer.

- It also recognises the potential of what has been called the 'extended enterprise': extending the capability of a firm by tapping into the resources and competences of other network contributors (for example, by outsourcing activities like call centres to partners better equipped to undertake them). These days some of this extended enterprise may well be 'virtual': that is, connected purely by ICT links, such as the Internet. (You might never know, when you speak to the customer services department of a 'local' bank or telecom provider, that you are actually speaking to someone in India or South Africa.)

Christopher et al (2002) argue that:

"The real competitive struggle is not between individual companies, but between their supply chains or networks. This view is sometimes challenged on the grounds that supply chains cannot truly compete since, because they frequently share common suppliers, for example, they are not unique configurations. But this view misses the point. What makes a supply chain or network unique is the way the relationships and interfaces in the chain or network are managed. In this sense, a major source of differentiation comes from the quality of relationships that one business enjoys, compared to its competitors." p 126

1.2 Types of distribution channel

KEY CONCEPT

concept

Channels of distribution are methods by which goods or services are transferred from producers to customers.

Physical distribution is concerned with the handling and movement of outbound goods from an organisation to its customers. Distribution might be **direct** or **indirect**.

Logistics, is concerned with inbound raw materials and other supplies, as well as with outbound goods. It also covers strategic issues such as warehouse location, materials management, stock levels and information systems.

ACTIVITY 1

evaluation

For many types of goods, producers invariably use retailers as middlemen in getting the product to the customer. Try to think of some of the disadvantages of doing this, from the producer's point of view.

The type of product or product service dictates a channel and its management as illustrated below

Figure 3.3 Different channels for different types of product

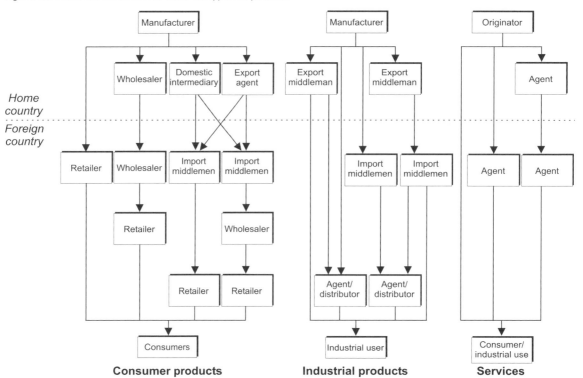

MARKETING AT WORK

concept

Fresh flowers from Africa to the UK require different channel management decisions than the export of machinery from Poland to the UK, because the flowers are more perishable and need to reach their destination quickly with little add-on cost.

Zara, the Spanish clothing retailer, relies on its European plants to create and respond quickly to new trends. Eschewing low cost Chinese or Indian labour, it has a design-to-shelf time of only two weeks, with lower transport costs to its European outlets from its European factories.

1.2.1 Intermediaries

Blythe (2009) comments:

"Intermediaries provide important services in smoothing the path between producers and customers, almost invariably reducing costs by increasing efficiency."

Companies may distribute direct to customers, or choose from a wide range of intermediaries: retailers, wholesalers, dealers, agents, franchisees and multiple stores.

KEY CONCEPT

concept

An **intermediary** is someone who 'mediates' or brings about a settlement between two persons: in this case between the original supplier and the ultimate buyer.

Some of the options, and the distribution channels they create, are illustrated in Figure 3.4.

Figure 3.4 Intermediaries

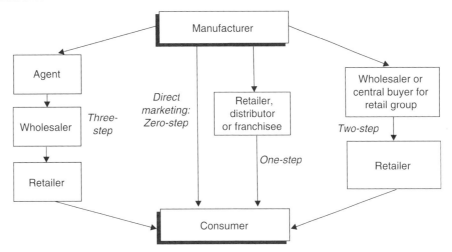

(a) **Retailers** are traders operating outlets which sell directly to households. They may be classified by:

- Type of goods sold (eg hardware, furniture, food, clothes)
- Type of service (self-service, counter service)
- Size and/or ownership
- Location (rural, city-centre, suburban or out of town shopping mall)

(b) **Wholesalers** stock a range of products from potentially competing manufacturers, to sell on to other organisations such as retailers. Many wholesalers specialise in particular products.

(c) **Distributors and dealers** contract to buy a manufacturer's goods and sell them to customers. Their function is similar to that of wholesalers, but they usually offer a narrower product range, sometimes (as in the case of most car dealers) the products of a single manufacturer. In addition to selling on the manufacturer's product, distributors often promote the products and provide after-sales service.

(d) **Agents** differ from distributors, in that they do not purchase and resell the goods, but sell goods on behalf of the supplier and earn a **commission** on their sales

(e) **Franchisees** are independent organisations which in exchange for an initial fee and (usually) a share of sales revenue are allowed to trade under the name of a parent organisation. For example, few of the Kall Kwik chain of High Street print shops are actually owned by Kall Kwik – most are run by franchisees.

 MARKETING AT WORK  application

Kodak Express Malaysia: Promotion of franchise opportunities

As a Kodak Express member, you will enjoy the following benefits.

- **Kodak Express Branding**: the right to use the Kodak Express logo for advertising and promotions in the store.

- **Quality Monitoring Service:** Kodak's engineers will advise and make recommendations on how to maintain our print quality according to international Kodak quality standards. With this support, your store will be able to provide quality prints to consumers.

- **Exclusive Rebates**: Exclusive only to you, these discounts and rebates will provide your business with a leading edge over the rest.

- **Training**: one of the best benefits in the franchise program. Each year, Kodak will organise at least four training sessions to help you improve your business performance.

- **Retail Shop Concept**: A new store concept for the Kodak Express shops is specially designed to project Kodak Express as a young, vibrant and professional retail store to consumers.

- **Stakeholder marketing**

- **360-degree Checklist Program**: your Business Support Executive will conduct checks and monitoring exercises in your store regularly. The quality of the photos processed, the visual displays and the quality of staff service will be measured to ensure that your store meets the quality requirements to stay competitive in the market.

- **Best Kodak Express Award**: designed to reward members who provide consistently good service and quality prints to consumers. Every year, the top ten Kodak Express Award winners will receive cash prizes and public recognition in local papers.

- **Newsletter**: one of the ways which you will be kept updated on the latest products, services and trends in the photo-retailing industry.

- **Advertisements**: you will benefit from the advertising plans and strategies initiated by Kodak.

- **Annual Conference**: an annual event where members will not only interact and discuss ways to improve the Kodak Express program, but also gain knowledge.

http://www.kodak.com/my

(f) **Multiple stores** (eg supermarkets, department stores) buy goods for retailing direct from the producer, sometimes under their 'own label' brand name.

(g) **Direct marketing** methods include:

- Mail order
- Telephone selling
- Door-to-door selling
- Personal selling in the sale of industrial goods
- Sales through retail outlets owned by the supplier
- TV shopping channels
- E-commerce (Internet selling via online marketing)

  KEY CONCEPT

concept

Direct marketing is marketing *without* intermediaries.

Direct marketing methods are covered in more detail in the chapter on the marketing communications mix.

1.2.2 Relationships with channel intermediaries

The Six Markets model (Peck et al, 1999) includes intermediaries as a sub-set of customers, since the marketing organisation is selling goods/services to them. All the principles of relationship marketing therefore apply as much to channel customers as to 'end user' customers.

However, channel intermediaries are businesses, and this highlights some particular issues.

- **Value exchange is likely to be more explicit**, because the intermediary has its own commercial objectives for doing business with the supplier. Intermediaries do not stock products or run promotions as a 'favour' to the supplier!

    - The terms of the relationship will need to be negotiated and contracted.

    - Intermediaries will need to be selected, prioritised and managed for long-term profitability; added value (eg provision of sales and customer information from electronic point of sale or EPOS systems); contribution to customer value (eg convenient access to the product, customer service); and compatibility with marketing strategy (eg matching the brand's positioning, targeting the right customer segments).

    - The benefits of the product or collaboration will have to be promoted to the distributor, through trade advertising, promotion and personal selling.

- Intermediaries may have equally committed **relationships with the firm's direct competitors** (eg a supermarket promoting both Pepsi and Coke). Marketers will need to differentiate their products and promotions, be discreet in sharing confidential information – and be aware of opportunities to gain useful competitor intelligence (eg a new product, or promotion plans).

- Intermediaries are in the front line of **contact with customers**. Marketers need to gather information from them as to customer buying patterns and preferences, and respect their advice as to what products/promotions will work (or not).

- Major retailers (eg supermarkets) have **considerable buying power** in their markets, and good working relationships must be preserved with them. This may come at the expense of profit (eg giving large supplier discounts or paying for point-of-sale display and promotions). It may also involve some loss of control over promotion (eg in-store display, price promotions) or distribution (eg granting a major distributor exclusive rights to sell the product).

- There may be significant mutual benefits from **promotional collaboration**. If the supplier promotes the product to customers through PR, advertising and customer incentives, the intermediary will benefit. If the intermediary promotes the product to customers – eg through in-store display and promotions – the supplier will benefit.

The Six Markets model is covered in more detail later in the text, in the context of external audiences for marketing communications.

 MARKETING AT WORK application

The vending machine is a familiar feature of the landscape – on railway platforms (for tickets or chocolate bars), in waiting rooms and anywhere that people may be passing by or simply passing the time. Vending machines can distribute anything from travel tickets and dry cleaning orders to food and drink, and offer the latest DVDs for hire. They can now even deliver clothing.

Japanese trainer shoe and sports fashion brand Onitsuka Tiger launched what it claims to be the UK's first trainer shoe vending machine. The machine, which can vend 24 pairs of trainers in 6 sizes, was launched in Carnaby Street, London. The brand intends to roll out the concept across the UK. As part of the launch, Onitsuka Tiger gave shoppers in the Carnaby Street area the chance to win a free pair of trainers for a limited period.

In March 2009, a vending machine was introduced in the Onitsuka Tiger store in Liverpool.

(Adapted from Kemp, 2008 and www.liverpool.com)

Relationships with channel partners are examined in more detail in Chapter 4.

1.3 Establishing channel strategies

 Blythe, J. (2009) noted:

"Managing the supply chain is by no means simple, and it is not always the role of the manufacturer to do so – many supply chains are managed by wholesalers, retailers or other members, using negotiation, coercion or reward to make the system operate more smoothly."

Choosing distribution channels is important for any organisation, because once a set of channels has been established, subsequent changes are likely to be costly and slow to implement. Distribution channels fall into one of two categories: **direct** and **indirect** channels.

 KEY CONCEPT concept

Direct distribution means the product going directly from producer to customer without the use of a specific intermediary. These methods are often described as **active**, since they typically involve the supplier making the first approach to a potential customer.

Indirect distribution means systems of distribution, common among manufactured goods, which use an intermediary (a wholesaler or retailer for example (as described in the previous section)). In contrast to direct distribution, these methods are **passive**, in the sense that they rely on customers to make the first approach by entering the relevant retail outlet.

Factors favouring the use of direct distribution	Factors favouring the use of intermediaries
(a) The need for an expert sales force to demonstrate products, explain product characteristics and provide after-sales service. Publishers, for example, use sales reps to keep booksellers up-to-date with new titles or to arrange for the return of unsold books.	(a) Insufficient resources to finance a large sales force.
(b) Intermediaries may be unwilling or unable to sell the product.	(b) A policy decision to invest in increased productive capacity, rather than extra marketing effort.
(c) Existing channels may be linked to other producers.	(c) The supplier may have insufficient in-house marketing 'know-how' in selling to retail stores.
(d) The intermediaries willing to sell the product may be too costly, or they may not be maximising potential sales.	(d) The product line may be insufficiently wide or deep for a sales force to carry. A wholesaler can complement a limited range and make more efficient use of his sales force.
(e) Where potential buyers are geographically concentrated, the supplier's own sales force can easily reach them (typically an industrial market).	(e) Intermediaries can market small lots as part of a range of goods. The supplier would incur a heavy sales overhead if its own sales force took 'small' individual orders.
(f) Where e-commerce is well established, potential buyers can be reached online.	(f) Large numbers of potential buyers spread over a wide geographical area (typically customer markets).

  ACTIVITY 2

application

One factor influencing the choice between direct and indirect methods is the average order size for a product. What do you think the relationship might be between average order size and the occurrence (or non-occurrence) of direct distribution?

Independently owned and operated distributors may well have their own objectives and these are likely to take precedence over those of the manufacturer or supplier with whom they are dealing. Suppliers may solve the problem by buying their own distribution route or by distributing direct to their customers. Direct distribution is common for many industrial and/or customised product suppliers. In some customer markets direct distribution is also common, particularly with the advent of e-commerce via the Internet.

1.3.1 Distribution strategy

There are three main strategies.

(a) **Intensive distribution** involves blanket coverage of distributors in one segment of the total market, such as a local area.

(b) Using **selective distribution**, the producer selects a group of retail outlets from amongst all retail outlets. The choice of selected outlets may be based on reflecting brand image (eg 'quality' outlets), or the retailers' capacity to provide after-sales service ('specialist' outlets).

(c) **Exclusive distribution** is where selected outlets are granted exclusive rights to stock and sell the product within a prescribed market segment or geographical area. Sometimes exclusive distribution or franchise rights are coupled with making special financial arrangements for land, buildings or equipment, such as petrol station agreements.

Discount factory shops, often situated on factory premises from where manufacturers sell seconds or retailers' returns, are well-established in the UK but developers have begun to group such outlets together in purpose-built malls.

What would you suggest are the advantages of this method of distribution for customers and manufacturers?

1.3.2 General principles

A number of considerations will determine the choice of distribution strategy

(a) The number of **intermediate stages to be used**. There could be zero, one, two or three intermediate stages of selling (as shown in Figure 3.4 above). In addition, it will be necessary to decide how many dealers at each stage should be used – ie how many agents should be used, how many wholesalers should be asked to sell the manufacturer's products, and what the size of the direct sales force should be.

(b) **The support that the manufacturer should give to the dealers**. It may be necessary to provide an efficient after-sales and repair service, or to agree to an immediate exchange of faulty products returned by a retailer's customers, or to make weekly, bi-weekly or monthly stock-checking visits to retailers' stores. To help selling, the manufacturer might need to consider advertising or sales promotion support, including merchandising.

(c) **The extent to which the manufacturer wishes to dominate a channel of distribution**. A market leader, wishing to ensure that its market share is maintained, might offer exclusive distribution contracts to major retailers.

(d) **The extent to which the manufacturer wishes to integrate its marketing effort up to the point of sale with the customer**. Combined promotions with retailers, for example, would only be possible if the manufacturer dealt directly with the retailer (and did not sell to the retailer through a wholesaler).

1.3.3 Factors in channel decisions

In setting up a channel of distribution, the supplier has to take several factors into account.

- Customers
- Nature of the goods or services
- Distributor characteristics
- Competitors' channel choice
- The costs associated with available channels
- The supplier's own characteristics

Customers

The **number** of potential customers, their **buying habits** and their **geographical proximity** are key influences. The use of mail order and Internet purchases for convenience as well as for those with limited time or mobility (remote rural location, illness) is an example of the influence of customers on channel design.

Different distribution strategies may be adopted for **customer** and **industrial** markets.

Industrial markets are generally characterised as having fewer, higher-value customers purchasing a complex total offering of products/services which fulfil detailed specifications. Industrial distribution channels therefore tend to be more direct and shorter, allowing partnership level relationships. There are specialist distributors in the industrial sector, which may be used as well as, or instead of, selling directly to industrial customers.

There have traditionally been fewer direct distribution channels from the manufacturer to the customer in the customer market. Even with the advent of e-commerce in some sectors, it is still more usual for companies in customer markets to use wholesalers and retailers to move their product to the final customer.

Nature of the goods or services

Some product characteristics have an important effect on design of the channel of distribution.

Characteristic	Comment
Perishability	Fresh fruit and newspapers must be distributed very quickly or they become worthless. Speed of delivery is therefore a key factor in the design of the distribution system for such products. Fragile items need extra care and minimal handling.
Customisation	Customised products tend to be distributed direct. When a wide range of options is available, sales may be made using demonstration units, with customised delivery to follow.
After-sales service/ technical advice	Extent and cost must be carefully considered, staff training given and quality control systems set up. Suppliers often provide training programmes for distributors. Exclusive area franchises giving guaranteed custom can be allocated, to ensure distributor co-operation; the disadvantage of this is that a poor distributor may cost a supplier dearly in a particular area.
Franchising	Franchising has become an increasingly popular means of getting products to the customer. The supplier gains more outlets more quickly, and exerts more control than is usual in distribution.
Value	High value items might be better suited to direct delivery.

ACTIVITY 4

application

How might a service organisation choose channels of distribution?

Distributor characteristics

The location, customer base, performance and reliability, promotion and pricing policies of different types of distributor, and specific distribution outlets, will have to be evaluated. Selling to supermarket chains in the UK, for example, is now very difficult as the concentration of grocery retailing into a few large chains has increased the power of the buyers. Some products (such as emergency medical supplies) will be dependent upon faultlessly reliable delivery systems.

Competitors' channel choice

For many customer goods, a supplier's brand will sit alongside its competitors' products. For other products, distributors may stock one brand only (for example, in car distribution) and in return be given an exclusive area. In this case new suppliers may face difficulties in breaking into a market because the distribution channel is in effect controlled by the competition.

Costs

There are considerable costs associated with distribution. In addition to the costs of importing goods from overseas suppliers, or exporting to overseas customers, products will often need to be stored (in warehouses for example) or held somewhere (such as on the shop floor, for the use of which rent will usually be payable) awaiting sale or collection. The cheapest method of transport (by road, as opposed to by air) will not always be the most effective.

Supplier characteristics

A strong financial base gives the supplier the option of buying and operating their own distribution channel: Boots the Chemist is a good example in the UK. The market position of the supplier is also important: distributors are keen to be associated with the market leader, but other brands may experience distribution problems.

1.3.4 Making the channel decision

Producers have to decide the following.

(a) **What types of distributor** are to be used (wholesalers, retailers, agents)?

(b) **How many of each type will be used?** This depends on what degree of market exposure is required.

- Intensive, blanket coverage
- Exclusive, appointed agents for exclusive areas
- Selective, some but not all in each area

(c) **Who will carry out specific marketing tasks?**

- Credit provision
- Delivery
- After-sales service

- Training
- Display

(d) How will the **effectiveness** of distributors be evaluated?

- In terms of cost?
- In terms of sales levels?
- According to the degree of control achieved?
- By the amount of conflict that arises?

1.4 Establishing channel needs

The participants in a trading channel have to provide certain services to the customer. A good trading channel will provide the following.

- Research and information feedback about the market
- Promotion of the goods and services
- Contact and negotiation with prospective buyers
- Storage, sorting, assembling and processing of orders
- Physical distribution
- Financing operations
- Speculative risk taking

The producer's problem is in ensuring that these activities will be carried out. It can be seen that where a weak distributive infrastructure exists within a country, the duties will fall on the exporter and the selected entry organisation, and thus care must be taken in the selection of any partner in international marketing.

1.4.1 Customers

Customer trading channels generally require a variety of goods in small quantities, and progressively the trading channel both accumulates a wider variety of goods and breaks down the trade quantities to smaller units. Thus whilst an importer may import wine in bulk and then sell it by the case to the retailer, the retailer will sell wine by the bottle and other associated goods that will appeal to the customer, and provide a sufficiently large order to make the cost of trading worthwhile. Because the discrepancy is so large, customer trading channels tend to be longer, with more intermediaries. In some underdeveloped countries, where the cost of even a standard pack may be prohibitive, the local market traders may even break open customer packs of goods like cigarettes and sell the contents in smaller units.

1.4.2 Organisations

Unlike customer trading channels, trading on a business to business basis usually requires a narrow variety of goods from specialist suppliers in larger quantities. Thus the problems of discrepancy of assortment are less and the trading channels shorter, often involving only one or two intermediaries between the originator and the end user.

Managing the supply chain varies from company to company. A company such as Unilever will provide the same margarine to both Tesco and Sainsbury. The way in which the product is delivered, transactions are processed and other parts of the relationship are managed will be different since these competing supermarket chains have their own ways of operating. The focus will need to be on customer interaction, account management, after sales service and order processing.

1.5 Developing distribution objectives

The choice of trading channel will also depend on what the company wants to achieve in a particular market. Three types of distribution objective are generally considered: coverage, market share and commitment required from intermediaries.

1.5.1 Coverage

There are three approaches to coverage, as we have already seen: exclusive, selective and intensive.

1.5.2 Market share

Where a company is content with a small share of the market, the use of a local distributor in a region of the market may be appropriate. In the UK most trading channels can provide national coverage, but in large countries such as the USA and India, the availability of national coverage through one or two organisations is almost impossible. Region by region dealerships need to be developed to obtain nationwide coverage.

1.5.3 Commitment

The desired degree of commitment will vary. Where an exporter either has little financial resources, or prefers not to invest that resource in a particular country, the preference will be for independent dealers that have no financial tie with the exporter. On the other hand, a greater degree of control in the channel can be exercised if the exporter has some degree of investment in the dealer network.

There is more detail on distribution objectives in the following chapter.

1.6 Approaches to international distribution

If an organisation has decided to enter an overseas market, its entry strategy is of crucial strategic importance. The mode of entry affects a firm's entire marketing mix and its control over the mix elements.

Do not forget the impact of digital marketing channels and the Internet. See Chapter 7 on planning the communications mix for a summary of the distribution uses of the Internet.

Broadly, three ways of entering foreign markets can be identified: direct exports, indirect exports and overseas manufacturing.

 KEY CONCEPT

concept

Indirect exports. These are sales to intermediary organisations at home which then resell the product to customers overseas. It is the outsourcing of the exporting function to a third party.

Direct exports. These are sales to customers overseas without the use of export houses etc. These customers may be intermediary organisations based abroad or end-users.

Overseas manufacture. A firm may set up its own production operation overseas or enter into a joint venture with an enterprise in the overseas market. As an example, a number of Japanese companies have established factories in the UK to manufacture for the UK and European markets.

Figure 2.5 Approaches to international distribution

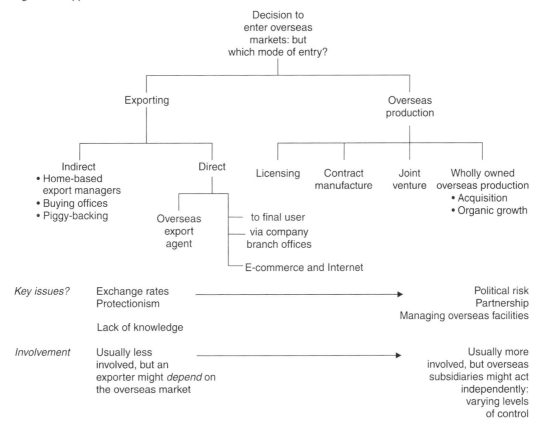

1.6.1 Selecting the method of entry to overseas markets

To choose a method of entry to a particular market, a firm should consider the following issues.

(a) **Firm's marketing objectives**, in relation to volume, timescale and coverage of market segments. Thus setting up an overseas production facility would be inappropriate if sales are expected to be low in volume, or if the product is only to be on sale for a limited period.

(b) **Firm's size**. A small firm is less likely than a large one to possess sufficient resources to set up and run a production facility overseas. Not only would the firm have to provide investment capital and organisational ability, but it would also have to support the costs of continuing operations.

(c) **Mode availability**. A firm might have to use different methods of entry to enter different markets. Some countries only allow a restricted level of imports, but will welcome a firm if it builds manufacturing facilities which provide jobs and limit the outflow of foreign exchange. In this case, overseas manufacture is a better option than direct export.

(d) **Method quality**. In some cases, all modes may be possible in theory, but some are of questionable quality or practicality. The lack of suitably qualified distributors or agents would preclude the export, direct or indirect, of high technology goods needing installation, maintenance and servicing by personnel with specialist technical skills.

(e) **Human resources requirements**. These vary according to which method of entry is used. When a firm is unable to recruit suitable staff either at home or overseas, indirect exporting or the use of agents based overseas may be the only realistic option.

(f) **Market information feedback**. In some cases a firm can receive feedback information about the market and its marketing effort from its sales staff or distribution channels. In these circumstances direct export or joint ventures may be preferred to indirect export.

One small UK company manufacturing and selling a range of leather goods decided to set up a direct export model using a sales subsidiary in France. Having done so they discovered from closer contact with the customers that the reason that one of their best selling lines in the UK was a flop in France was that French customers thought the regal red lining to their wallets was 'too vulgar'. A modest product change using a muted brown lining made the product very acceptable to French customers and sales rocketed.

(g) **Learning curve requirements**. Firms which intend a heavy future involvement might need to learn from the experience that close involvement in an overseas market can bring. This argues against the use of indirect exporting as the method of entry.

(h) **Risks**. Some risks, such as political risk or the risk of the expropriation of overseas assets by foreign governments, might discourage firms from using overseas production as the method of entry to overseas markets. Instead, firms might prefer the indirect export mode as it is safer. On the other hand, the risk of losing touch with customers and their requirements would encourage either direct export or overseas production.

(i) **Control needs**. Control over the marketing mix and the distribution channel varies greatly by method of entry. Production overseas by a wholly owned subsidiary gives a firm absolute control while indirect exporting offers virtually no control to the exporter.

1.6.2 Agents

Strictly speaking an overseas **agent** is an overseas firm hired to effect a sales contract between the principal (ie the exporter) and a customer. Agents do not take title to goods; they earn a commission. In practice, however, the phrase is often understood to include distributors (who do take title). Some agents merely arrange sales; others hold stocks and/or carry out servicing on the principal's behalf.

Advantages of overseas agents

(a) They have extensive knowledge and experience of the overseas market and the customers.

(b) Their existing product range is usually complementary to the exporter's. This may help the exporter penetrate the overseas market.

(c) The exporter does not have to make a large investment outlay.

(d) The political risk is low.

Disadvantages of overseas agents

(a) An intermediary's commitment and motivation may be weaker than the producer's.

(b) Agents usually want steady turnover. Using an agent may not be the most appropriate way of selling low volume, high value goods with unsteady patterns of demand, or where sales are infrequent.

(c) Many agents are too small to exploit a major market to its full extent. Many serve only limited geographical segments.

(d) As a market grows large it becomes less efficient to use an agent. A branch office or subsidiary company will achieve economies of scale.

As with all intermediaries, the use of an agent requires careful planning, selection, motivation and control.

1.6.3 Strategic alliances

These have become a popular model for global expansion. Some writers have argued that they are vital for survival in a world of fierce competition and shorter product life cycles.

 MARKETING AT WORK application

Globalisation is making the world too big for even the largest companies to conquer alone. The channels to market have become so complicated that the only way to cope is through forming partnerships and alliances.

As an example, Cable and Wireless has formed an alliance with Microsoft and Compaq to launch A-Services, an application services provider which draws upon the skills of, and provides market benefits for, all three organisations.

- C & W: telecoms
- Microsoft: software
- Compaq: hardware

Alliance participants tend to be competing firms from different countries, seeking to enhance their competencies by combining resources, but without sacrificing autonomy. The strategic alliance is usually concerned with gaining market entry, remaining globally competitive and attaining economies of scale. It has been suggested, they can be categorised as follows.

- Production based alliances – improving manufacturing and production efficiency
- Distribution based alliances – sharing distribution networks
- Technology based alliances – pooling R & D costs.

Many strategic alliances are within the high-technology sector. Jobber (2009) gives the following examples.

Companies	Competitive area
Nokia/Siemens	Broadband telephony, TV and wireless networks
Microsoft/Nokia	Mobile music
Sony/Ericsson	Mobile music
BP/TNK	Russian oil exploration and extraction
Google/Sun Microsystems	Electronic office systems
Toshiba/Microsoft	High definition DVD players
Sony/Matsushita	Blu-Ray DVD players
Motorola/Skype	Telephone calls over the Internet

Alliances may be **horizontal** (between two firms in the same industry) or **vertical**, involving collaboration between a supplier and a buyer. Sometimes, they involve firms with no such connection. Strategic alliances have mainly concentrated in manufacturing and high tech industries, and increasingly in services (notably airlines, such as the 'One World' alliance involving British Airways, Qantas and several other international collaborators).

A five-point checklist of 'Cs' has been suggested for choosing an alliance partner.

- Complementary skill sets and products
- Capability to enter new markets
- Clear understanding of the commercial arrangements
- Chemistry between the participants
- Shared intellectual capital

1.6.4 Joint ventures

 KEY CONCEPT

concept

A **joint venture** is an arrangement where two or more (often competing) firms join forces for manufacturing, financial and marketing purposes and each has a share in both the equity and the management of the business, sharing profits, risks and assets.

Forming a joint venture with a technologically advanced foreign company can lead to new product development, maybe at a lower cost.

Licensing, franchising and contract manufacture are loose forms of joint venture. However joint ventures are bound by much stronger formal ties. They essentially focus on a single national market. When based abroad, they usually involve partners of unequal strength, for example when a developed country multinational, contributing capital and technology, joins forces with a local firm in a developing country, offering local market knowledge and contacts.

 MARKETING AT WORK

application

Ford and Mobil Oil in the US announced a strategic alliance to work on new fuel systems for the automotive industry. Faced with threatened and actual new exhaust emission standards in California and, probably, the rest of the world, together with resource shortages in oil stocks possible in the foreseeable future, these two companies have chosen to pool R & D expertise to find a solution which can benefit both corporations.

US car manufacturers have acquired parts of Japanese firms to participate in small car development eg Ford and Mazda.

Coca Cola and Cadbury Schweppes bottle and distribute Coca Cola in Great Britain.

A joint venture is usually an alternative to seeking to buy or build a wholly owned manufacturing operation abroad and can offer substantial advantages.

(a)   As the capital outlay is shared, joint ventures are attractive to smaller or risk averse firms, or where very expensive new technologies are being researched and developed (such as the civil aerospace industry).

(b)   When funds are limited, joint ventures permit coverage of a larger number of countries since each one requires less investment by each participator.

(c)   A joint venture can reduce the risk of government intervention as a local firm is involved (eg Club Med pays much attention to this factor). The strong role of government in China means that nearly all foreign ventures in China are alliances with Chinese partners.

(d)   Licensing and franchising often give a company income based on turnover, and any profits from cost reductions accrue to the licensee. In a joint venture, the participating enterprises benefit from all sources of profit.

(e)   Joint ventures can provide close control over marketing and other operations.

(f)   A joint venture with an indigenous firm provides local knowledge. This is a big advantage for firms seeking to do business in difficult markets, such as Russia. Political know-how, site selection expertise and business connections are important.

(g)   In oligopolistic markets, where a few firms are dominant, a foreign firm may find the cost of market entry too high, and seek an alliance with an established competitor.

In 1995, Hungary became Tesco's first international market. Other Eastern European countries have since followed. Then in 1999 Tesco invested £130 million in developing a chain of hypermarkets in South Korea in partnership with Samsung.

Tesco said the move was part of a coherent long term strategy of expanding into underdeveloped markets. It has acquired 13 hypermarkets in Thailand. Outside the UK, Tesco now operates in countries with a total population of 170 million people, including Malaysia (opened in 2002) and China (in 2004). It also sources products from India, with trading offices in Delhi, Bangalore and Thirapur.

www.tesco.com

Partners in a joint venture do not necessarily hold equal shares, and the contribution from each partner may vary. Funding, technology, equipment and marketing organisation may be contributed. There are several forms of joint venture.

- Spider's web, which consists of many firms in a network
- Go-together then split after a period of time, either due to success or failure
- Successive integration

The major disadvantage of joint ventures is that there can be conflicts of interest between the different parties.

- Profit shares
- Amounts invested
- The management of the joint venture
- The marketing strategy

There is always a potential for conflict. There are ways to minimise it.

- Careful selection of partners
- Formulation of jointly beneficial contracts
- Pre arranging for arbitration to resolve any clashes that occur

Channel conflict is considered in more detail in a later chapter.

2 The internal and external environment

2.1 Factors influencing channel strategy

The following checklist can be used to assess the choice of a particular distribution channel.

(a) **Internal factors**

- Cost of ongoing distribution and margins to distributors
- Capital investment required
- Control over the channel
- Coverage of the market
- Character of the distribution: changes in the market
- Continuity in the relationship

(b) **External**

- Customers
- Cultural differences between channel members, expectations of each other
- Competitors: how do they distribute? What influence do they have?
- Company objectives
- Communications

2.2 International and global factors

Although, in domestic markets, firms often give some control over distribution to intermediaries, this problem is magnified in international terms. In some cases, a firm has no choice but to enter into a joint venture. For many firms, overseas operations means they are forced into meeting the aims of intermediaries, even though this may not be the ideal means of the satisfying the needs of the end customer.

As markets open to international trade, channel decisions become more complex. A company can export using host country middlemen or domestic middlemen. These may or may not take title to the goods. Implications of channel management in the case of exporters include a loss of control over product policies like price, image, packaging and service. A producer may undertake a joint venture or licensing agreement or even manufacture abroad. All will have implications for the power structure and control over the product.

2.3 Ethical considerations

Ethics are a set of moral principles or values about what constitutes 'right' and 'wrong' behaviour. They are shaped by social (and sometimes religious) assumptions and beliefs, and – more deliberately – by public and professional bodies, in the form of agreed principles and guidelines (ethical codes or codes of practice) which are designed to protect society's best interests.

 KEY CONCEPT

concept

Marketing ethics are 'the moral principles and values that guide behaviour within the field of marketing, and cover issues such as product safety, truthfulness in marketing communications, honesty in relationships with customers and distributors, pricing issues and the impact of marketing decisions on the environment and society.' (Jobber, 2009)

At the macro level, marketing itself has been subject to criticism from consumer, environmental and anti-globalisation groups for its harmful impacts: generating manufacturing activity and waste products which impact on the environment; encouraging over-consumption of scarce resources; encouraging consumption of harmful products (such as alcohol, tobacco and junk foods); invasion of privacy (eg through direct marketing and customer data collection); erosion of national cultures through globalisation and the exploitation of workers and consumers in less developed markets.

At the corporate level, ethical issues face a marketing organisation as it formulates policies about how it interacts with its various stakeholders. Some of these matters are covered by legislative requirements (eg in regard to product safety, truth in advertising or basic rights of employees). Others are subject to rules laid down by industry regulators, such as Ofcom for the communications industry, the Competition Commission (regulating merger and acquisition activity) and the Advertising Standards Authority (regulating media advertising).

An organisation may have a 'compliance based' approach to ethics which strives merely to uphold these minimal requirements. Alternatively, it may pursue a more proactive 'integrity based' approach, which pursues high ethical standards – whether or not they are illegal. (It is not currently illegal in the UK, for example, to promote extreme dieting among teenage girls, or to put genetically modified ingredients in food products – but both have been argued to be unethical, and leading brands have altered their policies accordingly.)

2.4 Intermediaries and competitors

As noted above, intermediaries will often have equally committed **relationships with the firm's direct competitors**, and this will influence strategy. For many customer goods, a supplier's brand will sit alongside its competitors' products and there is little the supplier can do about it. For other products, distributors may stock one name brand only (for example, in car distribution) and in return be given an exclusive area. In this case, new suppliers may face difficulties in breaking into a market if all the best distribution outlets have been taken up.

2.5 Environmental ('green') considerations

Issues relating to the natural environment have already had a considerable impact on marketing policies and this influence is expected to increase in the future. In the past there has been a tendency to regard marketing, and business activities in general, as incompatible with 'green' principles, but it is now recognised that the two can be complementary.

Much of the concern about companies' responsibilities focuses on their attitude towards environmental concerns of the public. The environment has come to people's attention for a number of reasons.

(a) The **entry** into **decision making** or political roles of the generation which grew up in the 1960s, where ecological issues became aired for the first time, has affected the political climate.

(b) The **growth in prosperity** after World War II has encouraged people to feel that **quality of life**, as opposed to material production and consumption, is no longer a luxury.

(c) **Expansion of media coverage** (eg of famines) and wider discussion of long-term environmental trends (eg the impact of global warming on the weather) has fuelled public anxiety. This has been particularly true in relation to third world issues such as rain forest destruction and drought.

(d) Some **notable disasters** (eg Chernobyl, oil slicks caused by the Exxon Valdez accident and the Gulf War) have aroused public attention.

(e) **Greater scientific knowledge** is available about the effect of productive activity on the environment. For example, it has only recently been possible to measure the hole in the ozone layer and assess its causes.

(f) **Longer-term cultural shifts** against the ideals of science and rationality have encouraged the idealisation of a 'natural' way of life. (Appeals to nature are common in advertising.)

It is possible to identify several ways in which the public concern with environmental issues will impinge on business.

- Consumer demand for products which appear to be **environmentally friendly**
- Demand for **less pollution** from industry
- **Greater regulation** by government
- Demand that businesses be charged with the **external cost** of their activities
- Possible requirements to conduct **ecological** (or environmental) **audits**
- Opportunities to develop products and technologies which are **ecologically friendly**

 MARKETING AT WORK   application

The increase in the use of recycled and recyclable packaging materials over recent years are examples of business recognising its responsibilities toward resource sustainability. The material usually carries a statement declaring it is or can be recycled. This demonstrates that organisations recognise that being considered a relatively 'green' organisation is advantageous to them.

2.6 Economic/financial considerations

Attempts should be made to establish the relative profitability of different distribution channels. An organisation may then be in a position to improve profitability by focussing on more profitable channels, or to improve the profitability of other channels (eg through cost improvement programmes or by increasing the minimum order size). The following example illustrates this.

Example: Jazz Ltd

Jazz Ltd sells two consumer products, X and Y, in two markets A and B. In both markets, sales are made through the following outlets.

- Direct sales to supermarkets
- Wholesalers

Sales and costs for the most recent quarter have been analysed by product and market as follows.

	Market A			Market B			Both markets		
	X	Y	Total	X	Y	Total	X	Y	Total
	£'000	£'000	£'000	£'000	£'000	£'000	£'000	£'000	£'000
Sales	900	600	1,500	1,000	2,000	3,000	1,900	2,600	4,500
Variable production costs	450	450	900	500	1,500	2,000	950	1,950	2,900
	450	150	600	500	500	1,000	950	650	1,600
Variable sales costs	90	60	150	100	100	200	190	160	350
Contribution	360	90	450	400	400	800	760	490	1,250
Share of fixed costs (production, sales, distribution, administration)	170	80	250	290	170	460	460	250	710
Net profit	190	10	200	110	230	340	300	240	540

This analysis shows that both products are profitable, and both markets are profitable. But what about the channels of distribution?

Further analysis of Market A reveals the following.

		Market A	
	Supermarkets	Wholesalers	Total
	£'000	£'000	£'000
Sales	1,125	375	1,500
Variable production costs	675	225	900
	450	150	600
Variable selling costs	105	45	150
Contribution	345	105	450
Direct distribution costs	10	80	90
	335	25	360
Share of fixed costs	120	40	160
Net profit/(loss)	215	(15)	200

This analysis shows that although sales through wholesalers make a contribution after deducting direct distribution costs, the profitability of this channel of distribution is disappointing, and some attention ought perhaps to be given to improving it.

  EXAM TIP  application

In the sample case study, there is a question on the key factors influencing the channel management strategy of Innocent Drinks. Candidates are expected to consider the following issues in their answers:

- Channel length
- Integration
- Logistics
- Distribution density
- Location
- Management of relationships

- Customers
- Cost considerations
- Positioning
- Competitor strategies
- Segmentation

Learning objectives	Covered
1 Determine and prioritise the key principles and purposes of innovative and effective distribution strategies in order to deliver the organisation's business and marketing objectives in a range of different contexts and different sectors to maximise customer requirements	☑ Types of organisational relationship (1.1) ☑ Types of distribution channel (1.2) ☑ Establishing channel strategies (1.3) ☑ Establishing channel needs (1.4) ☑ Developing distribution objectives (1.5) ☑ International distribution (1.6)
2 Critically analyse the implications, challenges and constraints arising from the internal and external environment in the context of the development of channel strategies	☑ Factors influencing channel strategy (2.1) ☑ International and global factors (2.2) ☑ Ethical considerations (2.3) ☑ Intermediaries and competitors (2.4) ☑ Environmental considerations (2.5) ☑ Economic and financial considerations (2.6)

1   Draw a diagram illustrating possible intermediaries between a manufacturer and a consumer.

2   The ideas in the table below are jumbled. Rearrange them into the proper order.

Product characteristic	Issue
Perishability	Training required
After-sales service	More sales outlets
Franchising	Demonstration units are used
Customisation	Speedy delivery

3   Why is it important for companies to have what is termed 'local knowledge' and how does this impact upon distribution choices?

4   An organisation has limited financial resources and a small assortment of products, but potentially a global market. Which type of distribution should it use?

5   Fill in the blank: '_____ distribution is common for many industrial and/or customised product suppliers.'

6   When would using 'surface' transport be preferable to using air freight over a long distance?

7   What is 'intensive distribution'?

8   Explain why the network concept may be more useful than the supply chain concept.

9   What is 'direct' marketing?

10   Why might a company choose to use an overseas agent?

1   Your answers might include some of the following points.

(a)   The middleman of course has to take his 'cut', reducing the revenue available to the producer.

(b)   The producer needs an infrastructure for looking after the retailers – keeping them informed, keeping them well stocked – which might not be necessary in, say, a mail order business.

(c)   The producer loses some part of his control over the marketing of his product. The power of some retailers (for example W H Smith in the world of UK book publishing) is so great that they are able to dictate marketing policy to their suppliers.

2   Other things being equal, if the order pattern is a small number of high-value orders, then direct distribution is more likely to occur. If there are numerous low-value orders, then the cost of fulfilling them promptly will be high and the use of intermediaries is likely.

3   Prices can be as much as 50% below conventional retail outlets, and shoppers can choose from a wide range of branded goods that they otherwise might not be able to afford. They can also turn a shopping trip into a day out, as factory outlet centres are designed as 'destination' shopping venues, offering facilities such as playgrounds and restaurants.

Manufacturers enjoy the ability to sell surplus stock at a profit in a controlled way that does not damage the brand image. They have also turned the shops into a powerful marketing tool for test-marketing products before their high street launch, and selling avant-garde designs that have not caught on in the main retail market.

4   Ideally they should look at the characteristics of the service and match these to the characteristics of the method of distribution. McDonalds for example is able to use a franchise method because they need to standardise their product and service experience.

Train companies however are complex cases because they need to use the existing railway infrastructure, and differentiate their point of service delivery (eg the train). They are also able to choose between a number of ticket sale mechanisms such as agents, direct booth sales and internet options.

1

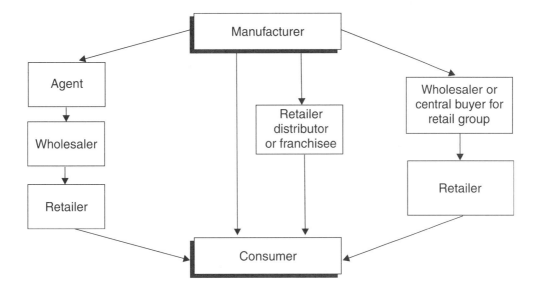

2

Product characteristic	Issue
Perishability	Speedy delivery
After-sales service	Training required
Franchising	More sales outlets
Customisation	Demonstration units are used

3   As production has tended to become centralised in pursuit of economies of scale, the need to understand and be 'close to' local markets has grown. This can mean that distributors who have knowledge of customers in a particular geographical area need to be chosen – very important when considering international distribution.

4   In theory the organisation should use an intermediary. However, effective internet distribution may make direct selling possible, especially if the product can be distributed over the internet (such as some software packages).

5   Direct.

6   When, for example, speed is not vital in delivering the product, or its weight makes air freight prohibitively expensive.

7   Intensive distribution involves blanket coverage of distributors in one segment of the total market, such as a local area.

8   The network concept portrays the complexity of business relationships more realistically. It raises the possibility of a wider range of connections and collaborations, and recognises the potential of the 'extended enterprise' to bring resources and competencies to the firm.

9   Marketing without intermediaries.

10 (a)   They have extensive knowledge and experience of the overseas market and the customers.

    (b)   Their existing product range is usually complementary to the exporter's. This may help the exporter penetrate the overseas market.

    (c)   The exporter does not have to make a large investment outlay.

    (d)   The political risk is low.

References

Blythe, J (2009) <u>Principles and Practice of Marketing</u>, 2nd edition, South-Western/Cengage Learning.

Blythe, J (2008) <u>Essentials of Marketing</u>, 4th edition, FT Prentice Hall.

Brassington, F and Pettitt, S (2006) <u>Principles of Marketing</u>, 4th edition, FT Prentice Hall.

Dibb S, Simkin L, Pride WM, Ferrell OC (2005) <u>Marketing: Concepts and Strategies</u>, 5th edition, Houghton Mifflin.

Jobber (2009) <u>Principles and Practice of Marketing</u>.6th edition, McGraw Hill Higher Education

Christopher, M (2005) <u>Logistics & Supply Chain Management</u> (3rd edition). FT Pitman, London.

Christopher M, Payne A & Ballantyne D (2002) <u>Relationship Marketing: Creating Stakeholder Value</u>, Elsevier Butterworth-Heinemann, Oxford.

Cox, A & Lamming, R (1997) *'Managing Supply in the Firm of the Future'* in European Journal of Purchasing & Supply Management. Vol 3, No 2.

Gummesson, E (2002) <u>Total Relationship Marketing</u> (2002) Elsevier Butterworth-Heinemann, Oxford.

Kemp, E (2008) *'Onitsuka Tiger Introduces trainer vending machine to London'* Marketing Magazine 14th April 2008.

Peck HL, Payne A, Christopher M & Clark M (1999) <u>Relationship Marketing: Strategy and Implementation</u>, Elsevier Butterworth-Heinemann, Oxford.

Chapter 4
Managing channel partners

Topic list

Introduction

Physical distribution is concerned with the movement of goods via road, rail, sea and air – ie all about organising transportation to move goods in a timely and secure way from producer to consumer, taking all factors into account including budget.

Logistics takes a holistic view of the process – it considers the entire process of delivering value to customers, starting with raw materials extraction. Logistics takes the whole transport problem and integrates it into a smooth system for moving goods from where they are produced to where they are needed.

Supply chain management has been described as the integration of business processes from end user through original suppliers to provide products, services and information that add value for customers.

Behind these definitions, and implicit in them, is a web of relationships between the organisations responsible, at various points in the chain, for delivering goods to customers. This chapter builds upon material covered earlier and examines those relationships in more detail.

Syllabus linked learning objectives

By the end of the chapter you will be able to:

Learning objectives	Syllabus link
1 Assess the nature and scope of intermediaries and determine criteria for selecting intermediary partners and the likely Return on Investment (ROI) they can achieve	2.3
2 Determine the level and scope of controls required for effectively monitoring and managing distribution channels	2.4
3 Determine the contractual requirements and service level agreements for engaging intermediary partners within the distribution channel	2.6

1   Selecting intermediary partners

Blythe has commented that:

"Wholesalers, agents, retailers and other intermediaries perform useful functions in ensuring that the right products reach the right customers at the right time and in the right condition."

1.1 Types of distribution intermediary

KEY CONCEPT

concept

As we have seen in an earlier chapter, there are basically two types of **intermediary**: those who take title to the goods (wholesalers and retailers) and those who don't (agents).

Firms may distribute products or services direct to customers, or they may choose from a wide range of intermediaries: wholesalers, dealers, agents, franchisees, retailers or multiple stores. Glance back at Figure 3.4 in Chapter 3 if you need a remainder of the options and the distribution channels they create.

1.2 Roles and responsibilities of distribution intermediaries

Intermediaries reconcile the needs of producers and customers:

- Producers manufacture a small range of goods in large amounts
- Customers need a wide range of goods in small amounts
- They make the goods accessible (as they are generally made a long way from where they will be consumed)
- They provide 'ownership utility' (goods available immediately)
- They can provide specialist services (aftersales, maintenance, installation, training)

Figure 4.1 Roles/responsibilities of intermediaries

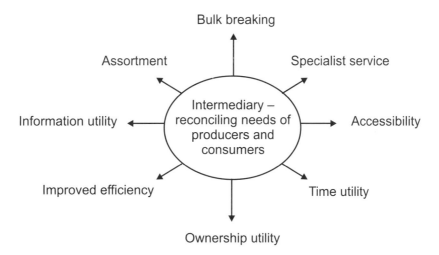

1.3 Criteria for selection

Some intermediaries (such as the large supermarkets in the European grocery sector) have more power in the supply chain than producers, so they can pick and choose where they do business. Retailers such as the large supermarkets are often the spokespeople for the customers – they gauge consumer need and translate that into purchases from wholesalers and manufacturers.

Channel strategy is all about choosing the right distributors. Selecting the right distributor depends upon a number of factors, related to the market, the producer, the product itself and competitors.

Figure 4.2 Factors affecting choice of distributor

If channel strategy is all about choosing the right distributors, then Innocent Drinks appeared to get it wrong in the eyes of some consumers when it chose to start selling its drinks in McDonalds outlets. Despite the obvious willingness of McDonalds to stock the product, and the potentially huge market that could be reached, many individual buyers perceived the decision as a 'sell out' of Innocent's values. Balancing issues of strategic fit with customer expectations proved to be problematic in this case.

1.4 Intermediaries and profitability

In practice, two main variables have to be weighed up in channel management. There is a trade-off between the total distribution cost, and the level of service to be given to customers. What are the revenue and margin gains to be derived from an improved level of service?

Effective supply chain management is a powerful tool for enhancing profitability and creating competitive advantage.

- Reduces costs
- Improves asset utilisation
- Reduces order cycle time
- Shuts out competitors by denying them access to the channel

All of these will have a positive effect upon profitability.

1.5 New and emerging channels

ICT has enabled direct marketing of products and services to consumers/business users, cutting short distribution channels, by:

- **Facilitating conventional direct sales**: offering sales force information linked to central databases, allowing personalised direct mail and online mail order catalogues.

- Empowering customers to **purchase direct from virtual stores and auctions**. e-commerce and its B2B equivalent (e-purchasing) via the Internet has exploded in many sectors over recent years, especially in markets such as music and books, travel products, banking services, groceries and specialist goods.

- **Facilitating home delivery** of goods, eg by allowing remote ordering, payment and tracking – and 'virtual' supply (eg by downloading information, software, books or music direct from the Internet).

- The **computerisation of purchase systems and record keeping**, covering stock control, purchase requisitions, purchase orders, expediting/tracking of deliveries, goods receipts and the generation of reports.

- **Electronic Data Interchange (EDI)** allows direct transfer of queries, information, orders, invoices and payments via cable or telecommunication link between supplier and purchaser.

- **Point-of-sale data capture systems**, such as bar-coding and electronic point of sale (EPOS) systems, which allow stock and sale information to be recorded in a database and processed as management information for retailers and suppliers.

- Warehousing data capture systems, using barcodes and scanners to carry out inventory checks and re-ordering.

Increasingly, the online shopping experience is simulating 'place', with familiar processes (eg 'shopping carts' and 'checkouts'), access to people (eg e-mail contact or voice/phone options) and physical evidence (eg downloadable/printable order confirmations, vouchers and brochures).

Direct distribution and e-distribution are growing trends, and represent significant cost savings for the organisation. They may be used as part of a relationship marketing strategy, as a way of establishing **direct contact with consumers** which can be developed into a relationship over time. Customers may, for example, have to register on a website in order to make a purchase, and may thereby be exposed to a range of membership benefits (as in the example of Amazon.com, say). Direct and e-distribution strategies may form key parts of brand identity, as with i-Tunes (digital entertainment downloads).

It is worth noting, however, that direct and e-distribution strategies may create issues in relationships with other stakeholders, for which **trade-offs** may have to be made. For example, they put the marketing organisation in the position of competing against its channel intermediaries for sales. This may damage relationships unless it can be carefully justified and mutual benefits negotiated (eg by including stockist lists on the website). Such strategies may also damage communities eg in the case of local bank branch closures (in favour of Internet banking), or impact on businesses (eg CD and video stores going out of business due to competition from downloadable formats).

It is worth noting, too, that while many products can be ordered on the Internet, they cannot all be delivered electronically.

 MARKETING AT WORK   application

Fulfillment or physical distribution of high-volume, global orders may cause problems for customer relationships. A US survey by the Boston Consulting Group found a variety of problems, which Internet marketers will need to overcome.

% respondents citing the problem

- Hard to contact customer service 20%
- Product took much longer than expected to arrive 15%
- Returned the product 10%
- Tried to contact customer service and failed 8%
- Ordered product that never arrived 4%
- Wrong product arrived and couldn't return it 3%

So much for sustained, value-adding, relationship-building service encounters!

The Internet is not expanding at the same rate in every sphere of business. The rate of growth is influenced by:

(a)   The degree to which the customer can be persuaded to believe that using the Internet will **deliver some added-value** – in terms of quickness, simplicity and price.

(b)   Whether there are 'costs' which the **customer** has to bear – not exclusively 'costs' in the financial sense, but also such 'costs' as the isolated online shopping experience.

(c)   The **market segment** to which the individual belongs. The Internet is largely the preserve of more affluent and technologically competent individuals.

(d)   The frequency of **supplier/customer contact** required.

(e)   The availability of **incentives** which might stimulate Internet acceptance. For example, interest rates on bank accounts which are higher than those available through conventional banks (Egg), the absence of any charges (Freeserve) or the creation of penalties for over-the-counter transactions (Abbey National).

 MARKETING AT WORK   application

Amazon, the online retailer, offers discounts to customers willing to reserve new products in advance. By tracking these advance sales, Amazon can develop more accurate demand forecasts.

2 Controls for monitoring and managing the distribution channel

2.1 Setting distribution objectives

The distribution system needs to be managed in such a way that overall objectives are achieved. Contributors to achievement of objectives include the following (Jobber, 2009):

(a) **Customer service**: 'What level of service should be provided?'

For example, 95% of orders to be delivered within one week of receipt. Higher standards tend to mean higher costs, such as stockholding, so customer service standards tend to become a key decision criterion.

(b) **Order processing**: 'How should orders be handled?'

Reducing the time between placing an order and receiving the goods can be achieved by careful analysis of the processes involved. Most companies are moving to computer-based systems to improve efficiencies in this area.

(c) **Inventory control**: 'How much inventory should be held?'

A balance needs to be struck between minimising stockholding costs and avoiding the danger of being out of stock of key items. '

Jobber, comments as follows

"To always have in stock every conceivable item that a customer might order would normally be prohibitively expensive."

(d) **Warehousing**: 'Where should the stock be held? How many warehouses should be used?'

Storage warehouses and distribution centres cost money. As always, it is a balance between customer service and cost considerations. Having numerous locally-based warehouses to hold stock will enable fantastic customer service, but will involve very high costs.

(e) **Transportation**: 'How will the products be transported?'

On time, and without damage, is the key goal. The five major transport methods are rail, road, air, water and pipelines for liquids and gases.

(f) **Materials handling**: 'How will the products be handled during transportation?'

These days there is generally a high level of automation, in order to reduce the incidence of human error. Two key developments are 'unit handling' (combining multiple packages) and 'containerisation' (combining many quantities into a single container). Packaging is important too. It needs to be rigorous enough to withstand potentially rough handling, balanced with issues of cost and appearance.

 MARKETING AT WORK   application

Tetley Tea developed new packaging materials to increase the density per pallet of its products by 50%, reducing the number of vehicle loads between the factory and the warehouse.

2.2 Managing third party relationships

In many ways, relationships with suppliers and distributors are the same as those with colleagues, customers, visitors and other business contacts and require many of the same features.

In other respects, however, relationships with suppliers and distributors are different to those with colleagues and visitors. As business relationships, they raise a number of other issues.

(a)   They involve dealings with other business organisations which have their own aims and objectives: these may or may not be congruent.

(b)   They involve dealings with representatives of other business organisations, who have a dual responsibility to you (as client) and (primarily) to their employers.

(c)   They are governed by legal terms and constraints, expressed in contracts.

(d)   They are subject to commercial and competitive pressures: if one party is not satisfied, they can break the relationship.

(e)   They are shaped by the operational requirements of the work for which the relationship was formed.

2.3 Evaluating channel members

The evaluation of channel members will lead to decisions on which ones to keep and which ones to drop. Reasons for poor performance might include:

(a)   A shortfall in skills (training may help here)

(b)   A lack of motivation (this may be improved by financial incentives or the adoption of a 'partner' approach)

Such evaluation is likely to be more frequent and wider in scope (and therefore more effective) when the balance of power is held by a manufacturer/producer with a strong brand and lots of distributors willing to be involved with the product. When the channel member holds all the cards, then the producer is likely to be relatively powerless. This tends to be the case with the large European grocery retailers.

Jobber (2009) sets out the following criteria for evaluating channel members.

- Sales volume and value
- Profitability
- Stock levels
- Quality/position of displays
- New accounts opened
- Sales and marketing capability
- Quality of customer service
- Market information feedback
- Ability/willingness to meet commitments
- Attitudes and motivation
- Personal capability

2.4 Benchmarking

 KEY CONCEPT Concept

Benchmarking is the establishment, through data gathering, of targets and comparators, through which relative levels of performance (and particularly areas of underperformance) can be identified.

Benchmarking essentially involves comparing your operations to somebody else's. There are four types of benchmarking.

- **Internal benchmarking**: comparison with high-performing units or functions in the same organisation. One division's marketing function might be benchmarked against another, for example, to lift standards and consistency within the organisation.

- **Functional benchmarking**: comparison with a best-practice external example of a function, regardless of industry. This is also known as operational or process benchmarking. An IT company might benchmark its marketing function against that of Apple Computers or Coca Cola, say, as a way of lifting its processes to best-practice level.

- **Competitor benchmarking**: comparison with a high-performing competitor in key areas which impact on performance: for example, Dell comparing its product reliability, time-to-market for innovation or B2B marketing with Hewlett Packard.

- **Generic benchmarking**: comparison of business processes across functional boundaries and industries. The organisation can benchmark itself against 'excellent' companies or an excellence framework (such as the EFQM), or an organisation with a reputation for learning, innovation, relationship marketing – or whatever the organisation is interested in pursuing.

2.4.1 Benefits of benchmarking

Some of the potential benefits claimed for benchmarking include the following.

- It enables the firm to **assess its existing performance** and position, and particularly its competitive strengths and weaknesses or areas in which it falls short of best practice.

- It focuses on **improvement in key results areas** (critical success factors) and sets targets designed to be realistic (since other organisations have achieved them) yet challenging (since the benchmarking organisation hasn't yet achieved them). This is the most effective combination for motivation.

- It replaces an ad hoc or subjective approach to performance measurement, improvement and competitive advantage-seeking with a set of **objective, systematic criteria**.

- The process is generally carried out by the managers who have to implement and live with the changes: this should help to secure **stakeholder buy-in** for improvement.

- It **stimulates research and feedback-seeking** about the organisation's strengths, weaknesses and core competences.

- It generates **new ideas and insights** 'outside the box' of the organisation's usual ways of thinking and acting. Analysis of competitor products and processes, for example, may give rise to ideas which can be learned from or imitated.

It should be noted that there are also **limitations and drawbacks** to benchmarking as an approach to performance measurement and improvement.

- It may suggest that there is **one best way** of doing business. However, the organisation needs to take a contingency approach to problem-solving, suitable to its own resources, strengths, weaknesses and environment – rather than an 'off-the-shelf' approach drawn from other organisations' experience.

- The benchmark may be **'yesterday's solution to tomorrow's problem'**. For example, a cross-channel ferry company might benchmark its activities against airlines and other ferry companies – however the Channel Tunnel has emerged as the main competitor for cross-channel ferry services.

- It is a reactive, **'catch-up' or 'me too' exercise**, which may not result in the seeking and development of unique, distinctive and hard-to-imitate core competences.

- It depends on **accurate and detailed information** about competitors (which may pose research and ethical challenges), and on appropriate analogies/comparisons in other industries (because of the need to compare like with like).

2.4.2 The process of benchmarking

Oakland (1991) puts forward a 15-step benchmarking process.

Plan	1	Select the function, unit or process to be benchmarked
	2	Identify the exemplar of best practice, key competitor or successful partner (using industry analysis, customer feedback or a benchmarking consultant)
	3	Identify the criteria to be benchmarked (based on critical success factors)
	4	Establish a benchmarking project team (clear roles, authority and resources)
	5	Plan methods for data collection (surveys, interviews, documents, visits)
	6	Conduct research
	7	Manage direct contacts with the target organisation (interviews, visits etc)
Analyse	8	Collate and analyse benchmark data to compare performance: identify performance 'gaps'
	9	Create a 'competence centre' and knowledge bank: document information
	10	Analyse underlying cultural, structural and managerial factors that enable performance to benchmark standard (ie not just performance measures)
Develop	11	Develop new performance standards, targets and measures to reflect desired improvements
	12	Develop systematic action plans (change management programmes, resource plans etc with time-scales, accountabilities and monitoring/review processes)
Improve	13	Implement the action plans
Review	14	Continuously monitor and/or periodically review progress and results
	15	Review the benchmark process for future learning.

2.4.3 Benchmarking against the competition

Benchmarks can be set on a variety of key performance indicators as an objective form of control.

(a) **Process benchmarking**, where data is exchanged between companies with similar administrative and manufacturing processes. For example, one of the factors affecting aircraft turnaround away from the home is the availability of spare parts required for routine maintenance. This process is very similar to the provision of field maintenance for office systems such as photocopiers and computers.

(b) **Competitor benchmarking** focuses on the performance and relative strengths of direct competitors using information from customer and supplier interviews and published data from any source available. A firm tries to be as good as its competitors.

In reality it is difficult to benchmark against competitors because it is often impossible to gain access to key measures. Belonging to relevant trade associations may be one way of overcoming this problem as competitors look to improve standards throughout the industry via the association which may promote more shared information. Typically areas where information may be shared relate to issues of social importance such as environmental awareness and health related issues.

 MARKETING AT WORK application

Several organisations in the processed foods industry benchmark against industry norms with regards to levels of salt, fat and sugars found within foodstuffs.

3 Contractual issues

3.1 Types of contract and typical terms

In basic terms, a contract or legally binding agreement exists between two parties if there is:

- The intention to create a legal relationship (as opposed to a purely personal one)
- Offer and acceptance (agreeing to supply or receive goods or services)
- Consideration (some payment given or promised for the goods or services to be supplied)

This covers most of the transactions you will come across in marketing activity. A contract does not have to be a formal legal document: it can be a letter, or even a strong verbal understanding (as long as the three basic elements can be proved).

A contract may set out express (clearly stated) terms.

- Delivery/completion dates

- Description of the goods/services to be provided

- Quality standards below which the goods/services will not be accepted

- The amount to be paid, and when, and what it covers and does not cover

- Any conditions and caveats either party wishes to impose: for example, that they will not be liable for errors arising from faulty components or information provided by the other party; that in the event of cancellation of the project, they will be paid for all work done up to the date of cancellation

3.1.1 Agent/distributor agreements

Some of the key contract areas that will need addressing in agent/distributor agreements are as follows:

- Applicable laws
- Taxes
- Duration of agreement
- Termination of agreement
- Records and communication
- Arbitration procedures
- Payment and compensation

- Access to facilities and personnel
- Inventory
- Confidentiality
- Trademarks, trade name etc
- Sale or service agreements
- Advertising and promotion decisions

 ACTIVITY 1

application

Get hold of a copy of the terms and conditions of any service supplier you may do business with. Note the main issues covered by contract terms and identify areas where your procedures and practices may need adjusting to comply more securely.

A contract also has implied terms, which are 'understood' from the context of the business relationship. If not expressly stated, for example, it is still implied that goods and services should be of reasonable quality, provided to specification and within a reasonable timescale.

When working with other organisations, it is helpful to exchange a contract, letter or purchase order, which:

- Is in writing (even if only to confirm a verbal agreement)
- Defines the products/services to be supplied, and the delivery schedule
- Defines the division of responsibility between the parties
- Confirms the negotiated terms and conditions for payment

The procedures to be followed will be dictated by the particular task or project in hand. Simply following recommended procedures correctly and efficiently is a major element in working smoothly and successfully with other organisations.

In general, however, a systematic approach to collaboration should include the following.

(a) Clear and specific briefing on requirements. Objectives, schedules, budgets and job specifications make everyone's job easier.

(b) Joint planning which clearly defines the scope and limit of activity, and establishes how to implement any recommendations.

(c) Negotiation of terms.

(d) Sharing of information and resources.

(e) Monitoring, checking and approval. Liaison and accountability is the way to ensure that objectives are met.

(f) Exchanging feedback. Developing on-going relationships requires mutual adjustment. Regular feedback meetings allow both parties to reinforce positive aspects, identify and solve problems and celebrate successes.

(g) Paying debts on time. Nothing sours a commercial relationship like non-payment or persistent late payment.

3.2 Contracting with overseas partners

Global B2B intermediaries can provide:

- Fast delivery
- Local credit
- Product information
- Assistance in buying decisions
- Anticipation of customer needs

They can also:

- Buy and hold stocks
- Combine the outputs of various manufacturers
- Share the credit risk
- Share the selling risk
- Forecast market needs
- Provide market information

Agreements tend to vary among firms and between markets. Even so, they normally include all or most of the following features.

(a) Identity of the parties

(b) The purpose of the agreement

(c) The products that are subject to the agreement and any future changes

(d) The agent's territory

(e) Exclusivity
　　(i) For the agent
　　(ii) For the producer

(f) Duties of the principal, such as promotional support and training of the agent's staff

(g) Duties of the agent such as minimum turnover required and after sales service

(h) Agent's commission, dealing with issues such as the percentage rate, any variation across markets and dates payable

(i) Duration and dates of contract period

(j) Provision for termination before expiry of contract (for example breach of contract and bankruptcy)

(k) Arbitration provisions for settling major disputes

(l)   Authentic text (that is evidence of which text is authentic if the agreement is written in two different languages)

(m)   Specification of the country whose law governs the contract

The above list should be treated as a skeleton checklist. Most of the points mentioned should be considered in far greater detail before any specific agreement is finalised.

MARKETING AT WORK

application

Jobber (2009) refers to a study finding that over 90% of producers carry out evaluations of their overseas channel partners, usually based upon sales-related measures. However, it also found that less than half of these producers used mutually agreed objectives as a basis for evaluating performance. If a partnership approach, based upon clarity of and commitment to objectives, is to prevail then there needs to be a move away from comparisons with past performance and towards a more mutual relationship with overseas channel partners.

3.3 Service level agreements (SLAs)

KEY CONCEPT

concept

A **service level agreement** is a formal statement of performance requirements, setting out the nature and range of the services to be provided, and the level of performance that is expected.

Service level agreements are covered in more detail in the chapter on Customer Service and Customer Care.

3.3.1 Determining service levels

A high, consistent and competitive level of customer service (seen as an on-going chain of satisfying service encounters or episodes) is a key to customer satisfaction and loyalty – and therefore to long-term relationships of mutual advantage – in many industries. It is also one of the main ways in which an organisation can add customer value.

There are many dimensions in service delivery, before and after the service encounter itself.

*   The creation of a **corporate culture** which expresses and models customer-focused values, and reinforces those values through its selection, appraisal and reward systems, and the messages it sends employees at every level.

*   The creation of service-supporting **internal relationships** and **internal marketing**: the recruitment of skilled customer-facing people; the supply of appropriate training; the empowerment of staff to take decisions that will satisfy and retain customers; and the reward and recognition of staff who deliver outstanding service.

*   Gathering, analysing, communicating and acting on **customer feedback**. Feedback and adjustment (addressing customer concerns and complaints) are crucial in minimising dissatisfaction and demonstrating commitment to customer value. Constructive handling of problems and complaints (sometimes called 'service recovery') may lead to restored satisfaction – and even strengthened relationship, because of the supplier's demonstrated commitment.

*   Establishing a **partnership approach** to relationships with customers, suppliers and intermediaries (distributors, retail outlets, call centres) in order to support high levels of service at all links in the value-delivery chain.

*   Ensuring **promise fulfilment** (Jobber, 2009): making realistic promises (to manage customer expectations); enabling staff and service systems to deliver on promises made; and keeping promises during service encounters.

*   Offering **support services** (eg warranties, servicing, user training and help-lines) to facilitate customers in using the product safely and satisfyingly, and support them through changes and difficulties.

*   Reinforcing loyalty with **customer incentives** and **rewards**, to show that the organisation values its 'valued customers'.

- Establishing **customer-friendly systems**. It is no good expecting staff to give great service to customers if the systems, procedures, technology and information flows do not support their efforts.

ACTIVITY 2

While high levels of customer service are essential for customer retention, they may not be sufficient. Why?

3.3.2 Effective service measures

Service levels should be:

- Reasonable (ie not unnecessarily high, incurring additional unnecessary costs)
- Prioritised by the customer
- Easily monitored (ie quantifiable as far as possible, and observable)
- Easy to understand

3.4 Establishing and monitoring key performance indicators (KPIs)

Key performance indicators can be drawn up to suit the needs of each particular service contract.

KEY CONCEPT

concept

Key performance indicators (KPIs) are specific measures of the performance of an organisation, against which performance can be evaluated.

KPIs need to be capable of direct and consistent measurement, and for this reason it is preferable that they are quantitative. They may for example be expressed in the following ways in the context of channel management.

- Cost, or cost savings
- Time
- Quantity of outputs (eg deliveries)
- Number of complaints
- Ratio of on-time deliveries

MARKETING AT WORK

application

KPIs for a food manufacturer might cover:

- Number of on-time deliveries
- Value of cost reductions or savings achieved
- Time taken to complete certain routes
- Number of drivers employed
- Food spoilt/wasted due to transport delays
- Extra costs incurred for emergency deliveries or non-routine items
- Customer satisfaction and feedback

3.4.1 Monitoring service levels

A wide range of techniques is available for monitoring service provision and service levels.

- Observation and experience
- Spot checks and sample testing
- Business results
- Customer feedback
- Electronic performance monitoring
- Self assessment by the service provider
- Collaborative performance review (ie shared by the customer and the service provider)

If it is to be applied effectively in improving service levels, the information obtained from these measures must be passed on to the managers with overall responsibility for performance.

ACTIVITY 3

evaluation

Suppose that a food manufacturer decides to use a specialist firm for the transport of its refrigerated goods to a wholesaler. What basic service level issues could be agreed upon and included?

Learning objective review

Learning objectives	Covered
1 Assess the nature and scope of intermediaries and determine criteria for selecting intermediary partners and the likely Return on Investment (ROI) they can achieve	☑ Types of distribution intermediary (1.1) ☑ Roles and responsibilities of intermediaries (1.2) ☑ Criteria for selection (1.3) ☑ Intermediaries and profitability (1.4) ☑ New and emerging channels (1.5)
2 Determine the level and scope of controls required for effectively monitoring and managing distribution channels	☑ Setting distribution objectives (2.1) ☑ Managing third party relationships (2.2) ☑ Evaluation (2.3) ☑ Benchmarking (2.4)
3 Determine the contractual requirements and service level agreements for engaging intermediary partners within the distribution channel	☑ Types of contract and typical terms (3.1) ☑ Contracting with overseas partners (3.2) ☑ Service level agreements (3.3) ☑ Establishing and monitoring KPIs (3.4)

1   Define 'intermediary'.

2   Give five functions of intermediaries.

3   How can effective supply chain management enhance profitability?

4   Why is inventory control an important part of distribution management?

5   Give six criteria that are useful in evaluating the performance of channel members.

6   How might a producer overcome a lack of motivation on the part of a channel member?

7   What is a service level agreement?

8   Can you see a reason why a firm might decide that its service levels can be 'reasonable', rather than 'high'?

9   Give some KPIs in the context of channel management.

10   What product factors may influence the choice of distributor?

1   This requires your own research.

2   High levels of service may even get taken for granted over time, and cease to be an incentive to loyalty, in the face of competitor offers.

3   •   How often is the transport service to be provided?

     •   During what hours can it be carried out?

     •   How many staff will be involved?

     •   How far will the service extend? For example, does it include the loading of the goods on to the trucks, or is that to be arranged by the manufacturer?

     •   What speed of response will be required by the transport company if the manufacturer needs to make a non-routine or urgent change to the delivery schedules? What extra cost might it incur?

     •   How can the manufacturer monitor the performance of the transporter?

     •   What rate will be paid?

1   An intermediary is someone who 'mediates' or brings about a settlement between the original supplier and the ultimate buyer.

2   Bulk breaking, specialist service, accessibility, time utility, ownership utility, improved efficiency, information utility, assortment.

3   It has the potential to reduce costs, improve asset utilisation, reduce the time taken to fulfill orders and shut out competitors.

4   Inventory control is important because there are significant costs associated with holding stock. A balance needs to be found between holding enough stock to satisfy customer demand, but not so much that working capital is tied up unnecessarily storing goods which may only be ordered infrequently.

5   Sales volume and value
Profitability
Stock levels
Quality/position of displays
New accounts opened
Sales and marketing capability
Quality of customer service
Market information feedback
Ability/willingness to meet commitments
Attitudes and motivation
Personal capability

6   Through additional financial incentives, or the development of a more inclusive 'partnering' approach.

7   A service level agreement is a formal statement of performance requirements, setting out the nature and range of the services to be provided, and the level of performance that can be expected.

8   A high level of service, which the customer may not expect anyway, is likely to incur unnecessarily high costs. It will be better for the firm to set reasonable service levels that are more easily attained and afforded.

9   Cost; time; quantity of deliveries; number of complaints; ratio of on-time deliveries.

10 Complexity of the product; its perishability; special handling needs.

References

Blythe, J (2009) Principles and Practice of Marketing, 2nd edition, South-Western/Cengage Learning.

Blythe, J (2008) Essentials of Marketing, 4th edition, FT Prentice Hall.

Jobber (2009) Principles and Practice of Marketing. 6th edition, McGraw Hill Higher Education

Sodhi, M.S. & Tang, C.S. 'Rethinking links in the global supply chain', FT.com Special Reports, 29 January 2009.

Chapter 5

Managing wider stakeholder needs

Introduction

Marketers need to identify and appreciate the different **needs**, **expectations, interests and drivers** of different stakeholders within the distribution channel. A 'one size fits all' approach will not work, given the multiple, differing – and sometimes conflicting – needs and expectations of different stakeholders.

This chapter begins with an analysis of what a 'stakeholder' is (section 1) and then examines the range of those needs and expectations within the marketing channel (section 2). Section 3 considers the importance of proper information and communication in managing the relationship with stakeholders.

Conflict is an expected part of business relationships, and section 4 examines some of the ways that it can arise, before suggesting strategies for dealing with it.

Syllabus linked learning objectives

By the end of the chapter you will be able to:

Learning objectives	Syllabus link
1 Assess the requirements for managing the various stakeholders' needs within the distribution channel, in particular, reviews, reporting, communications and conflict management	2.5

1   What are stakeholders?

For any given organisation, there will be a number of individuals and groups who have some kind of a relationship with it, or have invested in it in some way, or are affected by its activities – and who therefore have a legitimate interest or 'stake' in it.

These parties are called stakeholders.

KEY CONCEPT

concept

'**Stakeholders** are those individuals or groups who depend on the organisation to fulfil their own goals and on whom, in turn, the organisation depends.' (Johnson & Scholes, 2005, p179)

'**Stakeholders** are individuals and/or groups who are affected by or affect the performance of the organisation in which they have an interest. Typically they would include employees, managers, creditors, suppliers, shareholders (if appropriate) and society at large.' (Worthington & Britton, 2006, p220)

'A **stakeholder** of a company is an individual or group that either is harmed by, or benefits from, the company or whose rights can be violated, or have to be respected, by the company. Other groups, besides shareholders, who typically would be considered stakeholders are communities associated with the company, employees, customers of the company's products, and suppliers.' (Jobber, 2009)

1.1 Stakeholders in what?

The definitions of stakeholders quoted above come from influential textbooks on corporate strategy and management. In this context, stakeholders are regarded as having an interest in, and the potential to seek influence over, the broad purposes and plans of an organisation: managers are urged to take account of their expectations, concerns and possible positive or negative responses – or even to involve them in decision making – when developing and communicating strategic-level changes.

However, we can also speak about stakeholders in more specific contexts that might affect a marketer's role, and particularly the distribution function.

- There are stakeholders in particular organisational processes, activities and functions – such as distribution. Marketers need to consider the possible impacts of their plans on stakeholders; potential constraints on (or even resistance to) their plans arising from stakeholder groups; and – on the positive side – potential for stakeholders to support and add value to their plans. In the context of this syllabus, managing channel stakeholders will directly affect the processes that contribute towards value creation for customers.

- There are stakeholders in particular decisions, plans and projects. Huczynski & Buchanan (2001, p601) define a stakeholder as 'anyone likely to be affected, directly or indirectly, by an organisational change or programme of changes'. Examples that would affect the distribution function might include a new advertising campaign, a change in prices, the launch of a new product, or a rationalisation of the supplier base. You should be able to think of a number of individuals or groups who might be affected, positively or negatively, by each of these plans.

  EXAM TIP   concept

A task may focus upon the stakeholders of an organisation – but it may also focus more specifically on the stakeholders of particular marketing activities. Channel management strategy is the subject of a question on the sample case study.

The key point of stakeholder theory is that an organisation affects its environment and is affected by its environment. The boundaries of the organisation are highly permeable: influence flows from internal stakeholders outwards (eg through marketing) and from external stakeholders inwards (eg if a major customer pressures sales staff to represent its interests within the organisation, or more generally if a marketing-oriented organisation seeks to listen to its customers and meet their needs).

1.1.1 Process and outcome stakeholders

The distinction between process stakeholders and outcome stakeholders is often made in project contexts, and this may also be a useful way of ensuring that you think comprehensively about who may have a stake.

- **Outcome stakeholders** have an interest in the outcomes of a strategy, project or decision. So, for example, customers have an interest in the outcomes of marketing decisions: sales promotions, price rises, new products and distribution outlets.

- **Process stakeholders** have an interest in the process by which outcomes are reached. Customers are less likely to have an interest in how the marketing decisions are reached, but managers and departments in the organisation will have such an interest: they will have expectations and concerns around whether their viewpoint is taken into account, whether information is shared, who is responsible and accountable for the decision, whether clear goals and plans have been agreed and how progress is going to be monitored and measured. Other external parties may also be concerned that the processes of marketing are legal, fair and ethical (for example, that large marketing organisations have not colluded in setting prices, or that privacy has not been breached in gathering customer data).

1.2 Categories of stakeholder

There are three broad categories of stakeholder in an organisation, as you may remember from your earlier studies. This is just to recap:

- **Internal stakeholders**, who are members of the organisation. Key examples include the directors, managers and employees of a company – or the members of a club or association, or the volunteer workers in a charity. They may also include other functions of the organisation (eg production or finance) which have a stake in marketing activity, and/or separate units of the organisation (eg regional or product divisions) which have a stake in its plans.

- **Connected stakeholders** (or **primary** stakeholders), who have an economic or contractual relationship with the organisation. Key examples include the shareholders in a business; the customers of a business or beneficiaries of a charity; distributors and intermediaries; suppliers of goods and services; and financiers/funders of the organisation.

- **External stakeholders** (or **secondary** stakeholders), who are not directly connected to the organisation, but who have an interest in its activities, or are impacted by them in some way. Examples include the government, pressure and interest groups (including professional bodies and trade unions), the news media, the local community and wider society.

Cadbury Schweppes is an international confectionery and beverages company, selling chocolate, sweets, gum and beverages around the world. It uses different ways to communicate with different stakeholder groups.

Shareholders – Cadbury Schweppes has over 60,000 registered shareholders. These include private individuals as well as large institutional investors, such as pension funds and banks. All shareowners are also entitled to attend the Annual General Meeting, at which they have the opportunity to ask questions, discuss the company's performance and vote on certain issues.

Consumers – Consumers can contact the company by various means and Cadbury Schweppes deals with consumer enquiries on a daily basis. It performs market research to track changing consumer trends. Many parts of the business also use survey and market research panels to find out what consumers think of products.

Customers – The company has ongoing discussions with its customers. Wholesalers and retailers (intermediaries) provide the vital link to consumers and it is they who make Cadbury Schweppes' brands widely available.

Employees – Managers hold regular individual and team meetings to inform colleagues about the business and hear their views. The company also conducts surveys to check how its employees feel about working at Cadbury Schweppes. Internal newsletters, a group website and many local websites help employees keep up to date with what is going on.

Society – The company enters into regular dialogue with organisations such as national governments and international bodies such as the World Health Organisation (WHO), to discuss issues that affect the company. These issues can be anything from agricultural policy to education and skills.

1.3 Stakeholders in marketing

As we noted earlier, each function, unit and project of an organisation may be said to have stakeholders, whose needs and influence may have to be taken into account. For any given marketing activity or decision, it should be possible to identify relevant stakeholder groups.

- The owners or sponsor of the project or activity, who puts authority behind it, initiates it and sets its objectives (for example, the marketing manager or director).

- Customers, users or beneficiaries of the activity or its outputs: for example, internal departments who receive marketing advice or input, and external customers at whom products/services are targeted.

- The various target audiences of marketing messages: the customer base, consumer or industrial markets, the press, recruitment and financial markets.

- Other functions of the organisation, who may share marketing's overall aims (profitable and competitive business), but may have differing goals, priorities, technology, culture and timescales.

- Suppliers of goods and services used by marketing (eg advertising agencies and media, research consultants intermediaries) and suppliers of goods and services to the organisation in general, since they also contribute to the products and services it offers to its customers.

- External collaborators, partners or allies eg in joint promotions, sponsorship or knowledge-sharing networks.

- Secondary stakeholders impacted by marketing: for example, communities affected by the environmental and economic impacts of marketing plans (eg waste packaging or price changes) or interest groups concerned with the environment, trading practices, consumer rights and advertising standards.

2 Stakeholder networks and the marketing channel

All of those who make up the channel of distribution are stakeholders in it. The following questions need to be asked if the channel is to be managed successfully:

- Who are the stakeholders?
- What do they need?
- How important are they?
- What are their aims/objectives?

Stakeholder 'maps' indicate the primary relationships and patterns of interdependence within the marketing channel. These networks includes not only those organisations that make up the marketing channel but also aim to include all those other organisations that help channel members to satisfy customer needs.

Within the marketing channel, there are two primary stakeholder roles.

Performance – directly involved with adding value in the marketing channel (manufacturer, wholesaler, retailer). These are interdependent.

Support – banks, consultancies, government and so on, supporting the 'performing' members. These have no such interdependence.

  ACTIVITY 1 application

Identify the 'performance' and 'support' organisations that make up the network in the marketing channel used by your company, or one with which you are familiar.

Decisions are mainly focused on the interests of:

- **Target customer groups**: where and how they can best access the product or service.

- **The marketing organisation and its shareholders**: how the product/service can be delivered to customers most effectively, efficiently, competitively and cost-effectively; how information on customer behaviour can flow back to the organisation to improve planning.

- **Channel intermediaries and service providers**: how their resources and expertise can best be secured, utilised, supported and rewarded.

However, place decisions may also be targeted to the needs and concerns of wider stakeholder groups in various ways.

- Supporting '**reverse logistics**': that is, the return of products from the customer back to the manufacturer, for replacement or refund (eg in the case of a product recall due to safety concerns), repair or maintenance, or, at the end of the product's useful life, safe disposal or recycling. This requires relationship management with intermediaries who may have to mediate returns, exchanges or refunds. However, it is primarily seen as a benefit to customers and to wider society, mainly in terms of environmental responsibility (encouraging recycling and safe waste disposal).

- Allowing wider – and perhaps more equitable – **access to products and services**, through extending the distribution network to cover more areas or centres. This may further social policies of supporting remote communities and less-developed regions, and perhaps also enhance the national interest by establishing cultural and trading links with other nations (through international distribution).

- Giving wider access to products through **direct distribution** (supplying direct to customers, without intermediaries) and/or **e-distribution** (supplying products and services over the Internet: for example, downloadable books or music, or banking and e-learning services). This enables remote or un-serviced communities to access goods and services without having to find a retail outlet, and is of particular social benefit for some important services (eg banking, education, legal/medical advice). It may also support less mobile segments of the community, such as the elderly and disabled, in accessing goods and services through home or online delivery.

OTC Medicines

The distribution channel is often a crucial element in the success or failure of a product. In the case of over-the-counter (OTC) medicines, because of the unique features of the product, the situation and the constraints on marketers, the distribution channel plays a key role in customer decision making.

Medicines satisfy a powerful and basic need – relief from pain. As a consequence, products tend to be evaluated in terms of their strict efficacy, and the functions of branding or advertising are far less prominent than usual. According to Mellors Reay and Partners, who work on the marketing of OTC medicines, this is compounded by regulations and restrictions on the advertising and retail promotion of products. These include the following.

(a)   Strict regulation of claims and impact of advertising

(b)   Non-display of items on retailers' shelves

(c)   Restrictions on merchandising, discounting, the use of personality endorsement, loyalty schemes, cross promotions and free trials

(d)   Huge price rises when products transfer from prescription to OTC

(e)   Similarity between brand names because of reference to ingredients (for instance, paracetamol based analgesics include Panadeine, Panadol, Panaleve, Panerel, Paracets, and so on)

(f)   the influence of the pharmacist who can overcome or counter any promotional effect

The role of the pharmacist is crucial, and is becoming more ambivalent, as the old semi-medical professional role is combined with one as an employee of commercial and market-oriented enterprises. The increasing availability of OTC medicines previously only available on prescription only increases this power. Marketing OTC medicines directly to customers must involve, to some extent, countering the respect and trust of customers for pharmacists.

Yet brands can become established in spite of these problems. Nurofen, for example, an ibuprofen-based analgesic, has established a powerful presence by building a brand which is distinctive by using advertising which suggests both power and empathy, and also by visualising and emphasising in an imaginative way the experience and relief of pain.

Admap

ACTIVITY 2

evaluation

Can you think of some of the other ways in which place or distribution decisions may be adapted for greater corporate social responsibility, or the interests of wider stakeholder groups.

3 Information and communication

Again, we consider Blythe's comments

"Goods flow down the supply chain, but information flows up it, enabling the various members of the chain to plan around the reality of existing market conditions." ■

3.1 The role of information in channel management

Channel management is helped by channel co-operation. Members must co-operate if goods are to move along the channel and reach the customer. Information is critical for each member to be able to perform their role in the chain, so that channel partners are able to:

(a)   Agree on target markets
(b)   Define member tasks and avoid duplication

ACTIVITY 3

application

List the aspects of dealings with a supplier which need to addressed from the outset of a relationship to help to foster channel co-operation.

'Information' in the context of channel management covers both the operational day-to-day data flows (where information technology, such as EPOS scanning to update stock levels, is invaluable) and marketing communications. The brand manager and the PR manager tend to be those responsible for communications with channel members, such as the multiple retailers.

Information needs to be shared as far as possible without compromising commercial confidentiality on such topics as corporate strategy, new product development, customer details and other strategic areas. Because such information can be commercially sensitive, a lot of trust is required.

3.2 The importance of communication

Organisations group together when they cannot achieve their objectives independently. If a marketing channel is to function effectively, cooperation is paramount.

(a) A distribution system with a central core organising and planning marketing throughout the channel is termed a **vertical marketing system (VMS)**. Vertical marketing systems provide channel role specification and co-ordination between members. There is much more **interdependence** than is featured in a conventional system.

(b) In **corporate marketing systems** the stages in production and distribution are owned by a single corporation in a fairly rigid structure. This common ownership permits close integration and therefore the corporation controls activities along the distribution chain. For example, Laura Ashley shops sell goods produced in Laura Ashley factories.

(c) **Contractual marketing systems** involve agreement over aspects of distribution marketing. One example of a contractual marketing system that has become popular over the last decade is franchising.

(d) If a plan is drawn up between channel members to help reduce conflict this is often termed an **administered marketing system**.

3.2.1 Interorganisational communication

The management of communication is usually undertaken by a dominant member – the channel 'leader' or 'captain' who holds most of the power in the channel. In industrial markets where channel lengths are generally short, power often lies with manufacturers of products rather than 'middlemen'.

Communication within networks travels not only between levels of dependence (up and down the network) but also across, such as from retailer to retailer. Reflecting its role in the push strategy, it has the following roles.

- Provide persuasive information
- Foster participative decision making
- Provide for coordination
- Allows the exercise of power
- Encourages loyalty and commitment
- Reduces the likelihood of tension and conflict

Trust in and commitment to the network is crucial for success. Managing a channel through coercion rather than negotiation and co-operation is likely to lead to damaging conflicts that can affect the success of the channel's performance.

 KEY CONCEPT

concept

Trust: the degree to which partners are confident that each will act in the best interests of the relationship, with positive outcomes for all.

Commitment: the desire to maintain a valuable relationship.

 MARKETING AT WORK

application

The use of trade promotions and trade advertising by a company will be designed to keep the channel loyal. Techniques such as offering discounts to wholesalers, in return for extra promotion of the product, or extra shelf space, will help to increase sales as well (if the discount is passed on to the end customer). Trade advertising in the form of brochures, leaflets and samples should focus on aspects such as margins, turnover, shelf space profitability and the level of manufacturer - support.

4 Managing conflict

Conflict is the breakdown in cooperation between channel partners.

It has also been described as 'tensions between two or more social entities (individuals, groups or larger organisations) which arise from incompatibility of actual or desired responses'.

(Raven and Kruglanski (1970) quoted in Brassington & Pettitt (2006))

Blythe notes:

"Channel co-operation is an essential part of the functioning of channels....The problem is that conflict arises: although everyone agrees that co-operation is the best way forward for the overall success of the channel, each link in the channel has its own interests to consider, and short-term advantage might be gained at the expense of other members."

4.1 Conflict

One of the key points of stakeholder theory is that, inevitably, the interests of different stakeholder groups do not always coincide.

Johnson & Scholes (2005) note that:

"Since the expectations of stakeholder groups will differ, it is quite normal for conflict to exist regarding the importance or desirability of many aspects of strategy. In most situations, a compromise will need to be reached between expectations that cannot all be achieved simultaneously."

4.1.1 Sources of channel power

Channel stakeholders may have power to influence the channel in various ways. French and Raven (1958) classify the sources of power as follows.

- **Legitimate power**: legal/rational, formally conferred authority. This is often associated with a formal position or role: a marketing manager, for example, has influence over marketing decisions by virtue of delegated authority. Power may also be legitimised by law or agreed contract terms, such as those between a franchisor and franchisee.

- **Expert power**: the power of expertise or knowledge which is recognised and valued by the organisations making up the channel. This influence may be used by stakeholders such as professional marketing staff, wholesalers, experts in other functional areas (such as logistics management), specialist service providers (such as advertising agencies) and advisory bodies.

- **Resource power**: control over resources that are scarce and/or valued by the channel. In the broadest sense, this is the power of customers to withhold valued business from the marketing organisation or the power of suppliers to control access to critical supplies.

- **Referent power**: power emanating from an attractive and inspiring personality, image, or leadership quality. This may be exercised by a charismatic leader of the organisation; a supplier, distributor or competitor with a strong brand or reputation in an industry; or the opinion leadership of pressure groups, for example. This type of power calls for a high degree of respect and communication.

- **Coercive power**: the power to threaten sanctions, punishments or negative consequences. This may be exercised through the aggressive use of competitive leverage by a dominant supplier or customer (an accusation currently being levelled at large UK supermarket chains, for example).

As relationship marketing approaches become more widely used, large organisations might be expected to be relying less upon the wielding of power as a way of controlling the marketing channel in their favour. There is a need to focus upon stakeholder relationships rather than purely financial measures. In the case of the grocery sector in Europe, however, retailers have progressively taken over the marketing channels and their control is now almost total.

 MARKETING AT WORK   application

French wine makers knows the importance of the British market - the UK is the biggest importer of wine in the world. But the three-bottles-for-£10 supermarket offers that South African and South American suppliers can push at the moment are beyond the reach of most of them.

The director of the Syndicat des Vins de Pays D'Oc, the regional wine association that is the biggest single exporter in France, knows that times are bad.

'Britain is a market based on sharp changes of fashion in wines', she says. 'It's also a trend-setter for the world and that is why so many producers want to be part of it. But the fact that it is not part of the eurozone is a huge disadvantage to us. We cannot enter the bargain basement sales market - there will always be someone else to undercut us. And besides that, production costs in a country such as Spain are about 30% lower.'

Jean-Claude Mas runs a wine estate just outside the medieval town of Pezenas in France. His has been one of the most innovative and creative estates in marketing its wine in recent years. He produces multi-award winning bottles which retail for between five euros (£4.65) and €12 (£11.15) and, at the moment, he is using dwindling profits from markets inside the eurozone to subsidise his British business.

Effectively, he says, he is giving some of his wine away to Majestic and Waitrose in the hope that, if economic times improve, he can keep his crucial foothold in the UK market. 'The supermarkets and the buyers have all the power', Mr Mas says. 'We are squeezed dry by them and there is a limit to how long we can hold out.'

(*'French wine withers on the vine'* http://news.bbc.co.uk – accessed 29 March 2009)

4.1.2 Sources of conflict

Channels are subject to conflicts between members, particularly because the different types of power that can be present in the channel are very rarely equally shared. This need not be destructive as long as it remains manageable. The causes of conflict need to be identified, so that strategies can be formulated to repair any damage. Conflict stems from four main problems: differences in goals; differences in desired product lines; multiple channels and inadequacies in performance. Specifically:

- Failure to do the job as understood by the rest of the channel – who should do what?
- Incompatible goals, particularly when it comes to profit maximisation
- Disagreement over a policy issue, such as territory or margin
- Differing perceptions on how to get the job done
- Disagreements over resource allocation
- Conflict over who is in the best place to make marketing (or any other) decisions
- Inadequate communications and information flows

Brassington & Pettitt, 2006 noted:

"In any channel, there are likely to be periods of manifest conflict and periods of calm and cooperation. Similarly, there may be conflict in one area, for example profit-margin split, but cooperation in others, for example promotion.")

The following are just two examples of conflicting needs and expectations of key stakeholder groups.

- In order to maximise profits (in the interests of shareholders and investors), the organisation may downsize or limit pay levels (affecting employee interests); pressure suppliers to lower their prices, or pay them late to improve cash flow (affecting supplier interests); use low-cost suppliers or enter into mass markets, which may cause a decline in quality standards (affecting customer interests); or cut corners on controlling the environmental impacts of production (affecting the interests of local communities and environmental groups).

- Marketing may aim to make strong, attractive and high-profile promises to customers about product features, quality and delivery dates. This often conflicts with the agenda of the finance function (to manage or reduce costs) and the production/operations function (which may feel the promises are unrealistic!).

In addition, channel members may have relationships with many different firms at the same time, giving rise to conflicts of interest. A key to dealing with conflict is to not let it continue unresolved – at best the channel will become inefficient, and at worst there may eventually be legal problems to deal with. Strategies for dealing with conflict include:

- Regular meetings
- Frequent communication
- Ensuring that all parties are satisfied with negotiated outcomes
- Arbitration if required
- Management commitment to conflict resolution

 MARKETING AT WORK application

Clarks shoes distributes its products both through its own stores, and through other retailers. Conflict could arise if it failed to support these channels to the satisfaction of all parties concerned.

 EXAM TIP concept

A task may ask you to analyse the interests (and influence) of different stakeholder groups, and one of the outcomes of such an analysis will be to identify where different stakeholder interests conflict. This may be important for further tasks (such as planning a co-ordinated marketing mix for stakeholders), because it highlights the need for:

(a) The prioritising of stakeholders (because the interests of some will be more important than those of others)

(b) Trade-offs between different interests, in order to achieve acceptable outcomes for as many key stakeholders as possible

Learning objectives	Covered
1 Assess the requirements for managing the various stakeholders' needs within the distribution channel, in particular, reviews, reporting, communications and conflict management	☑ Definitions of stakeholders (1.1)
	☑ Categories of stakeholder (1.2)
	☑ Stakeholders in marketing (1.3)
	☑ Stakeholder networks and the marketing channel (section 2)
	☑ The role of information (3.1)
	☑ The importance of communication (3.2)
	☑ Conflict (4.1)

1 Distinguish between process and outcome stakeholders.

2 Distinguish between connected and external stakeholders.

3 Give an example of conflicting stakeholder interests.

4 What is 'reverse logisitics'?

5 What is a 'vertical marketing system'?

6 Give an example of referent power.

7 Give some examples of sources of conflict.

8 Why should conflict never be left unresolved?

9 What are the key areas that need to be agreed upon by channel partners?

1 Based upon your own research.

2 Reducing the environmental and social impacts of transport and logistics: eg efficient route planning to avoid unnecessary fuel use and pollution; transport planning to minimise traffic congestion at pick-up/delivery hubs; training and incentives for drivers to drive safely.

- Ensuring compliance with legislation and regulation in areas such as the transport, storage and handling of hazardous goods; the health and safety of warehouse workers; the monitoring of drivers' working hours.

- Distributing through small local retail outlets, which maintain the ambience and prosperity of local communities – rather than out-of-town mega-malls and retail chains.

- Ensuring that franchisees are adequately supported, to reduce the rate of small business failure and its local socioeconomic impacts.

- Ensuring, as far as possible, that intermediaries offer reliable supply and good levels of service to customers: offering sales and inventory management support, or staff training in demonstration or servicing of the product, if necessary. This will impact on the supplier's relationships not just with the intermediary, but also with customers, since point-of-sale, delivery and after-sales service are part of the total offering of value to the customer. Responsibility for such matters should be clearly apportioned by negotiation between suppliers and intermediaries, and performance monitored.

3 The following areas should be addressed at the beginning of a relationship with a supplier:

- Clear specifications, for fewer disputes and errors
- Efficient order processing procedures
- Fair procedures for awarding orders and evaluating tenders
- Ethical and sustainable dealings
- Timely and complete payment of debts
- Agreements on reasonable levels of profit taking
- Clear opportunities for development

1   Outcome stakeholders have an interest in the results of decisions, projects or processes: process stakeholders have an interest in the process by which they are arrived at.

2   Connected stakeholders have a direct legal or commercial connection with the organisation. External stakeholders do not: they are interested in the organisation's activities by virtue of their potential to impact on their interests or rights.

3   An example of conflicting stakeholder interests is shareholders' desire to maximise profits (and therefore returns on their investment), while this may work against the interests of customers (eg higher prices, lower quality).

4   The return of goods from the customer to the manufacturer.

5   A vertical marketing system is a distribution system with a central core organising and planning marketing throughout the channel.

6   Referent power is power emanating from an attractive and inspiring personality or quality. This may be exercised by a charismatic leader of the organisation or a supplier, distributor or competitor with a strong brand or reputation in an industry.

7   Differences in goals
Differences in desired product lines
Multiple channels
Inadequacies in performance
Failure to do the job as understood by the rest of the channel – who should do what?
Disagreement over a policy issue, such as territory or margin
Differing perceptions on how to get the job done
Disagreements over resource allocation
Conflict over who is in the best place to make marketing (or any other) decisions
Inadequate communications and information flows

8   If left unresolved, conflict can escalate to the level where legal action is required.

9   The key areas are likely to be the definition of target markets, and the agreement of 'who does what'.

Blythe, J (2009) Principles and Practice of Marketing, 2nd edition, South-Western/Cengage Learning.

Blythe, J (2008) Essentials of Marketing,4th edition, FT Prentice Hall.

Jobber (2009) Principles and Practice of Marketing.6th edition, McGraw Hill Higher Education

Brassington, F and Pettitt, S (2006) Principles of Marketing (4th edition), FT Prentice Hall.

French, J & Raven, B (1958) 'The bases of social power' in Studies in Social Power, Cartright D (ed). MI: Institute for Social Research, Ann Arbor.

Henley, P. 'French wine withers on the vine' http://news.bbc.co.uk [accessed 29 March 2009].

Huczynski, A & Buchanan, D (2001) Organizational Behaviour: An Introductory Text (4th edition), FT Prentice Hall, Harlow, Essex.

Johnson G, Scholes K & Whittington R (2005) Exploring Corporate Strategy: Text and Cases (7th edition), Pearson Education, Harlow, Essex.

Worthington I & Britton C (2006) The Business Environment (5th edition), Pearson Education, Harlow, Essex.

Chapter 6

Approaches to effective
marketing communications

Topic list

Introduction

Promotion is the process of communication by a seller to a market. This market or target audience may be:

- A consumer audience: purchasers of the product/service
- A channel audience: suppliers and intermediaries
- An all-stakeholder audience: all those who have an interest in the organisation's activities

Targeting the communications mix for stakeholders means identifying and using the appropriate communication media and the appropriate modes of communication.

There are several tasks facing those responsible for marketing communications:

- Who should receive messages
- What the messages should say
- What image of the organisation/brand receivers should retain
- How much is to be invested in the process
- How the messages are to be delivered
- What actions receivers should take
- How the whole process should be controlled
- How to determine what was achieved

It is important to note that effective communication is not a wholly 'one-way' flow. Producers need to understand customer motivations if they are to be able to 'talk' to them in an effective way and properly understand their market.

This chapter discusses the factors that need to be considered to ensure that marketing communications are effective. Influences on strategy, and the importance of the internal and external market, are discussed. This provides an introduction to the more detailed consideration of marketing communications methods that follows in a later chapter.

Syllabus linked learning objectives

By the end of the chapter you will be able to:

Learning objectives	Syllabus link
1 Determine marketing communications strategy and objectives to align with and deliver the organisation's marketing strategy and plans	3.1
2 Prioritise the internal and external marketing segments to be targeted for marketing communications in different organisational contexts and sectors	3.2

1 Determining marketing communications strategy

Schultz et al (2000)note:

"What exists in the mental network of the consumer or the prospect is truly where marketing value resides. [It] is what people believe, not what is true. [It] is what people want, not what is available; what people dream about, not what they know that really differentiates one product from another in a parity marketplace." ■

1.1 The role of marketing communications

Communications are essential to support relationship marketing.

- The organisation needs to use extensive contact, interaction and feedback to learn about (and from) customers, with the aim of continually adding value.

- The organisation needs to maintain direct and regular communication, through multiple points of contact and across a range of reasons for contact, in order to develop valuable relationship ties with customers.

- The organisation needs to maintain multiple exchanges with a number of stakeholders (network relationships) rather than a single focus on customers, in order to manage all links in the customer value delivery chain.

- Dialogue and developing trust provide a basis for the customisation and personalisation of contacts, messages and value-propositions, which further deepen stakeholder relationships.

- Communication is part of the relationship value offered to stakeholders: keeping them informed in areas of their interest or concern, guiding and supporting them through changes in the organisation's plans, communicating support for their causes and agendas.

Targeting the communications mix for customers (and other stakeholders) means identifying and using:

- Appropriate communication media and tools to target relevant groups, to suit their needs and characteristics, and to attract them to the message

- Appropriate modes of communication to express the message in a way that reflects their interests, motives and objectives – and in a way that establishes and maintains constructive, sustainable relationships with them.

1.2 Legal and ethical aspects of marketing communications

Laws and regulations governing marketing communications must obviously be observed. Each country will have its own set of restrictions which apply to advertising, packaging, sales promotion or direct marketing.

 MARKETING AT WORK application

In the EU alone, there are a number of significant differences regarding the regulation of advertising between member states. A Gossard TV commercial came under scrutiny in the UK for its risqué execution. In France, the problem was not the generous display of cleavage, but the fact that the advert was set in a bar where alcohol was being consumed. There is a ban on TV alcohol adverts and the Gossard ad needed to be re-edited to fall in line with French restrictions.

In some countries, restrictions apply to the use of non native models and actors. This can mean that advertising has to be reshot for specific countries.

Packaging regulations can vary. In a number of European markets, the push towards environmentally-friendly packaging has resulted in far more stringent rules than apply in the UK. In Denmark, soft drinks may not be sold in cans, only in glass bottles with refundable deposits.

Sweden forbids all advertising aimed at children under 10; Greece bans TV toy advertising between 7am and 10pm; some countries require ads for sweets to carry a toothbrush symbol; others have rules intended to curb advertisers from encouraging children to exercise 'pester power'.

The same maze of national rules exists when it comes to promoting alcohol, tobacco, pharmaceuticals and financial services.

Price advertising and discounting measures are so disparate that cross-border campaigns using discounts are all but impossible... In Germany, cash discounts are limited to 3% and the advertising of special offers is also restricted. Austria, Belgium and Italy also have strict regimes. In contrast, in Scandinavia, where the advertising law is more closely linked to consumer protection rather than unfair competition considerations, price advertising is encouraged – Swedish law, for example, promotes comparative price advertising between traders.

Critics of marketing argue that it is dedicated to selling products which are potentially damaging to the health and well-being of the individual or society. Examples include tobacco, alcohol, automobiles, detergents and even electronic goods such as computers and video recorders. It has been argued that even seemingly beneficial, or at least harmless, products, such as soft drinks, sunglasses or agricultural fertiliser, can damage individuals and societies. In traditional societies, new products can disrupt social order by introducing new aspirations, or changing a long established way of life.

How should the marketer react to these problems? There appears to be a clear conflict; what is profitable for a business organisation may well not be in the interest of the customer, or the society within which the transaction is taking place.

1.2.1 Ethics and the law

Ethics deal with personal moral principles and values, but laws are the rules that can actually be enforced in court. However, behaviour which is not subject to legal penalties may still be unethical. We can classify marketing decisions according to ethics and legality in four different ways.

- Ethical and legal (eg the Body Shop)
- Unethical and legal (eg 'gazumping')
- Ethical but illegal (eg publishing stolen but revealing documents about government mismanagement)
- Unethical and illegal (eg employing child labour)

Different cultures view marketing practices differently. While the idea of intellectual property is widely accepted in Europe and the USA, in other parts of the world ethical standards are quite different. Unauthorised use of copyrights, trademarks and patents is widespread in countries such as Taiwan, Mexico and Korea. According to a US trade official, the Korean view is that ' ...the thoughts of one man should benefit all', and this general value means that, in spite of legal formalities, few infringements of copyright are punished.

1.2.2 Ethics in marketing communications

Ethical considerations are particularly relevant to promotional practices. Advertising and personal selling are areas in which the temptation to select, exaggerate, slant, conceal, distort and falsify information is potentially very great indeed. Questionable practices here are likely to create cynicism in the customer and ultimately to preclude any degree of trust or respect for the supplier. It was because so many companies were acting unethically with regard to marketing communications that the Trade Descriptions Act 1968 came into being. Even taking into account the protection afforded to the consumer by such legislation, many think that persuading people to buy something they don't really want is intrinsically unethical, especially if hard sell tactics are used.

Also relevant to this area is the problem of corrupt selling practices. It is widely accepted that a small gift such as a mouse mat or a diary is a useful way of keeping a supplier's name in front of an industrial purchaser. Most business people would however condemn the payment of substantial bribes to purchasing officers to induce them to favour a particular supplier. But where does the dividing line lie between these two extremes?

1.2.3 Consumer and community issues

The consumer movement can be defined as a collection of organisations, pressure groups and individuals who seek to protect and extend the rights of consumers. The movement originated in a realisation that the increasing sophistication of products meant that the individual's own judgement was no longer adequate to defend against inappropriate marketing.

 MARKETING AT WORK application

Four basic consumer rights were identified by US President John Kennedy.

(a) The right to **safety**. Consumers expect that the products they purchase will be inherently safe to use. This right is bolstered in many countries by extensive product liability legislation.

(b) The right to **be informed**. It is not acceptable for marketing communications to suppress important information or make false claims.

(b) The right **to choose**. Companies should not attempt to stifle competition or make comparisons difficult by, for instance, restricting the information they make available.

(d) The right to **be heard**. Complaints should be dealt with fairly, effectively and speedily.

The main consumer protection body in the UK is the Office of Fair Trading. The Director of Fair Trading has a number of roles.

- To promote competition
- To encourage the adoption of codes of practice
- To curb anti-competitive practices
- To issue licences under the Consumer Credit Act
- To administer the Estate Agents Act

As well as government bodies, there are voluntary associations. Chief of these in the UK is the Consumers' Association (CA). Consumer protection legislation also exists to protect the consumer.

- Trade Descriptions Act 1968
- Fair Trading Act 1973
- Unfair Contract Terms Act 1977
- Food Act 1984
- Weights and Measures Act 1985
- Consumer Protection Act 1987

1.3 Global and international aspects

Companies operating outside their home markets have to be aware of the implications of cultural differences for all aspects of the marketing mix. Marketing communicators need to be particularly sensitive to culture if messages are to work in global markets.

We absorb the culture of our home society as we grow up. Our family, our religious institutions, and our education system all play a part in passing culture from one generation to the next. Some behaviours and customs learned early in life are likely to remain resistant to the best marketing or promotional efforts. For instance, attitudes and behaviour with respect to particular foodstuffs can be culturally ingrained.

Culture evolves. Although core cultural precepts are passed from one generation to the next, the values of society do change. Before the Second World War, a 'marriage bar' existed in white collar occupations such as clerical work and teaching. When a single working woman married, she was expected to give up her job to look after her husband.

Various dimensions of culture are relevant to the international marketing communicator.

- Verbal and non verbal communications
- Aesthetics
- Dress and appearance
- Family roles and relationships
- Beliefs and values
- Learning
- Work habits

1.4 Strategic aims

The nature of marketing communications strategy has to be viewed within the context of an overall marketing strategy, since a promotional strategy cannot exist in isolation. Prior to the promotional strategy being decided, the company will make a series of corporate and/or business unit decisions that will determine the nature of the overall marketing strategy. It is this which will then lay down the parameters within which a promotional strategy will be developed.

Each level of the organisation has a hierarchy of:

- Objectives
- Strategy
- Tactics

The tactics of the upper level then become the objectives of the next level down in the organisation. The levels we can usually consider are:

- Corporate (and then business unit, if separately managed)
- Functional (including marketing)
- Activity (including marketing communications)

The diagram below illustrates this '**planning hierarchy**'.

Figure 6.1 planning hierarchy (Simon Majaro)

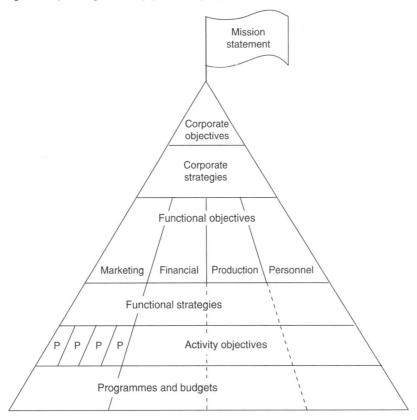

An organisation's **mission statement** is a description of long-term vision and values. Mission statements have become increasingly common because they can provide clear guidance to managers and employees on the future direction of the organisation. In particular the mission statement can be used to develop the hierarchy of objectives that link the long-term vision and values with specific objectives at each level of the organisation.

In order to deliver an effective plan, it is important to establish **marketing communications objectives**. These will involve variables such as perception, attitudes, developing knowledge and interest or creating new levels of prompted and spontaneous awareness.

It should be clear from the diagram below that for our purposes there are three different forms of objectives: corporate, marketing and marketing communications objectives. Collectively these are referred to as promotional goals or objectives.

Figure 6.2 Objectives

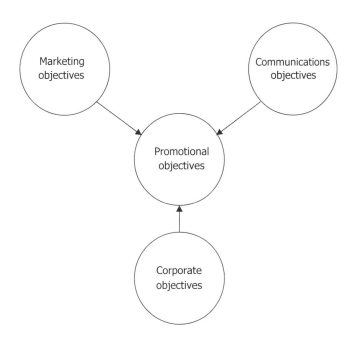

1.4.1 Communications objectives

Objectives need to be **specific** in that they must be capable of communicating to a target audience (who), a distinct message (what), over a specified time frame (when). Promotional objectives must therefore include:

- Identification of the **target audience**
- A **clear message**
- **Expected outcomes** in terms of trial purchase, awareness and so on
- A measurement of **results**
- Mechanisms for **monitoring and control**

The objectives need to be **measurable** and therefore quantifiable. Statements such as 'increase consumer awareness' are vague, whereas 'increase awareness of the 55 - 65 year age group from 40% to 80%' is more precise and capable of measurement.

Objectives need to be **achievable**. Purely from an internal company perspective, if sales are targeted to increase by 25% over a designated time period then manufacturing capacity will have to be secured to meet this target. Likewise, attempting to gain additional shelf space within a retail outlet will require that additional resources are devoted to the sales force, to sales promotions and to advertising.

Objectives need to be set with a degree of **realism** rather than on the basis of wild imagination. Otherwise, a company would be better off having no targets at all. An unrealistic target would tend to ignore the competitive and environmental forces affecting the company, the available resources at the company's disposal and the time frame in which the objectives have to be achieved.

Finally, objectives need to be **timed** over a relevant time period. Although a plan of action may be drawn up for a year, it will be the case that the plan will be reviewed against target, for example monthly or quarterly, so as to enable corrective action to be taken.

These principles of **SMART** (specific, measurable, achievable, realistic and timed) apply not only to the overall communication strategy but also to the setting of objectives for each tool within the promotional mix. Once the overall communication strategy has been set then individual (yet coordinated) plans need to be devised for each of the five main promotional tools. Using the SMART principle, objectives can be set for advertising, sales promotion, public relations, direct marketing and personal selling. These are examined in more detail in Chapter 7.

concept

The syllabus specifically mentions the importance of marketing communications in the achievement of competitive advantage. This might mean promoting sources of competitive advantage that competitors do not have access to (a strong brand, strongly developed distribution channels, loyal customers) or potential competitive advantage which will appeal to the organisation's target market (such as health benefits).

1.5 Marketing communications and customer relationships

Relationship marketing communications place a high emphasis on frequency, quality and personalisation of contact with customers and other stakeholders.

- Multiple on-going customer contacts, using multiple touch points within the marketing organisation: eg sales or direct marketing, customer research and feedback-seeking, customer service, after-sales service/maintenance, the web site, loyalty programmes, newsletters, product up-dates, maintenance reminders, invitations to launches and other events, notification of special offers

    Designated account managers or customer contacts may be used to focus initial contact on an individual touch point, to create personal familiarity and add value by having a single 'gatekeeper' to direct customer queries to other parts of the organisation.

- Two-way dialogue with customers: not just marketing messages (business-to-customer or B2C) but customer to-business (C2B) communication, through mechanisms such as feedback and suggestion seeking, the creation of customer communities and customer-generated web and advertising content.

    This may be augmented by encouraging customer-to-customer (C2C) communication via discussion boards, user groups and customer networking events. C2C happens anyway, so it makes sense for the organisation to monitor the exchanges in order to gather information on customers' perceptions and interests); create a sense of belonging or affiliation (adding a social benefit to the total product/service offering); and offer social/entertainment value which draws people repeatedly to the web site and other mechanisms (where they can be targeted with promotional messages).

- Personalised and customised contacts: making customers feel recognised and valued, and that their individual needs are being catered for. Examples include: customer 'recognition' by customer service staff (enabled by computer-telephony integration); the use of customer data to send birthday cards or service reminders (such as you might get from a dentist or car dealership); the personalisation of mailings, e-mail and web pages; and the customisation of offers on the basis of customers' previous purchases.

application

Amazon.com is a retail organisation specialising in books (and an increasingly diversified range of related leisure products). It has developed a world-leading relationship marketing strategy which utilises to the full the technological opportunities provided by online marketing and database management. Some of the relationship-building devices it uses include:

- Complete personalisation of the site for registered users

- The option to receive targeted e-mail recommendations, reminders and offers

- A virtual community of users through interactivity, notice boards, personal reviews and recommendations, blogs and customer home pages

- Customer choice as to communication/contact/privacy preferences

- Transparency about the sources and uses of personalised information

- Added-value site services such as free e-cards, gift certificates and out-of-print book searches

- Convenient and secure online purchase transactions, follow-up and order tracking

- A very friendly, personal, up-beat tone

2 Internal and external marketing

Internal marketing has been well summarised by Peck et al (2004):

"Internal marketing is concerned with creating, developing and maintaining an internal service culture and orientation, which in turn assists and supports the organisation in the achievement of its goals. The internal service culture has a vital impact on how service-oriented and customer-oriented employees are, and, thus, how well they perform their tasks... The development and maintenance of a customer-oriented culture is a critical determinant of long-term success in relationship marketing...

"The basic premise behind the development of internal marketing is the acknowledgement of the impact of employee behaviour and attitudes on the relationship between staff and external customers. This is particularly true where employees occupy boundary-spanning positions in the organisation... The skills and customer orientation of these employees are, therefore, critical to the customers' perception of the organisation and their future loyalty to the organisation." p 313

In other words, it is through internal marketing that all employees can develop an understanding of how their tasks, and the way they perform them, create and deliver customer value and build relationships.

KEY CONCEPT

 concept

Internal marketing may be defined as a variety of approaches and techniques by which an organisation acquires, motivates, equips and retains customer-conscious employees, in order to help retain customers through achieving high quality service delivery and increased customer satisfaction.

Berry and Parasuraman (1991) define it as: 'attracting, developing, motivating and retaining qualified employees through job products that satisfy their needs' – which relates it clearly to the conventional concept of the marketing exchange.

2.1 The role of internal communications

Organisations are made up of people (often referred to, these days, as the human resources of a business). When we talk about 'organisations' marketing to external customers/stakeholders, or establishing relationships with them, what we are really talking about is employees of the organisation implementing and carrying out these activities.

Employees and their employing organisations are mutually dependent. Employees need work and its financial rewards in order to live – and organisations need employees to implement their plans and carry out their activities.

Employees are therefore key stakeholders in the organisation, with both high interest and high (collective) power. Peck et al (1999) identify the internal market as a key component of their Six Markets Model (see below). It includes employees in all parts of an organisation with potential to contribute towards marketing effectiveness by delivering service excellence.

'There are two key aspects to internal marketing. The first is concerned with how staff work together across functional boundaries so that their work is attuned to the company's mission, strategy and goals. The second involves the idea of the internal customer. That is, every person working within an organisation is both a supplier and a customer.' (ibid p302)

Gummesson (2002, p198) similarly suggests that:

'The objective of internal marketing within Relationship Marketing is to create relationships between management and employees, and between functions. The personnel can be viewed as an internal market, and this market must be reached efficiently in order to prepare the personnel for external contacts: efficient internal marketing becomes an antecedent to efficient external marketing.'

2.2 Identifying key internal audiences

As the term suggests, the internal customer concept implies the following ideas.

- Any unit of the organisation whose task contributes to the task of other units (whether as part of a process or in an advisory or service relationship) can be regarded as a supplier of a product/service. In other words, there is an internal supply chain – and the 'next person to handle your work' is your internal customer.

- The objective of each unit and individual thus becomes the 'efficient and effective identification and satisfaction of the needs, wants and expectations of customers' (one definition of marketing) within the internal value chain – as well as outside it.

- Any given unit of the organisation must 'create, build and maintain mutually beneficial exchanges and relationships' (another definition of marketing) within the organisation, as well as outside it.

2.2.1 Segmenting the internal market

The internal marketing mix (like the external marketing mix) will need to be adapted to the needs and drivers of the target audience. The internal market can (like the external market) be segmented to allow targeting to the distinctive needs of each group.

Jobber (2007) suggests segmentation of internal customers into:

- **Supporters**: those who are likely to gain from the change or plan, or are already committed to it
- **Neutrals**: those who are likely to experience both gains and losses from the change or plan
- **Opposers**: those who are likely to lose from the change or plan, or are traditional opponents

The product (plan) and price may have to be modified to gain acceptance from opponents. Place decisions will be used to reach each group most effectively (eg high-involvement approaches such as consultation meetings for supporters and neutrals). Promotional objectives will also differ according to the target group, because of their different positions on issues.

Christopher et al (2002, p 109) suggest an alternative way of segmenting internal customers, according to how close they are to external customers:

- **Contactors** have frequent or regular customer contact and are typically heavily involved with conventional marketing activities (eg sales or customer service roles). They need to be well versed in the firm's marketing strategies, and trained, prepared and motivated to service customers on a day-to-day basis in a responsive manner.

- **Modifiers** are not directly involved with conventional marketing activities, but still have frequent contact with customers (eg receptionists, switchboard, the credit department). These people need a clear view of the organisation's marketing strategy and the importance of being responsive to customers' needs.

- **Influencers** are involved with the traditional elements of marketing, but have little or no direct customer contact (eg in product development or market research). Companies must ensure that these people develop a sense of customer responsiveness, as they influence the total value offering to the customer.

- **Isolateds** are support functions that have neither direct customer contact nor marketing input – but whose activities nevertheless affect the organisation's performance (eg purchasing, HR and data processing). Such staff need to be sensitive to the needs of internal customers as well as their role in the chain that delivers value to customers.

Who are the internal customers of the marketing function in your organisation, or any organisation? How should they be managed?

2.3 Internal communications methods

Peck et al (2004, p 324) identify the following range of inter-related activities thought to be critical in implementing internal marketing.

- **Organisational design**: eg drawing key employees together in cross-functional customer service or quality teams

- **Regular staff surveys**: assessing the internal service culture and attitudes

- **Internal customer segmentation**: adapting the internal marketing mix to different employee groups

- **Personal development and training**: focused on core competencies for internal marketing

- **Empowerment and involvement**: enabling staff, within defined parameters, to use their discretion to deliver better service to customers

- **Recognition and rewards**: based on employees' contribution to service excellence

- **Internal communications**: ensuring information flows to support cross-functional co-ordination, and all-employee awareness of their role and contribution to service

- **Performance measures**: evaluating each individual's and department's contribution to marketing objectives

- **Building supportive working relationships**: creating a climate of consideration, trust and support

2.4 Tools of internal communication

A very wide variety of communication media is used in formal internal communications, including: company reports, brochures and newsletters; corporate intranet (staff website); video- and web-conferencing; video and CD-ROM presentations and seminars; team meetings, briefings, presentations and conferences; one-to-one interviews; negotiating and consultative meetings (eg with employee representatives); letters, e-mail, memoranda and notices.

2.4.1 Email

The term 'electronic mail' or e-mail is used to describe various systems for sending messages electronically via a telecom or data network. E-mail has replaced letters, memos, faxes, documents and even telephone calls – combining many of the advantages of each medium with new advantages of speed, cost and convenience. E-mail offers many advantages for internal customer communication.

- Messages can be sent and received very fast (allowing real time message dialogue).

- E-mail is economical, especially for international communication: often allowing worldwide transmission for the cost of a local telephone call.

- All parties can print out a 'hard copy' of the message, for detailed perusal and repeated reference.

- Messages can be sent worldwide at any time: email is 24-7, regardless of time zones and office hours.

- The user can attach complex documents (spreadsheets, graphics, photos) where added data or impact are required.

- E-mail message management software (such as Microsoft Outlook) has convenient features such as: message copying (to multiple recipients); integration with an 'address book' (database of contacts); corporate stationery options; and facilities for mail organisation and filing.

From your knowledge of email, what might be some of the disadvantages of email for internal communication with colleagues in your own department or other departments.

2.4.2 Intranet

An intranet is an internal, mini version of the Internet, using a combination of networked computers and web technology.

'Inter' means 'between' and 'intra' means 'within'. This may be a useful reminder. The Internet is used to disseminate and exchange information among the public at large, and between organisations. An Intranet is used to disseminate and exchange information within an organisation: only employees are able to access this information.

The corporate intranet may be used for:

- **Performance data**: linked to sales, inventory, job progress and other database and reporting systems, enabling employees to process and analyse data to fulfil their work objectives

- **Employment information**: online policy and procedures manuals (health and safety, equal opportunity, disciplinary rules, customer service values and so on), training and induction material, internal contacts for help and information

- **Employee support/information**: advice on first aid, healthy working at computer terminals, training courses offered

- **Notice boards** for the posting of messages to and from employees: notice of meetings, events, trade union activities

- **Departmental home pages**: information and news about each department's personnel and activities, to aid crossfunctional understanding

- **Bulletins or newsletters**: details of product launches and marketing campaigns, staff moves, changes in company policy – or whatever might be communicated through the print equivalent, plus links to relevant pages for details

- **E-mail facilities** for the exchange of messages, memos and reports between employees in different locations

- **Upward communication**: suggestion schemes, feedback questionnaires, employee attitude surveys

- **Individual personnel files**, to which employees can download their training materials, references, certificates, appraisals, goal plans

Advantages cited for the use of intranets include the following.

- **Cost savings** from the elimination of storage, printing and distribution of documents that can instead be exchanged electronically or be made available online

- **More frequent use made of online documents** than printed reference resources (eg procedures manuals) and more flexible and efficient searching and updating of data

- **Wider access to corporate information**. This facilitates multi-directional communication and co-ordination (particularly for multi-site working). It is also a mechanism of internal marketing and corporate culture.

- **Virtual team working**. The term 'virtual team' has been coined to describe how ICT can link people in structures which simulate the dynamics of team working (sense of belonging, joint goals, information sharing and collaboration despite the geographical dispersion of team members in different locations or constantly on the move

2.4.3 Team meetings

Meetings play an important part in the life of any organisation.

- Formal discussions are used for information exchange, problem solving and decision making: for example, negotiations with suppliers, meetings to give or receive product/idea presentations or 'pitches', and employee interviews.

- Informal discussions may be called regularly, or on an ad hoc basis, for communication and consultation on matters of interest or concern: for example, informal briefings and marketing or project team meetings.

ACTIVITY 3

evaluation

Team meetings may appear to be relatively inconvenient, especially when compared to modern communications such as group emails. Why do you think that meetings are still held, and are still useful?

2.4.4 SMS

SMS text messaging is one of the 'hot' new advertising and direct marketing media. However, it is also a common tool of quick messaging in a variety of communication contexts, including internal. It is quicker and less intrusive than a phone call (since it does not need to be accepted or returned immediately), and enables mobile messaging for those without immediate access to e-mail (although SMS messages can also be sent from phones to computers and vice versa).

2.4.5 Informal communication channels

In addition to formal attempts by the organisation to communicate with its employees, there are informal communication channels such as the 'grapevine': friends, colleagues and contacts developing internal networks, sharing news, information and gossip. This is a fast and effective way of transmitting information: unfortunately, it is often inaccurate, subjective – and difficult for management to control. Marketers should feed plenty of information into informal networks, to avoid inaccurate speculation. They should also tap into these networks themselves, so that they know what is being said!

2.5 Identifying key external audiences

A number of influential models highlight the nature of a marketing organisation as a hub of relationships – and the positioning of marketing at the interface between the organisation and the other parties to those relationships.

2.5.1 The Six Markets model

The Six Markets model offers a helpful overview of the key categories of relationships for any given firm (sometimes called the 'core' or 'focal' firm, because we are looking at relationships from its point of view). It presents six role-related market domains or 'markets', each involving relationships with a number of parties – organisations or individuals – who can potentially contribute, directly or indirectly, to an organisation's marketplace effectiveness (Peck et al, 1999, p 5).

The model has developed since its formulation in 1991, to take account of changing views and priorities in marketing, but the most commonly used version of the framework is shown below. Note that the focal firm is not the centre of the relationship 'hub', although the model recognises that internal marketing supports relationships with all the other parties.

Rather, the customer is placed at the centre, 'to focus on the purpose of relationship marketing: the creation of customer value, satisfaction and loyalty, leading to improved profitability in the long term' (Peck, et al 1999).

Figure 6.3 Six markets model

Customer markets The concept of relationship marketing is based on the belief that firms must invest in building relationships with customers, in order to enhance profitability through customer retention and loyalty. The importance of customer relationships has long been recognised in professional and financial services, B2B marketing, and the market for regularly replaced consumer durables (such as cars). It is now 'catching on' in FMCG markets.

- For consumer goods or services, the customer market domain represents **end customers**, users and consumers.

- For B2B marketing, it also embraces channel **intermediaries**, including agents, retailers and distributors who are effectively 'customers' of the organisation, but operate between them and the end users.

Referral markets Referrals, recommendations and endorsements by existing customers are an important source of new business: either directing potential new customers to the supplier (eg B2B sales 'leads' and professional referrals) or guiding consumer choice (eg through word-of-mouth recommendations or endorsements by trusted third parties).

Potential sources of referrals must be cultivated and motivated. 'Given that satisfied customers will happily endorse the products or services of the supplier if prompted, relationships with existing customers are an unrecognised or underutilised facility for many organisations'. (Peck et al, op cit, p 7) Companies can create formal or informal cross-referral agreements between themselves and suppliers of complementary products (eg a weight loss consultancy and a local gym). Such referrals may also add value for customers, as part of a total service.

Internal markets The internal market comprises all employees, and other functions, divisions and strategic business units (SBUs) of the firm.

The concept of 'internal marketing', as we have already noted, argues that employees and units throughout an organisation can contribute to the effectiveness of marketing to customers: most notably, through value-adding customer service and communications. It has been shown that employee satisfaction and retention (the aims of internal marketing) correlate directly with customer satisfaction and retention (the aims of customer relationship marketing) in service businesses (Schlesinger & Heskett, 1991).

Recruitment markets The recruitment market comprises:

- The **external labour pool**, and more specifically, those with the attributes and competencies needed by the firm: that is, quality potential employees.

- **Third parties**, such as colleges, universities, recruitment agencies and other employers, who can give the firm access to those quality potential employees. Relationships with these markets must be cultivated in order for the firm to be able to compete with other employers to attract the best people, particularly in times, regions and disciplines in which there are acute skill shortages.

Influence markets

- Customers' buying decisions are often made with input from a group of key influencers, referred to as a **'decision making unit' (DMU)**.

- A range of **external third parties** also exercise influence over consumers – and over the marketing organisation itself. These influencers include governments and government agencies, the press/media, investors and pressure groups. Relationships with these markets can be exploited to generate positive PR (and/or minimise negative PR); influence public opinion in the organisation's favour; gain access to markets (eg through cause-related marketing); and enhance or replace other marketing activities (as in The Body Shop's exploitation of referral, media and pressure group relationships, in place of advertising).

'While relationships with these parties may not directly add value to a product or service, they can directly influence the likelihood of purchase or prevent an offer from even reaching the market' (Peck et al, 1999).

Supplier and alliance markets The supplier market refers to the relationships that the firm must cultivate with its supply chain or network, in order to enable reliable, flexible, value-adding, cost effective flows of supplies into and through the firm to the end customer. The concept of supply chain management recognises the need for long-term, collaborative relationship development with a small number of suppliers, particularly for strategic or critical items – rather than hard-bargaining, adversarial, one-off transactions (which may still be used for routine items, where price is the main criterion).

The alliance market recognises a wide range of opportunities to add value through collaborative relationships between the core firm and partners (other than its immediate suppliers) in joint promotions, strategic alliances, joint ventures, knowledge sharing networks and 'virtual' collaborations.

 MARKETING AT WORK application

Coutts Bank: It's not just about clients

Coutts considers the way it services five distinct markets, in addition to its traditional client market, to make sure it maintains consistent, high quality relationships with them.

- **Internal markets**: Coutts communicates with all staff – client account managers, product managers and support staff – about its relationship management priorities. The aim is to ensure there is no weak link in the chain that makes up the Coutts service offering.

- **Referral markets**: Lawyers, consultants and financial advisers are a significant source of new business for the bank: they meet prospective clients every day and advise them on how best to invest their wealth. Coutts contacts these sources regularly and delivers regular, tailored information to them so that the bank is in their minds when they are advising their clients.

- **Supplier markets**: Although the bank is a service provider, it needs to ensure that its tangible offerings –brochures, events, premises or staff lapel badges – match its service quality image. It works closely with a few suppliers who, over time, get to know its ways and standards.

- **Recruitment markets**: In banking, new client account managers can often bring a portfolio of business with them, so Coutts works hard to sustain its quality image among its peers, and to be an organisation that people want to work for, in order to attract the best recruits.

- **Influence markets**: One of Coutts' key influence markets is the governments and financial authorities in the countries in which it operates. They may actively seek the bank's views on legislative changes and new product opportunities that might attract investment to their countries.

2.5.2 Market relationships

Market relationships are the externally-oriented relationships between the suppliers, customers, competitors and intermediaries who operate in a market, which have traditionally been the focus of marketing.

- **Classic market relationships** are the focus of traditional mainstream marketing management: the supplier/customer dyad; the triad or three-way relationship of supplier-customer-competitor; and the distribution network.

- **Special market relationships** focus in on certain aspects of the classic relationships, such as:

  - The interfaces between two parties: eg multiple contact points between suppliers and customers (especially in B2B marketing); and interfacing through full-time marketers (who directly create customer relationships) and other business functions (which indirectly influence them)

  - The various means through which parties interact: eg the service encounter (the interaction between a customer and front-line personnel), customer membership of loyalty programmes, and electronic relationships (interaction via IT networks)

  - The status and condition of relationships: eg distant and close relationships, and relationships with dissatisfied customers

  - The basis of relationships: eg relationship with objects (such as an i-Pod) and symbols (such as brands and corporate identity); law (contracts and compliance); non-commercial objectives (in the public/voluntary sectors and families); and green relationships (based on environmental and health issues)

2.5.3 Non-market relationships

Non-market relationships are relationships outside the market, but which indirectly influence the efficiency of the market relationships.

- **Mega relationships** those which exist 'above' the immediate marketplace, in the economy or society in general. These include:

  - Personal and social networks, friendships and ethnic bonds, which often determine business networks (and can be exploited eg for word-of-mouth marketing and recruitment)

  - Non-market networks (relationships with governments, legislators and influential individuals) and megamarketing (eg lobbying and public relations activity) to support marketing on an operational level

  - Mass media relationships, which can be supportive or damaging to marketing

  - Alliances (relationships and collaboration between companies) and knowledge relationships (since knowledge acquisition is a key reason for forming alliances)

  - Mega-alliances (alliances beyond single companies, industries or nations: for example, the EU or North America Free Trade Agreement) which shape the macro environment of marketing

- **Nano relationships** exist 'below' the market relationships. They involve internal (intra-organisational) relationships, which may support or undermine the firm's external (inter-organisational) relationships and marketing. Examples of nano-relationships include:

  - Relationships between internal customers and internal suppliers in an organisation: how different tiers, functions and business units interact with one another as members of an internal supply chain

  - Concepts (eg total quality management) and organisational structures (eg matrix, product or account management) which can be used to build bridges between different functions, supporting integration and customer focus

  - Internal marketing: relationships with the 'employee market' which support external customer relationship marketing

Learning objectives	Covered
1 Determine marketing communications strategy and objectives to align with and deliver the organisation's marketing strategy and plans	☑ The role of marketing communications (1.1)
	☑ Legal and ethical aspects (1.2)
	☑ Global and international aspects (1.3)
	☑ Strategic aims (1.4)
	☑ Marketing communications and customer relationships (1.5)
2 Prioritise the internal and external marketing segments to be targeted for marketing communications in different organisational contexts and sectors	☑ The role of internal communications (2.1)
	☑ Identifying key internal audiences (2.2)
	☑ Internal communications methods (2.3)
	☑ Identifying key external audiences (2.4)

1   Why are ethics important in marketing communications?

2   What sits at the 'top' of the planning hierarchy, and what is its function?

3   What are 'SMART' objectives?

4   How might C2C communication be encouraged?

5   Which group makes up the key target for internal marketing initiatives?

6   How do Christopher *et al* classify internal customers?

7   Name the elements of the Six Markets model.

8   What are 'referral' markets?

9   Give an example of a 'nano-relationship'.

10   Which elements make up the classic triad, or three-way relationship?

11   What are the advantages of intranets?

12   Name some elements of culture that are of relevance to the international marketer.

1   With supporters, existing positive attitudes should be reinforced, and support (especially from key influencers) mobilised.

With neutrals, rewards and benefits should be emphasised, and downsides de-emphasised. Supporters may be used to 'win over' neutrals.

With opposers, promotion may be used to counter their objections, discredit or marginalise their position (if this can be done without causing negative relationship effects), or negotiate/bargain to lower resistance.

2   The disadvantages of e-mail include:

- The legal effect: firms can be sued for libellous, offensive or misleading remarks made in e-mail.

- E-mail can be used excessively, to the exclusion of other tools that might be more appropriate, or can simply create time-wasting information/message overload. Excessive personal use (or abuse) is also an issue for many organisations (as it has been with the telephone).

- E-mail is not private, and remains on the server. There are thus risks in using it to send confidential messages.

- E-mail is impersonal: it is often difficult to get the 'tone' right for sensitive interpersonal messages.

3   By gathering people together in a physical location, team meetings are an excellent tool of internal communication. Face-to-face discussion can be particularly effective in exchanging information and developing relationships.

1   Advertising and personal selling are areas in which the temptation to distort the truth is potentially very great, creating cynicism in the customer.

2   The company's mission statement, which is a description of long-term vision and values, providing guidance to managers and employees on the future direction of the organisation. It can be used to develop the hierarchy of objectives that link the long-term vision and values with specific objectives at each level of the organisation.

3   Specific, measurable, achievable, realistic and time-bounded

4   Via discussion boards, user groups and customer networking events. These can be used to gather information on customers' perceptions and interests; create a sense of belonging; and offer social/entertainment value which draws people to a website or other mechanisms (where they can be targeted with promotional messages).

5   The key target tends to be employees who need to be made aware of the importance of the customer, in order to help retain customers through achieving high quality service delivery and increased customer satisfaction.

6   *Contactors* have frequent or regular customer contact and are typically heavily involved with conventional marketing activities, eg sales staff.

   Modifiers are not directly involved with conventional marketing activities, but still have frequent contact with customers, eg receptionists.

   Influencers are involved with the traditional elements of marketing, but have little or no direct customer contact, eg product developers.

   Isolateds are support functions that have neither direct customer contact nor marketing input, eg HR staff.

7

8   This market consists of referrals, recommendations and endorsements by existing customers. They are an important source of new business, perhaps through sales 'leads' or word-of-mouth recommendation.

9   Relationships between internal customers and internal suppliers in an organisation, as members of an internal supply chain. Such a relationship supports the organisation's external relationships.

10 Supplier, customer and competitor

11 Cost savings from the elimination of paper documents   Wider access to corporate information
    More frequent use made of online documents   Virtual team working

12 Verbal and non verbal communications   Beliefs and values
    Aesthetics   Learning
    Dress and appearance   Work habits
    Family roles and relationships

Berry, L.L. & Parasuraman, A. (1991) <u>Marketing Services: Competing Through Quality</u>, Free Press, New York.

Blythe, J (2009) <u>Principles and Practice of Marketing</u>, 2nd edition, South-Western/Cengage Learning.

Blythe, J (2008) <u>Essentials of Marketing</u>,4th edition, FT Prentice Hall.

Brassington, F and Pettitt, S (2006) <u>Principles of Marketing</u>, 4th edition, FT Prentice Hall.

Dibb S, Simkin L, Pride WM, Ferrell OC (2005) <u>Marketing: Concepts and Strategies</u>, 5th edition, Houghton Mifflin.

Jobber (2009) <u>Principles and Practice of Marketing</u>.6th edition, McGraw Hill Higher Education

Christopher M.G., Payne A.F. & Ballantyne D. (2002) <u>Relationship Marketing: Creating Stakeholder Value</u>, Butterworth-Heinemann, Oxford.

Gummesson, E. (2002) <u>Total Relationship Marketing</u> (2nd edition), Elsevier Butterworth-Heinemann, Oxford.

Kotler, P. (2001) <u>Principles of Marketing</u>, FT Prentice Hall, Harlow.

Peck H.L., Payne A., Christopher M. & Clark M. (1999) <u>Relationship Marketing: Strategy and Implementation</u>, Elsevier Butterworth-Heinemann, Oxford.

Schlesinger, L.A. & Heskett, J.L. (1991) *'Breaking the cycle of failure in services'*, Sloan Management Review, Spring, pp 17-28

Schultz, D.E., Tannenbaum, S. & Lauterborn, R.F. (2000) Integrated Marketing Communications: Putting It Together & Making It Work, illustrated edition, McGraw-Hill Contemporary, London.

Chapter 7
Planning the communications mix

Topic list

1   Advertising strategy
2   Developing the marketing communications plan
3   Measuring marketing communications activities

Introduction

This chapter examines the marketing communications mix. In a market-orientated business (following relationship marketing principles) there is a two-way dialogue, where the buyer's response is as important as the seller's message: hence the term 'marketing communications'.

This chapter outlines some of the tools used in an optimal communications mix (sections 1 and 2) and the process for developing the marketing communications plan (section 3). There have been major changes in the way organisations communicate with their audiences. New technology, new media and changes in the way that people spend their time (working from home, shopping habits and leisure patterns etc) have meant that companies have to find new ways to reach people.

A vital part of the communications process is the measurement of how effective those communications have been. This is discussed in section 4.

Syllabus linked learning objectives

By the end of the chapter you will be able to:

Learning objectives	Syllabus link
1 Critically evaluate a range of communications mixes and recommend appropriate creative, innovative, sustainable and co-ordinated approaches to communications activities and creating the optimal mix for internal and external marketing activities	3.3
2 Develop and manage a co-ordinated marketing communications plan, in the context of the strategic marketing plan, in order to establish and build relationships appropriate to the needs of customers, stakeholders and prospects in different organisational contexts and sectors	3.4
3 Recommend appropriate methods for measuring marketing communications activities and successful delivery of the marketing communications strategy	3.7

The range of promotional tools continues to grow. The variety of media that can be used for 'above the line' campaigns has expanded, both in the printed advertising field and in the broadcast field. There are literally thousands of publications aimed at different target groups. In the broadcast field the number of television stations steadily increases through satellite, cable and digital television, and the number of commercial radio stations has also grown considerably.

1 Advertising strategy

Here's what Jobber (2009) says about advertising

"Advertising can create awareness, stimulate trial, position products in consumers' minds, correct misconceptions, remind and reinforce, and provide support for the salesforce."

KEY CONCEPT

concept

Advertising is 'any paid form of non-personal presentation and promotion of ideas, goods or services by an identifiable sponsor'.

(American Marketing Association)

1.1 Why advertise?

(a) To **promote sales**

Advertising is particularly good at raising awareness, informing and persuading. It can be used to stimulate primary demand for a product (eg in the introduction of a new product) and selective demand for a particular brand (eg in competition with other brands). This works in intermediary markets (eg selling in to retailers) as well as consumer markets, effectively 'introducing' the product in advance of a sales call. One example of a different sort of response is recruitment advertising: promoting the organisation and the job within the recruitment market, in order to secure applications from the best potential recruits. The same kind of approach may be used to advertise for suppliers (eg by putting a contract out to tender).

(b) To **create an image**

Institutional advertising is used by companies to improve their public image, and by not-for-profit and public sector organisations to promote their programmes (eg persuading people not to drink and drive, to support a pressure group or donate to a charity). Marketing organisations often use advertising to promote their corporate social responsibility credentials to the wider stakeholder audience. Innocent Drinks, the subject of the sample case study, is an example of such an approach.

(c) To **support sales staff**

Advertising can support personal selling, for example, by raising customer (consumer or intermediary) awareness of the product/service, motivating them to contact sales representatives. The company's sales promotions, presence at exhibitions, website and other communication channels can also be brought to the target audience's attention by advertising.

(d) To **offset competitor advertising**

Companies often attempt to defend their market share by responding aggressively to competitors' advertising campaigns. Advertisements may also be used to counter negative public relations messages and alter public opinion (eg correcting negative impressions given by critical incidents such as a product recall, or countering negative pressure group statements).

(e) To **remind and reassure**

Advertising reinforces the purchase decision and repeat purchase, by reminding consumers that the product continues to be available – and offers benefits – and reassuring them that they have made the right choice. In industrial markets, advertising may add credibility to sales visits by demonstrating professionalism and expenditure.

1.2 Developing an advertising strategy

Jobber (2009) suggests the following framework for developing an advertising strategy.

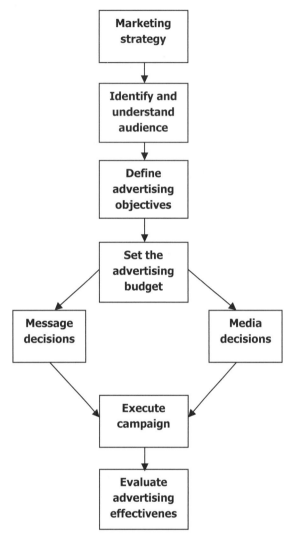

As indicated by the diagram, the planning of an advertising campaign includes:

(a) **The identification of the target audience**: Who are they? Where are they? Which demographic group do they fall into? What are their interests, media consumption habits, buying patterns, attitudes and values?

(b) **The specification of the communication or promotional message**: What do you need to say, and in what way, in order to impact on the audience is such a way as to achieve your marketing objectives?

(c) **The setting of targets**: What is the marketing goal to which the advertising can contribute? What do you expect the ad to achieve, and at what cost? What aspects of the audience's thinking or behaviour do you wish to change, and how will you recognise and measure that change if and when it occurs?

When it comes to media decisions, the general criteria for selecting the appropriate medium to convey the promotional message to the audience are as follows:

- The advertiser's specific objectives and plans
- The size of the audience that regularly uses the medium
- The type of people who form the audience for the medium
- The suitability of the medium for the message
- The cost of the medium in relation to its ability to fulfil the advertiser's objectives
- The susceptibility of the medium to testing and measurement

ACTIVITY 1

All other things being equal, and subject to detailed research, at what time of day, or in what kind of programme, might you advertise the following products on TV?

(a)   Shoe polish

(b)   Home disinfectant

(c)   Car repairs

(d)   Chat/introduction lines

1.2.1 The size and type of the audience

Each medium reaches a certain number and 'type' (demographic group, market segment, interest group) of people. There is a trade-off between the size and relevance of the available audience.

(a)   General interest, national mass-market media (such as national newspapers or TV) will have the highest circulation figures, but may not reach the highest percentage of the target market segment.

(b)   Segmentation may be possible through the scheduling and placing of ads in large-scale media (for example, in special-interest sections of supplements in the press, or by programme preference on TV).

(c)   Targeted media may reach a smaller population, but a higher percentage of the target audience.

- Local or regional media
- Specialist magazines and journals
- Media which fit with the 'media habits' of the target audience

1.3 Direct response advertising

KEY CONCEPT

Direct response advertising appears in the prime media (TV, press etc) and is designed to elicit 'an immediate response from the consumer in terms of purchase, or request for a brochure, or a visit to the shop.' (Blythe, J. (2008)). This may include a freephone telephone number, or a website address. It does not involve the use of intermediaries.

Direct response advertising may involve traditional advertising in a newspaper or magazine with a cut out (or stuck on) response coupon; loose inserts with response coupons or reply cards; direct-response TV or radio advertisements, giving a call centre number or website address to contact.

Advertising on interactive TV includes a 'pop up' button which gives you the option to interact by transferring to a website. DRTV (home shopping) is presently conducted mainly through the use of television commercials or infomercials (which combine information with a commercial), which direct customers to a website or telephone order lines. In the UK, cable and satellite also provide a number of channels exclusively devoted to shopping.

Direct response advertising enables detailed measurement of the effectiveness of ads on different stations, at different times, in different formats.

Direct mail tends to be the main medium of direct response advertising. The main reason for this is that other major media such as newspapers and magazines are familiar to people for advertising in other contexts. Direct mail has a number of strengths as a direct response medium.

(a)   The advertiser can target down to **individual level**.

(b)   The communication can be **personalised**. Known data about the individual can be used, while modern printing techniques mean that parts of a letter can be altered to accommodate this.

(c)   The medium is good for **reinforcing interest** stimulated by other media such as TV. It can supply the response mechanism (a coupon) which is not yet available in that medium.

(d)   The opportunity to use **different creative formats** is almost unlimited.

(e)   **Testing potential is sophisticated**: a limited number of items can be sent out to a 'test' cell and the results can be evaluated. As success is achieved, so the mailing campaign can be rolled out.

1.4 Personal selling

Personal selling encompasses a wide variety of tasks including prospecting, information gathering and communicating as well as actually selling.

Jobber (2009) identifies the following elements in the modern selling role:

*   Customer relationship management
*   Database and knowledge management
*   Marketing the product
*   Problem solving
*   Satisfying needs and adding value

 KEY CONCEPT    concept

Personal selling is the presentation of products and persuasive communication to potential clients by sales staff employed by the supplying organisation. It is the most direct and longest established means of promotion within the promotional mix.

Personal selling, or sales force activity, must be undertaken within the context of the organisation's overall marketing strategy. For example, if the organisation pursues a '**pull**' strategy, relying on massive consumer advertising to draw customers to ask for the brands, then the role of the sales force may primarily be servicing, ensuring that retailers carry sufficient stock, allocate adequate shelf space for display and co-operate in sales promotion programmes.

Conversely, with a '**push**' strategy, the organisation will rely primarily on the sales force to persuade marketing intermediaries to buy the product.

1.4.1 Sales roles

A salesperson might perform any of six different activities.

Activity	Salesperson's role
Prospecting	Gathering additional potential customers
Communicating	Communicating information to existing and potential customers about the company's products and services can take up a major proportion of the salesperson's time
Selling	Approaching the customer, presenting benefits, answering objections and closing the sale
Servicing	Providing services to the customer, such as technical assistance, arranging finance and speeding delivery
Information gathering	Feedback and marketing intelligence gathering
Allocating	Allocating products to priority customers, in times of product shortages

1.4.2 The selling process

Personal selling is part of an integrated promotional strategy. It will be supported by a range of other activities such as advertising and PR, lead generation and sales support information.

Elements of the selling process can be depicted as follows.

Figure 7.2: Elements of personal selling

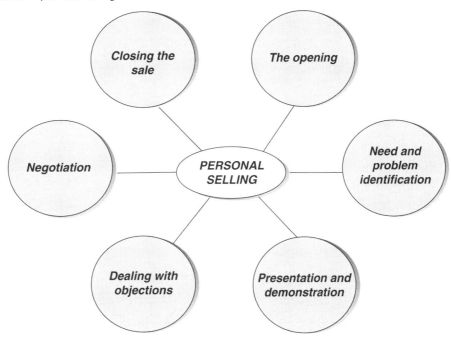

The stages need not occur in any particular order. Objections may occur during the presentation; negotiation may begin during problem identification; and if the process of selling is going well, the salesperson may try to close the sale.

The salesperson's job begins before meeting the buyer. **Preparation** could include finding out about the buyer's personal characteristics, the history of the trading relationship, and the specific requirements of the buyer and how the product being sold meets those requirements. In this way, the salesperson can frame sales presentations and answers to objections.

At the other end, the selling process does not finish when the sale is made. Indeed, the sale itself may only be the start of a long-term **relationship** between buyer and seller.

Personal selling will be **supported** by a range of other marketing communication activities.

(a)   **Product advertising, public relations and sales promotion**, drawing consumer attention and interest to the product and its sources *and* motivating distributors/retailers to stock and sell the product.

(b)   **'Leads'** (interested prospective customers) generated by contacts and enquiries made through exhibitions, promotional competitions, enquiry coupons in advertising and other methods.

(c)   **Informational tools** such as brochures and presentation kits. These can add interest and variety to sales presentations, and leave customers with helpful reminders and information.

(d)   **Sales support information**: customer/segment profiling; competitor intelligence; access to customer contact/transaction histories and product availability. (This is an important aspect of customer relationship management, enabling field sales teams to facilitate immediate response and transactions without time-lags to obtain information.)

1.4.3 The advantages and disadvantages of personal selling

Personal selling is often appropriate in **B2B markets**, where there are fewer, higher-value customers who are looking for a more complex total offering tailored to a more specific set of requirements.

A number of advantages are associated with using personal selling when compared to other promotional tools.

(a)   Personal selling contributes to a relatively **high level of customer attention** since, in face-to-face situations, it is difficult for a potential buyer to avoid a salesperson's message.

(b)   Personal selling enables the salesperson to **customise the message** to the customer's specific interests and needs.

(c)   The two-way communication nature of personal selling allows **immediate feedback** from the customer so that the effectiveness of the message can be ascertained.

(d)   Personal selling communicates a larger amount of **technical and complex information** than would be possible using other promotional methods.

(e)   In personal selling there is a greater ability to **demonstrate** a product's functioning and performance characteristics.

(f)   Frequent interaction with the customer gives great scope for the **development of long-term relations** between buyer and seller.

The main disadvantage of personal selling is the **cost** inherent in maintaining a salesforce. In addition, a salesperson can only interact with one buyer at a time. However, the message is generally communicated more effectively in the one-to-one sales interview, so the organisation must make a value judgement between the effectiveness of getting the message across against the relative expense.

According to Jobber (2009) there are forces at work that are changing the face of selling in the 21st century.

*   Rising customer expectations
*   Customer avoidance of traditional 'buyer versus seller' negotiations
*   Expanding power of major buyers
*   Globalisation of markets
*   Fragmentation of markets
*   Technological forces

1.5 Direct marketing

 KEY CONCEPT   concept

Direct marketing creates and develops a direct relationship between the consumer and the company on an individual basis.

(a)   The Institute of Direct Marketing in the UK defines direct marketing as 'The planned recording, analysis and tracking of customer behaviour to develop relational marketing strategies'.

(b)   The Direct Marketing Association in the US defines direct marketing as 'An interactive system of marketing which uses one or more advertising media to effect a measurable response and/or transaction at any location'.

Although it originated in direct mail and mail order catalogues, direct marketing today involves use of a wide variety of media to communicate directly with the target market and to elicit a measurable response. Such media include telemarketing, DRTV, the Internet and online shopping.

1.5.1 Features of direct marketing

It is worth studying these definitions and noting some key words and phases.

(a) **Response**. Direct marketing is about getting people to respond by post, telephone, e-mail or web form to invitations and offers.

(b) **Interactive**. The process is two-way, involving the supplier and the customer.

(c) **Relationship**. Direct marketing is in many instances part of an on-going process of communicating with and selling to the same customer.

(d) **Recording and analysis**. Response data are collected and analysed so that the most cost-effective procedures may be arrived at.

Direct marketing helps create and develop **direct one-to-one relationships** between the company and each of its prospects and customers. This is a form of **direct supply**, because it removes all channel intermediaries apart from the advertising medium and the delivery medium: there are no resellers. This allows the company to retain control over where and how its products are promoted, and to reach and develop business contacts efficiently.

1.5.2 Tools of direct marketing

No longer synonymous with 'junk mail', direct marketing tools include direct mail, e-mail, text message, DRTV advertising and telemarketing.

Direct marketing is the fastest growing sector of promotional activity. It now embraces a range of techniques, some traditional – and some based upon new technologies.

(a) **Direct mail (DM)**: a personally addressed 'written offering' (letter and/or sales literature) with some form of response mechanism, sent to existing customers from an in-house database or mailing list.

 MARKETING AT WORK application

Computers now have the capacity to operate in three new ways which will enable businesses to operate in a totally different dimension.

Customers can be tracked individually. Thousands of pieces of information about each of millions of customers can be stored and accessed economically.

Companies and customers can interact through, for example, phones, mail, E-mail and interactive kiosks. For the first time since the invention of mass marketing, companies will be hearing from individual customers in a cost-efficient manner.

Computers allow companies to match their production processes to what they learn from their individual customers - a process known as 'mass customisation' which can be seen as 'the cost-efficient mass production of products and services in lot sizes of one'.

There are many examples of companies which are already employing or experimenting with these ideas. In the US Levi Strauss, the jeans company, takes measurements and preferences from female customers to produce exact-fitting garments. The approach offers the company tremendous opportunities for building learning relationships.

The Ritz-Carlton hotel chain has trained staff throughout the organisation to jot down customer details at every opportunity on a guest preference pad. The result could be the following: You stay at the Ritz-Carlton in Cancun, Mexico, call room service for dinner, and request an ice cube in your glass of white wine. Months later, when you stay at the Ritz-Carlton in Naples, Florida, and order a glass of white wine from room service, you will almost certainly be asked if you would like an ice cube in it.

(b) **E-mail**: messages sent via the internet from an e-mail database of customers. E-mails can offer routine information, updates and information about new products: e-mail addresses can be gathered together via enquiries and contact permissions at the company's website.

(c) **Mobile phone text messaging (SMS)**. Messages can be sent via mobile phone to a captive audience, catching them wherever they are. This form of marketing is still in its infancy, but with the proliferation of mobile phone usage it is likely to be very significant, at least in terms of numbers reached. It is also becoming increasingly sophisticated, with '3G' (third-generation) mobile phone technology. SMS marketing is governed by the Mobile Marketing Association in the UK.

(d) **Direct response advertising** as described above.

(e) **Mail order**. Mail order brochures typically contain a selection of items also available in a shop or trade outlet, which can be ordered via an order form included with the brochure and delivered to the customer. Mail order extends the reach of a retail business to more (and more geographically dispersed) customers.

(f) **Catalogue marketing** is similar to mail order, but involves a complete catalogue of the products of the firm, which typically would not have retail outlets at all. Electronic catalogues can also be downloaded on the internet, with the option of transferring to the website for transaction processing, and on CD-ROM.

(g) **Call centres** and **telemarketing**. A call centre is a telephone service (in-house or outsourced by the marketing organisation) responding to or making telephone calls. This is a cost-effective way of providing a professionally trained response to customer callers and enquirers, for the purposes of sales, customer service, customer care or a contact point for direct response advertising.

 KEY CONCEPT

concept

Telemarketing is the planned and controlled use of the telephone for sales and marketing opportunities. Unlike all other forms of direct marketing it allows for immediate two-way communication.

 MARKETING AT WORK

application

A survey of recent direct mail campaigns includes the following creative ideas to overcome 'junk mail' resistance and marketing fatigue.

- **Great Ormond St Hospital, (UK)**
  How do you make it clear that a new ultrasound scanner would mean that surgeons could avoid unnecessary surgery when diagnosing children? Send a donation request in a clear package, that asks 'If you could see inside every envelope, would you open every one?'

- **Oroverde, Tropical Rainforest Founding (Germany)**
  How do you remind potential donors of the precarious state of the world's rainforests? Send them a paint-by-numbers kit with only one colour included: black.

- **Genesis Energy (New Zealand)**
  How do you let customers know you're there to help them save on their energy bills? Print your energy-saving tips in fluorescent ink, so they can read them with the lights off.

- **First Direct bank (UK)**
  How do you show customers that you're still the most thoughtful bank? Send them a single sock that they can marry to the odd one we all have in our sock drawer.

1.6 Technological developments and online marketing

KEY CONCEPT

concept

Digital marketing has been defined by Jobber (2009) as follows: ' the application of digital technologies that form channels to market (the Internet, mobile communications, interactive television and wireless) to achieve corporate goals through meeting and exceeding customer needs better than the competition.

ICT is adding impact, speed, interactivity and fun to the full range of promotional methods and tools. **Digital technologies** and the imaginative use of **websites** are creating endless possibilities.

(a) **Advertising**: using direct response advertising, web-advertising, CD-ROM and video packages, and mobile phone advertisements, ranking on Internet search engines

(b) **Direct marketing**: using e-mail or mobile text messages instead of conventional mail shots

(c) **Sales promotion**: online vouchers, discounts, loyalty schemes, 'SMS to win', competitions

(d) **Public and media relations**: corporate image on websites, posting of online press releases, special areas of the website for trade/press/client publics, news bulletins, crisis management, publicity for exhibitions and events

(e) **Point of sale display** at online shopping sites

(f) **Personal selling**: connecting mobile sales forces to customer/product databases and sales tools (eg video or computer modelling on the sales person's laptop, demonstrating product use or performance)

(g) **Relationship marketing**: generating multiple contacts via website, e-mail, phone 'remembering' customer details and preferences; allowing customer service staff to 'recognise' callers with relevant data

(h) **Customer loyalty programmes**: value-added benefits that enhance the Internet buying experience, user home page customisation, virtual communities (chat rooms etc), SMS messaging

1.6.1 Internet marketing

Brassington & Pettitt (2003) itemise the marketing uses of the Internet.

As a research and planning tool

- Obtain market information
- Conduct primary research
- Analyse customer feedback and responses

Distribution and customer service

- Take orders
- Update product offerings
- Help the customer to buy
- Process payments
- Raise customer service levels
- Reduce marketing and distribution costs
- Distribute digital products (music, software etc)

Communication and promotion

- Generate enquiries
- Enable low-cost direct communication
- Reinforce corporate identity and present company in a good light
- Produce and display product catalogues and product information
- Entertain, amuse and build goodwill
- Inform investors, suppliers and employees of developments

Jobber (2009) talks about how the evolving digital business environment has facilitated 'many-to-many' communications. See his book for more on marketing in the digital age.

 EXAM TIP

You should of course be aware of these technological developments, but also realistic about their current application. It is important for marketers to be aware of what ICT – especially the internet – can't do. It may be able to deliver some products/services in 'real time', or very fast: information, music and images, educational material and banking transactions. However, many products will still have to be physically delivered. The Internet is global in its reach, and so products will have to be delivered internationally. This takes resources, logistics, infrastructure and time.

Because of the promotional strengths of the internet, there is great potential for customer disappointment if the product does not live up to the sophistication of the promises – or if it cannot be delivered in a reasonable condition or within a reasonable period of time.

1.7 Sales promotion

Sales promotion techniques add value to a product in order to achieve a specific marketing objective.

 KEY CONCEPT

concept

The Institute of Sales Promotion (ISP) defines **sales promotion** as 'a range of tactical marketing techniques, designed within a strategic marketing framework, to add value to a product or service, in order to achieve a specific sales and marketing objective'.

Sales promotion activity is typically aimed at increasing short-term sales volume, by encouraging first time, repeat or multiple purchase within a stated time frame ('offer closes on such-and-such a date'). It seeks to do this by adding value to the product or service: consumers are offered something extra – or the chance to obtain something extra – if they purchase, purchase more or purchase again.

 EXAM TIP

application

It is worth being aware of the potential for confusion between the terms '**promotion**' (used as another way of saying 'marketing communications' in general) and '**sales promotion**' (which is a specialist term reserved for the techniques involved). In an exam, especially if you are reading through questions fairly quickly, it is all too easy to answer the 'wrong' question.

1.7.1 Objectives of sales promotion

The following are examples of consumer sales promotion objectives, stated in broad terms.

- Increase **awareness and interest** amongst target audiences
- Achieve a **switch in buying behaviour** from competitor brands
- **Incentivise consumers** to make a forward purchase of your brand
- **Increase display space** allocated to your brand
- **Smooth seasonal dips** in demand for your product
- Generate a **customer database** from mail-in applications

Sales promotion objectives will link into overarching marketing and marketing communications objectives. For example:

Marketing objective	Increase 'Brand X' market share by 2 percentage points between January and December 20XX
Marketing communications objective	To contribute to brand share gain of 2% in 20XX by increasing awareness of 'Brand X' from 50% to 70% among target consumers
Sales promotion objective	To encourage trial of 'Brand X' among target consumers by offering a guaranteed incentive to purchase

1.7.2 Consumer sales promotion techniques

Consumer promotion techniques include reduced price, coupons, gift with purchase and competitions and prizes.

The range of consumer **sales promotion techniques** can be depicted as follows.

Figure 7.3 Consumer sales promotion techniques

- **Price promotions**: for example discounted selling price or additional product on current purchase, or coupons (on packs or advertisements) offering discounts on next purchase

- **'Gift with purchase'** or **'premium'** promotions: the consumer receives a bonus, gift or refund on purchase or repeat purchase, or on sending in tokens or proofs of multiple purchases

- **Competitions and prizes** for example, entry in prize draws or 'lucky purchase' prizes, often used both to stimulate purchase (more chances to win) and to capture customer data

- **Frequent user (loyalty) incentives** for example, Air Miles programmes, points-for-prizes cards

 MARKETING AT WORK application

It is reckoned that two-thirds of purchases result from in-store decisions. Attractive and informative point-of-sale displays are therefore of great importance in sales promotion.

Point of sale materials include product housing or display casing (such as racks and carousels), posters and leaflet dispensers. Their purpose is to:

- Attract the attention of buyers
- Stimulate purchase in preference to rival brands

- Increase available display and promotion space for the product
- Motivate retailers to stock the product (because they add to store appeal)

1.8 Public relations

Public relations aims to enhance goodwill towards an organisation from its publics. According to Jobber (2009) it 'creates an environment in which it is easier to conduct marketing'.

 KEY CONCEPT concept

The Institute of Public Relations has defined **public relations** as 'the planned and sustained effort to establish and maintain goodwill and mutual understanding between an organisation and its publics'.

This is an important discipline, because although it may not directly stimulate sales, the organisation's image is an important factor in whether it attracts and retains employees, whether consumers buy its products/services, whether the community supports or resists its presence and activities and whether the media reports positively on its operations.

An organisation can be either reactive or proactive in its management of relationships with the public.

- **Reactive public relations** is primarily concerned with the communication of what has happened and responding to factors affecting the organisation. It is primarily defensive.

- In contrast, **proactive public relations** practitioners have a much wider role and thus have a far greater influence on overall organisational strategy. The scope of the PR function is much wider, encompassing communications activities in their entirety.

1.8.1 Scope of public relations

Organisations will have to deal with more than one public, including consumers, business customers, employees, the media, financial markets and wider society.

The scope of PR is very broad. Some frequently-used techniques are as follows.

(a) **Consumer marketing support**

- Consumer and trade press releases (to secure media coverage)
- Product/service literature (including video and CD-ROM)
- Special events (celebrity store openings, product launch events etc)
- Publicity 'stunts' (attention-grabbing events)

(b) **Business-to-business communication**

- Corporate identity design (logos, liveries, house style of communications)
- Corporate and product videos
- Direct mailings of product/service literature and corporate brochures
- Trade exhibitions and conferences

(c) **Internal/employee communications**

- In-house magazines and employee newsletters (or intranet pages)
- Recruitment exhibitions/conferences
- Employee communications: briefings, consultation, works councils

(d) **Corporate, external and public affairs**

- Corporate literature

- Corporate social responsibility and community involvement programmes: liaison with pressure and interest groups

- Media relations: networking and image management through trade, local, national (and possibly international) press

- Lobbying of local/central government and influential bodies

- Crisis and issues management: minimising the negative impacts of problems and bad publicity by managing press/public relations

(e) **Financial public relations**

- Financial media relations
- Design of annual and interim financial reports
- Facility visits for analysts, brokers, fund managers
- Organising shareholder meetings and communications

1.9 Exhibitions

There are differing views on the value of exhibitions, but Jobber (2009) writes:

"... exhibitions appear to be an important part of the industrial promotion mix. One study into the relative importance of promotional media placed exhibitions as a source of information in the industrial buying process second only to personal selling, and ahead of direct mail and print advertising."

Shows, exhibitions and trade fairs offer numerous marketing opportunities.

- **Public relations** either through visitors or media coverage

- **Promoting and selling** products and services to a wide audience of pre-targeted potential customers, particularly where demonstrations or visual inspection are likely to influence buyers

- **Networking** within the industry and with clients

- **Testing the response** to new products

- **Researching competitor products** and promotions

- **Researching suppliers' products** and services and making contacts along the supply chain

Most industries are catered for by at least one annual or bi-annual exhibition in the UK, as well as internationally. The events themselves are set up by exhibition organisers who are responsible for booking and preparing the venue, registering participants and organising seminars and events, issuing catalogues of standholders and events, providing stand construction services, and organising facilities, promotions and press coverage. Exhibiting is a demanding and expensive exercise, which should only be undertaken after research and cost-benefit analysis.

MARKETING AT WORK   application

New media is having an impact on the exhibitions industry. The Internet can be used to attract visitors to shows and for post-show marketing via email.

In addition, some exhibitors are using webcast technology to broadcast their shows live on the Internet. While this is not the same as being there, such facilities are still useful for communicating information about exhibited products to those who cannot attend the show. Online visitors can view just the stands that they are interested in.

The Director General of the Association of Exhibition Organisers says 'The growth of exhibitions will go hand in hand with the growth of electronic media' . Visitors can use the Internet to book exhibition tickets, flights, accommodation and meetings.

KEY CONCEPT

concept

Sponsorship involves supporting an event or activity by providing money (or something else of value, such as prizes for a competition), usually in return for naming rights, advertising or acknowledgement at the event and in any publicity connected with the event. Sponsorship is often sought for sporting events, artistic events, educational initiatives and charity/community events and initiatives.

Sports sponsorship is by far the most popular sponsorship medium as it tends to offer high visibility through extensive television and press coverage.

Sponsorship is often seen as part of a company's socially responsible and community-friendly public relations profile: it has the benefit of positive associations with the sponsored cause or event. The profile gained (for example in the case of television coverage of a sporting event) can be cost-effective compared to TV advertising, for example. However, it relies heavily on awareness and association: unless additional advertising space or 'air time' is part of the deal, not much information may be conveyed.

Marketers may sponsor local area or school groups and events – all the way up to national and international sporting and cultural events and organisations. Sponsorship has offered marketing avenues for organisations which are restricted in their advertising (such as alcohol and tobacco companies) or which wish to widen their awareness base among various target audiences.

- There is wide corporate involvement in mass-support sports such as football and cricket.

- Cultural sponsorship (of galleries, orchestras or theatrical productions) tends be taken up by financial institutions and prestige marketing organisations.

- Community event sponsorship (supporting local environment 'clean-up' days, tree planting days, charity fun-runs, books for schools programmes) is often used to associate companies with particular values (for example, environmental concern, education) or with socially responsible community involvement.

1.10.1 The purpose of sponsorship

The objective of the organisation soliciting sponsorship is most often financial support – or some other form of contribution, such as prizes for a competition, or a prestige name to be associated with the event. In return, it will need to offer potential sponsors satisfaction of *their* objectives.

The objectives of the **sponsor** may be:

- **Awareness creation** in the target audience of the sponsored event (where it coincides with the target audience of the sponsor)

- **Media coverage** generated by the sponsored event (especially if direct advertising is regulated, as for tobacco companies)

- Opportunities for **corporate hospitality** at sponsored events

- **Association** with prestigious or popular events or particular values

- Creation of a **positive image** among employees or the wider community by association with worthy causes or community events

- Securing **potential employees** (for example, by sponsoring vocational/tertiary education)

- **Cost-effective** achievement of the above (compared to, say, TV advertising)

- Creation of **entertainment opportunities** (in the sample case study, Innocent Drinks sponsors an annual music and comedy festival in London)

Sponsorship as a promotional technique also has limitations.

- Sponsorship by itself can only communicate a restricted amount of information (unless integrated with advertising and other initiatives).

- Association with a group or event may also attach negative values (such as sports-related violence and alcohol abuse).

ACTIVITY 2

application

List some examples of sporting, artistic, educational and community sponsorships that you are aware of in your country (or internationally).

- What image of the sponsoring company or brand does association with that particular event/group/cause create?

- How much promotional coverage (advertising, publicity) does the sponsor get as a result of sponsorship: how much information about the organisation or brand is conveyed?

1.11 Online forums, blogs and social networks

Web 2.0 is a term describing the trend in the use of Internet technology for purposes of creativity, information sharing and user collaboration. The recent and explosive development of web-based communities and hosted services, such as social-networking sites (Facebook, MySpace) and blogs has accelerated this trend.

MARKETING AT WORK

application

Facebook, the hugely popular social networking site, was begun in a Harvard University dorm room . In October 2007 Microsoft paid $240m for a mere 1.6% stake. Facebook hopes to become an advertising magnet by substantially increasing its current audience of nearly 500 million active users. That makes it the world's third largest 'country' by population. It is being criticised more and more over privacy concerns that may threaten its position. However, it seems that there is no limit to what some people are willing to share about themselves.

Fail to take your customers' online habits into account and you may regret it! Firms have long sought their customers opinions on products and services, but now those opinions are showing up on the web. Any experience somebody has with a firm – usually negative – can be posted on the web for all to see. This is going to prove a massive challenge for CRM over the next several years.

People are increasingly conditioned to having their opinions and thoughts listened to, and regard companies who ignore them as arrogant and 'last century'. According to BT customer experience consultant Dr Nicole Millard, savvy customers can be a boon to CRM. Customers were calling into BT contact centres asking how to use gaming consoles with their broadband service. Agents in the contact centres didn't know the answer, but other customers had already solved the problem. So BT started a web-based forum called Hubbub, which allows customers to share solutions with other users, and provide contact centre staff with another source of information. This was a benefit both for the customers and BT staff.

2 Developing the marketing communications plan

Marketers cannot control all the information that customers gather and process about products, but nevertheless marketing organisations must use these principles of communication in order to develop an effective coordinated marketing communications plan, and thereby exert some form of control.

Such plans are vitally important in the modern market, because the marketing mix variables on which marketers have traditionally relied to distinguish themselves from their rivals (product design, lower prices, distribution channels etc) have been changed by the march of technology. Competitors can copy what is done quicker than ever before.

It could be that marketing communications is one area where it is still possible to differentiate your product or service – making the customer believe what you want him to believe about your company, product, brand or service. Communications are therefore essential in supporting customer (indeed all stakeholder) relationships.

- The organisation needs to use **extensive contact**, interaction and feedback to learn about (and from) stakeholders, with the aim of continually adding value. 'In order to leverage relationship marketing, marketers need to move from monologue to dialogue with customers [and other stakeholders].' (Allen *et al*, 2001)

- The organisation needs to maintain direct and regular **stakeholder communication**, through multiple points of contact and across a range of reasons for contact, in order to develop relationship ties with stakeholders.

- The organisation needs to maintain **multiple exchanges with a number of stakeholders** (network relationships) rather than a single focus on customers, in order to manage all links in the customer value delivery chain.

- **Dialogue** and **developing trust** provide a basis for the customisation and personalisation of contacts, messages and value-propositions, which further deepen stakeholder relationships.

- Communication is part of the **relationship value offered to stakeholders**: keeping them informed in areas of their interest or concern, guiding and supporting them through changes in the organisation's plans, communicating support for their causes.

2.1 The communications plan

The nature of the prevailing market conditions is an important context that needs to be considered when planning and developing marketing communications activities.

Like all other areas of business activity, marketing communications needs careful housekeeping. The amount of money available is the key constraint on marketing communications, and there is growing pressure on total communications expenditure. This is because of fluctuating world economies, increasing media costs and also because methods of measuring the effectiveness of spending have been improved, and wastefulness is more transparent.

2.2 Communications planning frameworks

Each marketing communications programme is developed in unique circumstances. It is vitally important that the contextual conditions are analysed in order that any factor that may influence the content, timing or the way the audience receives and interprets information, be identified and incorporated within the overall plan.

In order to help provide for a systematic appraisal of the prevailing and future conditions, a context analysis is recommended when formulating a marketing communications programme. This consists of a review of the various sub-contexts.

Figure 7.4 Sub-contexts

The Business Context
The Customer Context
The Organisational Context
The Stakeholder Context
The External Context

2.2.1 The elements of context analysis

The business context

This part of the analysis involves a consideration of the markets and conditions in which the organisation is operating, which are of prime concern for the coordinated marketing communication programme.

Competitors' communications, general trading conditions and trends, the organisation's corporate and marketing strategies, a detailed analysis of the target segment's characteristics and a brand audit are the primary activities associated with this context.

The customer context

Here the emphasis is upon understanding buyer behaviour and the decision-making processes that buyers in the market exhibit. The objective is to isolate any key factor in the process or any bond that customers might have with the product/brand. This can then be reflected in any communication.

The stakeholder context

Coordinated marketing communications recognise that there are audiences other than customers, with whom organisations need to communicate. For example, members of the marketing channel, the media, the financial community, local communities and shareholders all seek a dialogue with the focus organisation. The strength and duration of the dialogue may vary but messages need to be developed and communicated and the responses need to be understood and acted upon wherever necessary.

The organisational context

The characteristics of the organisation can impact heavily on the nature and form of the communications they enter into. It is important, therefore, to consider the culture and the strength of identity the workforce has with the organisation. This is of absolute importance if truly coordinated communications are to be forged. In order to appreciate the strength of this sub-context, think about the way the staff of different companies communicate with you as a customer. Internal and external audiences communicate with each other and this is a significant part of coordinated marketing communications.

The external context

Coordinated marketing communications are influenced by a number of factors in the wider environment. These political, economic, social and technological elements are largely uncontrollable by organisations, for example economic conditions or laws and regulations. Nevertheless, they can shape and determine what, when and how messages are communicated to audiences.

  EXAM TIP concept

Marketing communications occur in particular contexts. It is very helpful when developing strategy and writing communication plans to understand the prevailing contextual conditions. It is also good exam practice to imagine the different forces and restraints operating on marketers. Consider for example the following circumstances.

- Launching new products
- Reviving a flagging brand
- Price competition
- Introducing a new variant
- A new competitor enters the market (such as giant PepsiCo and its Tropicana smoothie range, challenging Innocent in the sample case study)
- Regulations change
- Promotional budget is slashed

2.2.2 Outline marketing communications plan

The following is not a standard or compulsory model: it is just a suggested framework for thinking about the issues. (We have, for example, left out more detailed implementation aspects such as media scheduling, budgeting and agency briefings.

MARKETING COMMUNICATIONS PLAN FOR
[IDENTIFIED CUSTOMER if relevant]

1	**Communications objectives**	• What problem/need the communication plan is designed to address
		• What the communications plan is intended to achieve (SMART objectives if possible)
		• Co-ordinating marketing mix strategies within which the plan has been developed
2	**Target audience**	• Stakeholder group targeted by the plan
		• Key needs, concerns, interests and drivers of the group
		• Information needs of the group (either in general or in relation to the specific problem/situation)
		• Media and communication tools most used by and influential for the stakeholder group
3	**Core message(s)**	• Purpose of the message: desired stakeholder response
		• Content: key points of the message, and how best conveyed (eg text, multi-media)
		• Style: informative, persuasive, personal etc.
		• How the message fits within the co-ordinated marketing mix: consistency, synergy
4	**Communication media and tools**	Which media and tools will be used (with brief explanation/justification of each, if required):
		• Advertising
		• Direct Marketing
		• Public Relations
		And so on...
5	**Timetable**	• Period over which communication will be required
		• Timescales for review and measurement
6	**Resource allocation**	Estimated expenditure (or basis on which budget should be set: see later section of this chapter)
7	**Monitoring and control**	How progress and results will be monitored, reviewed and measured against objectives (see later section of this chapter)

2.3 Identifying and gaining new prospects

In order to achieve a sale, each buyer must move, or be moved, through a series of steps. These steps are essentially communication-based stages whereby individuals learn more about a product and mentally become more disposed towards adjusting their behaviour in favour (or not) of purchasing the item.

Awareness is an important state to be achieved as without awareness of a product's existence it is unlikely that a sale is going to be achieved! To achieve awareness people need to see or perceive the product, they need to understand or comprehend what it might do for them (benefits) and they need to be convinced that such a purchase would be in their best interest and to do this there is a need to develop suitable attitudes and intentions.

Analysis of the organisational context will have determined the extent to which action is required to communicate with members and non-members. Corporate communications, particularly with employees, and corporate branding to develop the image held by key stakeholders, should be integral to such coordinated marketing communication campaigns. These tasks form a discrete part of the communication programme.

In addition to this, it is the responsibility of the communication programme to communicate the mission and purpose of the organisation in a consistent and understandable form. And, the organisation needs to be able to listen and respond to communications from their stakeholders in order that they are able to adjust their position in the environment and continue to pursue their corporate goals.

2.4 Communications planning in different contexts

2.4.1 B2B

An organisation's interaction with the various markets in which it operates is, of course, crucial. In order that its marketing communications be effective it is necessary to understand the conditions and elements that prevail in specific markets.

- Is the market expanding or contracting?
- What are the values and beliefs held by the target audience towards the firm's products and those of competitors?
- What are the attitudes of intermediaries?
- What is the nature of competitive communications?

Most of our discussion so far has tended to concentrate upon the marketing of goods by businesses to consumers (B2C). Although the principles of marketing communications are the same for both consumer and industrial markets, there are significant differences in the details of how promotion is carried out. In particular, the targets in industrial markets are usually more specific and promotional budgets are usually more limited.

Perhaps the most significant differences are the nature of the buying motivation and the linked nature of the buying decision process. In industrial buying there are many motivations. These stem partly from the technical use of the product but also from financial, security of supply and, to a lesser degree, emotional reasons.

Decision makers	Buying motivation
Operations Manager	Uses the product in the organisation's processes - wants efficiency and effectiveness
Technical Manager	Often has to test and approve the product – wants reliability
Managing Director	May approve major expenditure or change of supplier
Purchasing Manager	Approves conditions of purchase
	Monitors supplier performance
Legal Manager	Draws up or approves legal contracts with supplier
Finance Manager	Approves expenditure and controls debt payment
Health and Safety Manager	May have a role to play with hazardous supplies

It will be obvious that marketing communications strategy for industrial marketing must reflect this considerably more complex decision-making process.

The variety of products in business markets is extremely large. Business products vary from product inputs to items for resale. They can be broken down into three main types.

- Capital equipment (major purchases of fixed assets)
- Production inputs (becoming part of the buyer's process)
- Business supplies/services (ongoing use by the buyer)

Again, each type of purchase will need a different communications strategy.

The range of promotional methods is described below.

Method	Comment
Personal selling	This is a major component of industrial marketing because of the need to deal with technical and other issues on a face to face basis.
Internal selling	Increasingly it is recognised that a salesperson has an internal role to play in representing his customers' needs to the company.

Method	Comment
Internet	The use of the internet for e-commerce is perhaps more highly developed in industrial marketing than in the consumer sector. Advertising and online catalogues are just two of the ways that it can be used. Many companies have also set up electronic links with suppliers and customers for such functions as automatic ordering.
Advertising	A wide variety of publications exist which can be used to target individual market sectors including: (i) trade journals (ii) business press (iii) directories
Telemarketing	Telemarketing has been proved to be a very cost effective method of order processing, customer service, sales support and account management.
Direct mailing	Direct mail, another form of direct marketing, has been used by industrial marketers for a long time but its use has substantially increased. It can be used to provide information and generate enquiries. It can be tailored to individual customer needs.
Public relations	Sometimes in industrial markets this is referred to as publicity. It often focuses on getting editorial coverage in appropriate magazines but it has a wider role of building customer relations.
Sales promotion	Sales promotion is an important area of communication in industrial markets. There are a wide range of methods that are of well established use in industrial campaigns. • Literature • Exhibitions • Videos • Discounting • Events • Business gifts • Trade shows

2.4.2 Not-for-profit communications

Categories of not-for-profit (NFP) communications include the following.

- Political party communications
- Social cause communications
- Charitable communications
- Government communications
- Religious communications
- Professional body communications
- Other private non-profit communications (hospitals, universities, museums and so on)

The major principles of marketing communications for non-profit organisations are the same as for consumer and industrial marketing. There are, however, considerable differences of emphasis. The sum of money available for organised communication may be less. Public scrutiny of policies may be higher.

 MARKETING AT WORK

application

In the face of a severe shortfall in revenue (due to wildly optimistic forecast visitor numbers) the amount of grant funding to the New Millennium Experience Company rocketed to £628 million. Sir John Bourne of the National Audit Office said in a report:

'Building and opening the Millennium Dome on the very short timescale required was a tremendous achievement. But the New Millennium Experience Company has experienced severe financial difficulties this year and has required considerable additional lottery funding.

The main cause of these difficulties is the failure to achieve the visitor numbers and income required. The targets were highly ambitious and inherently risky leading to a significant degree of financial exposure on the project. In addition, the task of managing the project has been complicated by the complex organisational arrangements put in place from the outset, and by the failure to establish sufficiently robust financial management.'

What went wrong? The whole issue illustrated the need for proper marketing communications planning. Strong negative word-of-mouth also had an impact. The following general points should have been considered.

- Promotional strategies to attract visitors (pull strategy), communication with those issuing tickets (push strategy), and promotion of the image of the 'Dome' and that of the Millennium Experience Company (Profile Strategy) should have been fully coordinated.

- Messages should have been adapted to the various audiences.

- Promotional strategies should have taken into account financial constraints imposed by the fact that this was funded in the main through public money. Sales were likely to fall short of targets if insufficient money and time was invested in marketing.

Almost certainly there will be a different set of communication objectives.

- Making target customers aware of a product, service or social behaviour
- Educating consumers about the offer or changes in the offer
- Changing beliefs about negative and positive consequences of taking a particular action
- Changing the relative importance of particular consequences
- Enlisting the support of a variety of individuals
- Recruiting, motivating or rewarding employees or volunteers
- Changing perceptions about the sponsoring organisation
- Influencing government bodies
- Preventing the discontinuity of support
- Proving benefits over 'competitors'
- Combating injurious rumours
- Influencing funding agencies

Once the non-profit marketer has developed the broad objectives for the communications plan the next step is to decide specific messages. Three types of message may be developed.

(a) Rational, emotional and moral framework

- Rational messages pass on information and serve the audience's self interest, for example messages about value, economy or benefits.

- Emotional messages are designed to develop emotion to shape the desired behaviour, for example with fear, guilt, shame to stop doing things like smoking, drinking, taking drugs or overeating.

- Moral messages directed at the audience's sense of right or wrong, for example to support a cleaner environment or equal rights or help the under-privileged.

 MARKETING AT WORK application

EShopAfrica.com is a website dedicated to selling the wares of African craftsmen. As well as the products themselves, the site features information about tribal traditions and personal stories about the craftsmen.

Difficulties with credit card payments to Africa (the financial infrastructure is relatively underdeveloped) and the fact that the products can be obtained far more cheaply from bulk import/export businesses has meant that the site has struggled to break even. According to the site's founder, this misses the point of the venture.

The site is aimed at improving the lot of the craftsmen, and its avowed primary goal is to create sustainable businesses for five artisans a year. It aims to tap the snobbery market, and specifically that customer segment that is social/ego oriented and which seeks out the original and unusual at a premium price. This premium price can be seen by the customer to directly benefit an African craftsman and so the customer can feel good about him or herself.

Method	Comment
Paid advertising	Non-profit organisations may have limited funds but this can still be an effective route even on low budgets, as the Save the Children Fund campaign showed. Alternatively the budget may be boosted by obtaining commercial sponsorship.
Unpaid (public service) advertising	Media owners may provide airtime or press space on a free of charge basis as a public service. However, there is little control over this and the times or spaces may occur at unpopular times or places.
Sales promotions	Short-term incentives to encourage purchases or donations. Market control is strong and promotions are often newsworthy (for example Red Nose day or Poppy day promotions).
Public relations	Many of the stories of non-profit organisations are of considerable interest. They may feature in the press or the broadcast media. Control over the message is good and feedback is possible.
Personal selling and communications	Staff at all levels of the non-profit organisations should be trained in personal communications. They will often have the opportunity to 'sell' to their supporters and possible benefactors.

3 Measuring marketing communications activities

3.1 Setting marketing communications objectives

In order to deliver an effective plan, it is important to establish marketing communications objectives. These will involve variables such as perception, attitudes, developing knowledge and interest or creating new levels of prompted and spontaneous awareness. As we have seen, they also need to be SMART.

Ultimately, communications are designed to meet three objectives.

Awareness   Increase brand awareness and establish brand recognition
Trial   Stimulate trial purchase
Reinforcement   Stimulate and reinforce brand loyalty

3.1.1 Sales goals

If you ask most people what the goal of marketing communications is, then most will respond 'to increase sales'. Ultimately this (and profit) is an important outcome, but ask yourself this: are sales generated by marketing communications alone? What role does each of the other elements of the marketing mix play? How will sales vary if a competitor reduces its prices or you increase yours? What impact do marketing channel and product availability play in sales performance? Marketing communications is important but it is not the sole contributor to marketing success or failure.

Sales goals are important and performance can be determined in terms of sales volumes, sales value or revenue, market share, or profitability measures such as return on investment (ROI). They are a useful management aid as they are easy to comprehend and measurement is straightforward.

3.2 Influences on the effective audience

The effective audience for a medium, and therefore the competitiveness of different media, is influenced by the following factors.

(a) **Opportunity to use the medium**. The potential audience will not be able to use TV during working hours, or magazines while driving, or cinema over breakfast. Radio in the morning and TV in the evening have bigger effective audiences.

(b) **Effort required to use the medium**. People usually use the medium that will cost them least effort. Print media require the ability to read and concentrate: television is comparatively effortless.

(c) **Familiarity with the medium**. People consume media with which they are familiar: hence the survival of print media, since the education system is still predominantly print-orientated. Electronic media are however gaining ground.

(d) **Segmentation by the medium**. The print media currently has the greatest capacity for segmentation into special-interest audiences. Commercial television segments to a limited extent through programming, and cable/satellite television to a greater extent, through the proliferation of channels. Some media only charge in proportion to the segment you are targeting, which is more cost effective than paying for the full circulation.

 ACTIVITY 3

What opportunity, effort and familiarity issues might you consider when appraising the following media?

(a) A newly launched radio station

(b) Daytime television

(c) Posters on buses

(d) Web pages

3.3 Measuring effectiveness

To succeed in achieving their goals, communications must:

- Gain attention
- Communicate a message
- Improve attitude to the brand
- Reinforce the already positive attitude to the brand
- Obtain the readers'/listeners'/viewers' liking for the message and its execution

 ACTIVITY 4

Brainstorm a list of media which might be suitably targeted (by factors in the media themselves, or in the media habits of the target audiences) for effective advertising of the following products/services.

(a) A local garage offering car service, maintenance and parts

(b) An up-market restaurant

(c) A software package for use by accountants (based on UK law and regulation)

(d) A new brand of washing powder

(e) A microchip for use in engineering applications

3.3.1 How to assess the effectiveness of communications campaigns

Principle	What it means
Value linkage	Communication must represent the value of the brand.
Sense making	Communications must be meaningful and relevant.
Simplification	Strict simplification is necessary in view of the avalanche of information.
Acceleration	The message must be transmitted in a few seconds.
Visualisation	We must communicate visually first and foremost.
Humanisation	Communication must relate to the lives and dreams of real people.

Principle	What it means
Emotionalisation	Communications should activate the receiver's feelings more.
Conditioning	Effective use requires strong, unambiguous, vivid stimuli.
Refreshment	Receivers can become bored or tired of campaigns.
Branding	The brand has to be a coordinated part of communications.
Entertainment	Entertainment can be extremely effective in some cases.
Consistency	Consistency has been the mainstay of major brands.

The difficult part is measuring the effectiveness of the marketing communications process. The following are some possible techniques.

Marketing communications methods	Examples of measurement
Personal selling	Sales targets
Public relations	Editorial coverage
Direct marketing	Enquiries generated
Advertising	Brand awareness
Sales promotion	Coupons redeemed
Exhibitions	Contacts made

3.4 The role of market research

When measuring marketing effectiveness, three key questions exist:

1   How can we satisfy customer needs?
2   How do we ensure we are competitive within the market?
3   What external factors are likely to affect us?

To address these questions the organisation needs to gather information on customers, competitors and the marketing environment. This is **market research**. The table below outlines the broad issues and then focuses on some of the detail that marketers will need to consider.

Customer information required	Information required on competitors and other organisations	Information required about the marketing environment
Who are our customers?	**Competitor activity**	**Macro environment**
Can our customers be segmented in any way?	Who are our competitors?	What are the PESTEL factors to impact us?
Are customers B2B or individual consumers or both?	What are their core competences?	Is our market growing or in decline?
Do we have groups of key customers or a broad market appeal?	What share of the market do they have?	Are we likely to remain profitable in the current and future market conditions?
	What additional threat do they pose?	
Where are customers found?	**Performance benchmarking**	**Micro environment**
Location?	Who should we measure ourselves against?	How effective is our internal market?
Frequent visitors to where?	What metrics should be used to provide a meaningful analysis?	Are we working with the right partners, suppliers etc?
Online presence, sites visited?		Internally are we organised as best as we can be to meet customer needs?
Where can we be available at their convenience?		Do our people understand our customers and how to best meet their needs?

Customer information required	Information required on competitors and other organisations	Information required about the marketing environment
How do we build a relationship with customers?	**Partner organisations and marketing networks**	
Are our customers exclusively loyal?	What referral markets should we belong to?	
Are we part of a portfolio of brands that our customers purchase?	Are we making the most of the networks that we belong to?	
How do our customers like to communicate with us?	How can we partner with other organisations for mutual gain?	
What is our history with our customers?		
How do customers perceive us?		
How do customers make purchases?		
What is the decision-making process for consumers?		
What reference groups are important?		
What decision-making units are involved in the purchase?		
Do customers regard purchases as high or low involvement?		
How do we satisfy customers needs?		
Have we correctly identified what customer needs are?		
How does our offering meet their needs?		
What are satisfaction levels?		
How can satisfaction levels be improved?		
What are the behaviour patterns of customers?		
Do customers relate to our product/service individually or within a group?		
What is the influence of third parties on the behaviour of customers with regard to our product/service?		

Learning objectives		Covered
1	Critically evaluate a range of communications mixes and recommend appropriate creative, innovative, sustainable and co-ordinated approaches to communications activities and creating the optimal mix for internal and external marketing activities	☑ The range of tools
2	Develop and manage a co-ordinated marketing communications plan, in the context of the strategic marketing plan, in order to establish and build relationships appropriate to the needs of customers, stakeholders and prospects in different organisational contexts and sectors	☑ The communications plan ☑ Communications planning frameworks ☑ Identifying and gaining new prospects ☑ Communications planning in different contexts
3	Recommend appropriate methods for measuring marketing communications activities and successful delivery of the marketing communications strategy	☑ Setting marketing communications objectives Measuring effectiveness The role of market research

1   What criteria can be used to select advertising media?

2   List three techniques of:
    (a) sales promotion, and
    (b) trade promotion.

3   Identify four activities involved in personal selling.

4   Define:
    (a) public relations, and
    (b) sponsorship

5   List three applications of corporate hospitality.

6   Why is it important to co-ordinate or integrate the promotional mix?

7   Put the following terms into the first column in the table inappropriate space: consumer marketing support, B2B, internal communications, public affairs, financial relationships.

PR technique	Example
	Shareholder meeting
	In-house magazine
	Celebrity store opening
	Trade exhibition
	Government lobbying

8   How can new digital technologies assist with relationship marketing?

9   Why is television the favoured medium for launching new products and building brands?

10 What are the disadvantages of internet advertising, when evaluating it against other media?

1   (a)   Assuming mainly professional male buyers: next to business news, news or evening/weekend sports

     (b)   Assuming mainly female buyers/decision makers: daytime (cost effective), home/lifestyle programmes, prime time soaps (eg for launch)

     (c)   Assuming car-owner buyers, not during commuting hours: driving/car programmes, motor sports, home/lifestyle (women buyers)

     (d)   Assuming single buyers: late-night television

2   This will depend on your own research. You might have considered sports sponsorship, especially of large international events that are guaranteed to have huge audiences. The public has a high level of acceptance of sponsorship, with many recognising that if there is no sponsorship, there will be no sports event at all. Spiralling costs have meant that sponsors are increasingly prepared to consider involvement at the grass roots level rather than the higher cost, 'glamour' events. This in turn encourages the development of sport over the long term, and appeals to today's socially responsible consumer who is looking for genuine involvement to overcome his cynicism about corporate motives. The Football Association in the UK, for instance, now has a limited number of sponsorship partners, who are expected to get involved at all levels of the game.

3   (a)   Opportunity and effort are good with radio: effortless background, portable etc. Familiarity may be a constraint where station newly launched: listeners may not want to switch from old favourites, may not be able to recall frequency.

     (b)   Daytime TV minimal effort and good familiarity with regular users, but limited opportunity if target audience includes workers/school-age viewers/commuters.

     (c)   Bus posters: minimal effort (depending on size, length of copy, sight lines: can be a strain to read bus posters), good familiarity, good opportunity because moving around (outside posters) but limited to bus users only (inside).

     (d)   Web pages: high effort (to search, wait, use queries etc, requires technological know-how), improving familiarity (biased towards computer-literate), limited opportunity by virtue of technology, access and expertise required.

4   Here are some suggestions.

     (a)   Local radio (in car), bus stop, poster sites (driver visibility), local paper 'Auto' section.

     (b)   Local cinema (evening session, adult-appeal film), local paper 'Food' section, Good Food Guide (regional listing), local radio (classical music/news programmes?)

     (c)   UK accountancy journals (various), Underground Station posters in financial districts, direct mail.

     (d)   Commercial TV (especially daytime for housewives), poster sites (shopper visibility), women's and household magazines (assuming mainly female buyer decision.)

     (e)   Trade engineering journals, website of inventor

1   Criteria used to select advertising media include: size of audience, type and targeting of audience, suitability of the medium for the message, and cost.

2   Sales promotion techniques include: price promotions, gift with purchase (or premium) promotions, competitions and frequent user (loyalty) incentives. Trade promotion techniques include: trade discounts, baker's dozen packs, collaborative promotion, point of sale support, competitions and awards for sales, and business gifts.

3   Personal selling involves communicating, selling, servicing and information gathering.

4   Public relations is the planned and sustained effort to establish and maintain goodwill and mutual understanding between an organisation and its publics. Sponsorship involves supporting an event or activity by providing money or some other value, in return for naming rights, advertising or other form of association with the event.

5   Corporate hospitality may be used for building or cementing relationships with stakeholders; rewarding or motivating suppliers, intermediaries or staff; wooing potential employees; encouraging networking; or showing a presence at events.

6   It is important to co-ordinate the promotional mix in order to maximise the use of resources; maintain coherence and clarity of messages, and maintain consistency of messages.

7

PR techniques	Examples
Financial reasons	Shareholder meeting
Internal communications	In-house magazine
Consumer marketing support	Celebrity store opening
B2B	Trade exhibitions
Public affairs	Government lobbying

8   Generating contacts via website; use of targeted e-mail; 'remembering' customer details using a database.

9   Television has very high exposure and strong audio-visual impact.

10 • Generally poor viewership

    • Consumer confidence in its is security low (but improving)

    • Possible to direct audience to information, but can be difficult to gain large audience without support from other media

    • Not yet a mainstream media with broad customer appeal – user expertise may be limited

    • Speed of access depends on sophistication of technological link

    • No universal computing language yet agreed

References

Allen C, Kania D & Yaeckel, B (2001) <u>One to One Web Marketing</u> (2nd edition), Wiley, New York.

Blythe, J (2009) <u>Principles and Practice of Marketing</u>, 2nd edition, South-Western/Cengage Learning.

Blythe, J (2008) <u>Essentials of Marketing</u>,4th edition, FT Prentice Hall.

Brassington, F and Pettitt, S (2006) <u>Principles of Marketing</u>, 4th edition, FT Prentice Hall.

Dibb S, Simkin L, Pride WM, Ferrell OC (2005) <u>Marketing: Concepts and Strategies</u>, 5th edition, Houghton Mifflin.

Jobber (2009) <u>Principles and Practice of Marketing</u>.6th edition, McGraw Hill Higher Education

Chapter 8
Managing communications agencies

Topic list

Introduction

To assist with the planning and implementation of marketing communications programmes, there are many suppliers of marketing related services, providing advice on or implementation of market research, advertising, promotions, PR, direct marketing, brand identity, sponsorship, creative process and many other areas.

This chapter examines some of the operational, procedural and contractual aspects of working with suppliers of marketing services such as advertising agencies or PR consultancies, from selection of the most appropriate supplier to the management of the relationship.

Syllabus linked learning objectives

By the end of the chapter you will be able to:

Learning objectives	Syllabus link
1 Critically evaluate and select the most appropriate marketing communications agency for the utilisation of marketing communications capability against agreed criteria	3.5
2 Recommend and justify an approach to managing agency relationships including reporting, monitoring and measuring performance	3.6

1   Using an agency

1.1 The role of marketing agencies in marketing communications

According to Jobber (2009) an advertiser has four options when developing a campaign.

(a) Small companies may develop advertising in co-operation with people from the media. Copy might be written in-house, for example, with artwork and final layout designed by the publication

(b) The advertising function may be carried out in-house, but its media buying power will be low

(c) Many advertisers opt to work with an advertising agency because of the specialist skills that are needed

(d) A fourth alternative is to use in-house staff for some of the work and specialists for the rest. Such specialists often hold large buying power, or special creative talent in the form of 'hot shops'.

Most companies which advertise use an advertising agency. There are a number of reasons why a company might want to use **external marketing services**, rather than plan or carry out marketing activities in-house.

(a) Professional marketing agencies specialise in communications, media and consumer trends, and stay up-to-date.

(b) They have wide experience with a range of clients, which they can bring to bear on problems and opportunities.

(c) They supply specialist organisational and creative talent with specialist facilities (for example, for filming, sound recording and editing).

(d) They are objective about the client's needs and position, and may be better able to view the product from the consumer's point of view.

(e) The cost of using external services, past a certain level of sophistication, is usually cheaper than attempting to perform the same functions in-house.

In the last few decades, marketing techniques have increased dramatically in range and complexity. Standard 'above-the-line' marketing (where media space is paid for), handled by large advertising agencies, has been augmented by 'below-the-line' (promotional) activities. Agencies specialising in sales promotion, direct marketing, e-marketing and PR have sprung up as independent operations and divisions of large advertising agencies. Many companies now use more than one agency to handle a portfolio of techniques above- and below-the-line, or to cover local and on-going work as well as national strategic campaigns.

In addition, the complexities of new media (such as e-marketing) have created technical specialisms such as Web page design, datamining, and digital media buying.

1.2 Marketing service providers

Here we will briefly outline some of the service providers with whom a marketer may have to deal.

1.2.1 Market researchers

Market researchers can be commissioned to gather and analyse information on any aspect of the business, market or environment.

1.2.2 Advertising agencies

 KEY CONCEPT
concept

Advertising agencies are still the most commonly-used marketing service. Agencies come in a range of sizes and specialisms to reflect an increasingly fragmented and diverse range of media.

(a) 'Media only' service (where the agency selects, schedules and books advertising space at a discount, which is then passed on to the client)

(b) 'Full service' (where the agency creates the whole campaign from concept through production to press/air)

Many larger, integrated agencies now have divisions specialising in various areas:

- Sales promotion
- Direct marketing
- Public relations
- E-marketing (Internet, SMS, podcasts etc)
- Design

1.2.3 Promotion agencies

Promotional activities – collaborations between brands, competitions and incentives – have been a huge growth area in marketing. Some agencies specialise in these areas:

- Sourcing promotional incentive products and merchandise
- Devising links and negotiating deals between brands
- Organising competitions
- Designing and producing promotional packaging and information material

PR consultancies handle several areas.

(a) **Media or press relations** – keeping the media informed, in order to manage the company's image and secure favourable coverage

(b) **Corporate relations** – promoting a corporate image to the public, market and business world

(c) **Marketing support** – promoting specific products or services via publicity, events and press coverage

(d) **Government relations** – lobbying on behalf of the company's interests

(e) **Community relations** – targeted at the general public or local residents, via communication and social programmes, community involvement, sponsorship

(f) **Financial relations** – communicating with shareholders, financial media, the stock exchanges

(g) **Employee relations** – communicating with staff

PR agencies are less easy to manage than advertising agencies, because their activity and output is often less tangible. The major cost is their time plus expenses. In order to make cost effective use of their services a marketer must consider the following:

- Set clear objectives for the plan or project
- Set a project fee where possible
- Brief comprehensively
- Monitor activity
- Monitor expenditure

1.2.4 Direct marketing services

Direct marketing agencies offer a range of services from database and mailing list development, analysis and segmentation to telemarketing, direct mail package design, copywriting, mailing and fulfilment – and their electronic equivalents such as email and SMS.

1.2.5 Brand identity

There are specialist agencies which perform specific brand-related services:

- Designing and producing product packaging and display
- Orchestrating brand updates
- Researching, devising, testing and registering new brand names

1.2.6 Sponsorship

Agencies undertake negotiations for:

- Sponsorship agreements
- Product endorsements by celebrities
- Product placement in films or TV programmes

1.2.7 Creative services

Agency, freelance and corporate help is also available with:

- Design and layout, artwork and illustration
- Concept development and copy writing
- Print buying and print production
- Photography
- Film, video and audio production
- Web page design

1.2.8 Other services

In addition to all of the above, the marketing department may deal with many providers of services related to promotional events and activities:

- Event organisers, venue managers, hotel and restaurant staff
- Exhibition organisers, stand constructors and removalists
- Postal services
- Model/talent agencies, costumer hirers etc

Here are two small ads. What sort of companies/products might use these services?

Market Research Limited
Trade Research Specialists

- Retail audits
- Product availability surveys
- Mystery shopping
- Customer interviews
- Consumer research

- Tailor made studies
- Overnight pricing checks
- Shop testing
- Trade interviews

CHILDREN AND YOUTH
BRITAIN AND CONTINENT

GB *Core Sample:* 1200 7 - 19 year olds with bi-monthly extensions to include ages 3 to 6 and 20-24. Any age range within these limits.

Field dates: every 2 - 4 weeks.

Rates: from £290 per question according to age range covered.

Continent: Five country child and youth surveys

1.3 How agencies are structured

1.3.1 Who's who in the agency?

The simplest form of **agency structure** is as follows.

Figure 8.1 Agency structure

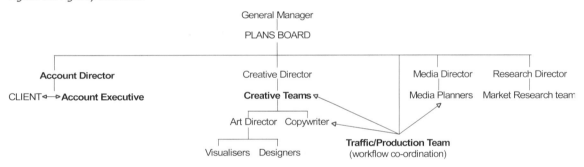

- The **account executives** service the clients on a day to day basis

- The **account director** monitors work on given accounts

- The **creative team** 'produces' the ad

- The **traffic/production team** plans and schedules agency workflow, monitors progress against deadlines and 'chases' work

The account director/manager is vitally important because a full service agency will provide the services of not fewer than 20 departments, and these need to be co-ordinated around a client focus. His role is to liaise with client staff and to brief, supervise and co-ordinate the appropriate agency staff at appropriate times. The departments commonly found in a **full service agency** are as follows.

- Creative
- Typography
- Presentation
- Studio
- Account management
- Economic forecasting
- Research

- TV and radio production
- Press production
- Press buying
- Print buying
- Art buying
- TV and radio buying
- Sales promotion

- Marketing
- Media planning
- Market intelligence
- Personnel
- Finance
- Administration
- Management

1.3.2 Internal structure of an agency

The internal structure of an agency can best be explained by considering how the agency handles a piece of client work.

(a)   **The client problem**

A client and agency who have been together for some time will have built up a good working relationship. The agency will understand the client's business, and the motivations and decision-making processes of end consumers. A new product or service, new situation or changing market conditions may provide the starting point for a new role to be performed by advertising. The client needs to brief the account executive on the task in hand.

(b)   **The internal briefing**

The account executive will brief the members of the account team who work on the client's business. These members are:

(i)   An **account planner**, responsible for using market research to develop advertising strategy for the clients.

(ii)   A **creative team** or duo of art director and copywriter, responsible for conceiving a creative idea which meets the advertising brief and working that idea up into visual form and written copy.

(iii)   A **media planner/buyer**, responsible for recommending an appropriate media strategy and ensuring media is bought cost effectively.

(c)   **The client presentation**

The account executive will present back to the client. He will show examples of how the final advertising execution will look, using rough visuals or storyboards and will explain the rationale for the ideas presented. Depending on the client's reaction to the team's interpretation of the brief, the team will either be asked to go ahead in developing the work, or will be asked to rework their ideas.

The go-ahead stage may include a decision to test the advertising in research prior to full production of the advert.

(d)   **Production of advert(s)**

Some simple advertising executions will be carried out almost entirely in-house by the advertising agency. For more complex executions, the agency will buy in specialist functions on behalf of the client.

Whilst production is ongoing, the media department will be involved in the actual commitment of the media budget. Dates, times and positions will be agreed with media owners.

During this stage, there will be continuous liaison between the account executive and the client. The client is likely to attend some of the key production stages such as filming or photography of the commercial.

If time allows, further research may take place to identify the need for any additional changes.

(e)   **The campaign appears**

The time span between the briefing of the account executive by the client and the campaign appearing can be as little as six or eight weeks for a simple photographic newspaper execution, to 20 weeks plus for an animated TV commercial. Once the campaign has appeared, it is important that it is properly evaluated against the objectives initially set.

Members of the account team, who work directly on the client's business in creating a campaign, are those the client is most likely to come into contact with, although the main point of contact will of course be the account executive. There are other behind the scenes staff with whom the account executive must liaise but who will not have direct client contact.

- **Accounts department**, responsible for billing the client and paying agency invoices
- **Vouchers department** checks that press adverts appear
- **Traffic department** ensures that jobs are taken through their different stages on time.
- A large agency may additionally have an **information** or **library service**, and **legal department**.

An IPA (*Institute for Practitioners in Advertising*) booklet 'Getting the most out of the client–agency partnership' suggests the following checklist of questions.

1 Are the client's **corporate objectives**, and the **marketing objectives** that derive from them, entirely clear to both parties? Have the marketing and communications tasks been quantified, together with their financial and profit implications?

2 Are the marketing and communications planners fully informed about **relevant factors in the commercial environment**, particularly:

- Actual and potential customers
- Product advantages and limitations
- Competitors
- Current or predictable marketing problems
- Product and marketing development plans?

3 Has sufficient **lead-time** been allowed for planning purposes?

4 Has the agency's **creative policy** been fully thought through and discussed in relation to the defined communications tasks?

5 Do the various creative manifestations (whether advertisements in paid media, explanatory literature, direct mail shots, audio-visual and other sales aids, exhibition stands or press publicity) **express the policy** effectively?

6 Have the **media plan and budget** been fully thought through and discussed? Are both agency and client convinced that they are as cost-effective as available information will permit?

7 If **results** in one area have not come up to expectations, has there been a serious effort to find out *why*, instead of shrugging it off or explaining it away?

8 Is there sufficient readiness not just to change for change's sake, but progressively to **improve performance** within an agreed long-term policy?

9 Is the level of **financial and administrative control** satisfactory on both sides?

10 Is the level of **client-agency communications** – in both directions – as good as it should be?

11 Is there **mutual understanding and respect** between the individuals working on the account, on the client and on the agency side?

1.4 Agency selection

1.4.1 The selection procedure

The stages of the selection procedure are as follows.

- Define the campaign requirements
- Develop a list of suppliers
- Assess their credentials
- Issue the brief to a short list of candidates

Figure 8.2 Agency brief

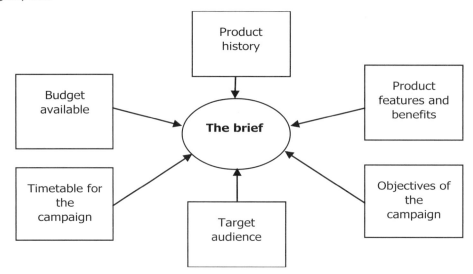

- Presentation
- Analysis
- Selection of the chosen agency
- Agree contract details

 ACTIVITY 2

concept

Explain the significance of the elements of the creative brief.

1.4.2 Criteria for assessment

It is essential that each agency is judged by the same criteria. The criteria should be established by the client in advance, and they must be understood and agreed by all who will be part of the selection team.

Criteria for assessing an agency	
Item	**Comment**
Present work	• Is it exciting/interesting?
	• Is it effective? What proof is there?
	• It is allied to our marketplace?
Present clients	• Are there any clashes that will worry us or the agency or the other client(s)?
	• Do previous clients come back for more or are agency/client relationships short lived?
Chemistry	• Will we feel able to trust the agency?
	• Will the trust be reciprocated?
Staffing	• Will the people who worked on the pitch work on the account?
	• How stable will our account team be?
	• What depth of experience can the account team offer?
Evidence	• Have we seen evidence of creativity, of production, of media planning, of management, of the particular skills we need?
The pitch	• Is it a package or tailored specially?
	• Does it arouse us to buy?

Criteria for assessing an agency	
Item	**Comment**
The agency	• Is its size, age and structure suitable?
	• Does it have to have international capacity?
	• Is it a full service agency or a specialist?
	• What is its workload? Does it have time for us?
	• Does it possess the necessary business skills? For example, has it negotiated a fee for specialised work necessary to meet the requirements of our invitation to pitch for the account?)
Specialised knowledge	• Has it demonstrated realistic and satisfactory understanding of our organisation and market?
Price	• Does the asking fee represent value for money when the above points are taken into account?
	• Does the agency know its value to us?
Judgement	• Is this the agency for us?

1.4.3 Final selection

The final selection will involve a judgement about how well the client believes the agency has responded to the brief in terms of the strategic thinking involved, the creative work (if presented) and the agency's all round understanding of the client's industry. Courtesy dictates that the client should inform both the successful agency and the unsuccessful ones in a prompt manner.

1.4.4 Criticism of the formal selection process

The formalised process is now being questioned, especially because with the arrival of new media and Internet technology, campaigns are having to be resolved in days rather than weeks. The pitching process can lead to tensions, especially on the part of unsuccessful agencies who may have invested a great amount of time and effort for no reward. Perhaps most significantly for them, they will have shared their ideas, over which they will have no subsequent control .

The pitching process also gives little insight into subsequent working relationships.

1.5 Fees and fee structures

1.5.1 Payment of creative agencies

Historically, agencies have earned their money through commission on media space purchased for their clients. The practice arises from the time when the advertising agent was a media broker who also provided other services. This method of payment also highlights the agency's legal standing. The agency is liable for bills to the media if the client defaults on payment. Nearly 50% of agency income still comes from commission. Retainers are also sometimes paid to agencies by a client. A retainer will ensure that the agency is available to comment on behalf of the client and there may be a base rate of work agreed in return for the agreed monthly fee. PR agencies are most likely to be employed on a retained basis. Clients increasingly try to avoid retainer based arrangements.

1.5.2 Agency commission

15% used to be the standard rate of agency commission. This is now no longer the case. Some large clients have argued that they should pay the agency a discounted rate of commission, because of the volume of media throughput that the agency handles. Other clients, themselves under pressure to make advertising money work harder, have argued for commission rates of 10% or 13%.

1.5.3 Fee payment

Some advertisers and their agencies prefer to work on a project by project fee system. This ensures the agency earns money, whether or not the work is media based. About 40% of agency income is earned in this way.

MARKETING AT WORK

application

David Ogilvy is on record as saying 'I pioneered the fee system but I no longer care how I get paid, providing I make a reasonable profit. With a fee system the advertiser pays only for the services he wants, no more and no less. Every fee account pays its own way. Large profitable accounts do not subsidise small, unprofitable ones. Cuts in client's budgets do not oblige you to cut staff. When you advise a client to increase his advertising he does not suspect your motive.'

It is essential for the agency to have an efficient system to capture accurately and promptly all data relating to the allocation of staff time, and the utilisation of other resources. It is reasonable for a client to expect to be shown the control method in use, but not to have access to the agency's detailed profitability. A typical fee calculation is shown below.

Advertising agency: typical fee calculation

	Actual hours	Amount £
*Direct time cost**		
Account management	1,000	40,000
Creative	1,500	60,000
Media	300	12,000
Production	400	16,000
Research and planning	750	30,000
	3,950	158,000
Overheads at 110% (including secretarial, managerial, accounting and administration payroll; also establishment and general costs)	-	173,800
Direct expenses (including directly attributable travel and presentation costs)	-	14,000
Total hours/cost	3,950	345,800
Gross profit at 25%	-	86,450
Total (£109.50 per hour)	3,950	432,250

* Includes direct and indirect payroll costs of all staff who allocate their time.

The sums charged per hour will obviously vary from agency to agency and over time. The hours needed, however, should remain constant. It will be seen that a new product development can occupy many hours. Even more hours will be used within the client, but they are unlikely to be controlled as rigorously. There is therefore considerable unquantified investment in any new creative development. The only party able to account for its involvement accurately is the agency. (Unfortunately for the agency, its efficiency in this respect means that is likely to be the first target in any cost-cutting exercise!)

1.5.4 Payment by results

Payment by results schemes have been used mainly in the USA, although they are becoming more common in the UK. With performance-related payment, the agency is judged on the effect its advertising has on client company sales. Different rates of commission then come into force, depending on performance to target, over-achievement or under-achievement. The major drawback to this method of remuneration is that it pre-supposes a direct correlation between advertising effort and sales.

Payment might be based upon

- Increased awareness levels
- Improved brand image

- Increased intentions to buy

- Achievement of communication objectives

- Achievement of sales targets

application

Jobber cites the example of Holsten Pils paying its agency TBWA London by the volume of lager sold. No other form of payment is made. Procter & Gamble ties its agency's remuneration to global brand sales.

2 Managing agency relationships

2.1 Managing agencies locally and internationally

The specialist agencies providing support services (advertising, public relations, sales promotion, research) usually all work to much the same principles. There will be an account director directly responsible for the client's account and working directly with the client brand manager. Thus all contact between client and agency is via the conduit established by these two individuals.

2.1.1 Client's responsibilities

(a) The advertising co-ordinator (or marketing department head) briefs the agency.

(b) The marketing department head approves the agency's assessment of the advertising objective, strategy, schedule and cost estimates.

(c) The advertising co-ordinator provides the agency with all available materials and information to help the creative team to produce effective ads.

(d) The advertising co-ordinator is the first one to see work that comes back from the agency at each stage of production (copy, story boards, sketches), and will probably check, correct and recommend any necessary changes before the ad is finally approved by the marketing department head.

(e) The ad is returned to the agency for typesetting, final art, filming and sound production.

(f) The advertising co-ordinator carries out final checks, and gets final approval before giving the agency clearance to release the ad to the media.

Establishing a relationship with a creative agency takes time. The end result has to be an on-going relationship based upon mutual understanding and respect. Therefore both the selection process and the day-to-day relationships have to receive very careful attention.

A creative agency should be a full member of the client's marketing team. As such, members of the agency have to be trusted with market information and, to some extent, with profit information as well. If they are not, then information will be withheld and the relationship will suffer. The creative work will suffer too, and sales and profitability will fall. If an agency understands the costing of a package it is less likely to spend time devising a promotion that the client will not be able to afford, and so keeping working data from an agency is counter-productive, morale sapping and expensive.

The only reason an agency is engaged is because it can do a job or provide a service better (and more quickly) than the client can do it for himself. It follows that the client should not meddle with their work. If the client does not like it, of course, he must say so, but the test must be 'will it work with the target audience?'.

2.1.2 Key principles for managing the relationship

1   Management is by the client.

2   The agency team must work closely within the client's marketing department.

3   Briefings must be specific and unambiguous.

4   All research data and management control information available to the brand manager must be provided to the agency.

5   The agency should sit in on the client's strategic planning meetings as an equal member, and of right.

6   Time and cost requirements must be reasonable and must be accepted by the agency.

7   The client should not meddle in the creative process and the agency should not interfere with the production of the package, although both may make an input, as appropriate, as part of the strategic planning process.

8   Full credit must be given when the agency is successful, and shared responsibility must be accepted as appropriate.

9   Fees and commissions should be agreed in advance and accounts should be paid promptly.

10 Copy should never be changed once it has been approved. It should be fully checked before it is signed off. Changes after that stage are not only expensive but, more importantly, they are damaging to the brand manager's personal credibility with the agency.

Given that the agency is accepted as part of the marketing communications team it should take full responsibility for the production of cost-effective work that meets the brief and hits time targets.

2.1.3 International agencies

Over the last forty years, as companies have expanded their operations internationally, so too have advertising agencies. Many of the large agencies have developed internationally, either by setting up branch offices in foreign countries or by merging with or acquiring local agencies.

Despite the increasing presence and power of international advertising and media networks, **independent local agencies** exist in the markets of most countries. Some companies prefer to retain country by country agency arrangements, believing local agencies to be **creatively closer** to their own markets.

Some agencies expanding abroad prefer to establish international networks or alliances where local offices are not wholly controlled. The argument is that local partners with a stake in the agency will be motivated to produce superior work.

Media independents have mirrored the pattern of agency development and many belong to international media planning and buying groups.

The trend amongst clients is towards the centralisation of advertising. Many large companies believe international brands are best served by an agency operating internationally.

Selecting an international advertising agency will follow a series of well defined stages. Locating suitable agency candidates is the first step in the process.

(a)   **Initial search.** Prospective clients will probably be aware of the large multinational agencies based within their own country.

(b)   A **shortlist** of agencies will then be drawn up, usually on the basis of their current work and past track record.

(c)   The **client will then visit** the local offices of those agencies for a series of credentials presentations. These initial visits will help to form an opinion about which candidates should be requested to formally pitch for the client's business. All agencies involved in the pitch should be given the same written brief to follow.

(d)   The **agency's response to the brief** will usually involve a formal presentation backed by a written proposal document with several important features.

- The agency's interpretation of the client's advertising problem
- The creative and media strategy which will ensure objectives are met
- Control mechanisms to be used
- Timing schedules
- Allocation of responsibilities
- Costings
- Terms and conditions of business

(e)   The **final selection decision** will have to take into account many client side factors such as the client's organisational structure and management style, the number of brands to be advertised and the degree to which brands penetrate different markets.

Other criteria for selection would include the following.

- The types of advertising and other communications services offered
- Level of **expertise** in the client's field of work
- The agency's **international creative track record**
- The **balance** within the agency of campaigns handled for local clients and those handled for international ones
- Whether the agency has **strong local offices** in the client's home and other key markets
- The extent to which the agency's **culture and management** style fits with that of the prospective client
- The **potential conflict** with existing business handled within the agency network
- The **control and co-ordination** procedures in place

  ACTIVITY 3

 evaluation

Your company is about to launch a group of new consumer toiletries products in the Middle East. What sorts of assurance would you want from an advertising agency pitching for this account?

2.1.4 The advantages of using an international agency

- Less duplication and dilution of effort on the part of agency and client
- Centralised control of all advertising effort
- Speedy response across markets
- Pooling of talent and ideas from the entire agency network
- Specialised resources available
- Standardised working methods by the agency
- Reduced costs due to economies of scale

2.2 Management and control issues

External factors, such as market diversity, segmentation and competition affect the type of co-ordination chosen. Internal factors, unrelated to the market, can also dictate the management and co-ordination of international promotions.

(a)   **Organisation structure**

   (i)   **Local autonomy**. Each subsidiary of an international agency may act as a separate profit centre, attracting its own clients in the home market. Upon appointment, the subsidiary which has brought in the client takes the role of lead agency office, with overall supervision of the client's account.

   (ii)   **Central control**. Alternatively, an agency may exert strong central control on regional offices from its headquarters base.

(b)   **Organisation culture**. Managers may have different assumptions as to how advertising ought to be done, and it might be a basic hidden assumption that decisions are taken at the top or, on the other hand, by giving local managers their head.

(c)   The need for **coordinated marketing communications**; firms with worldwide exposure may need central control of marketing communications to ensure they are, in fact, coordinated.

2.2.1 Current client/agency issues

As markets expand, clients are likely to forsake traditional, vertical organisational structures where brands are managed on a country by country basis, in favour of a horizontal structure which cuts across country divides. This implies brand and product management at a centralised level and may result in a preference for centralised agencies. Consequences might be as follows.

(a) **Clients** are likely to become more demanding of their agencies, as clients strive to ensure that their advertising is accountable and effective. In America, the trend is already towards payment by results. Clients are also likely to demand a larger base of expertise in terms of communications and research services provided.

(b) **Agencies** will continue to expand internationally to meet the needs of their clients. This may lead to a concentration in advertising agency ownership as the large agencies seek to expand still further by way of acquisition and merger.

(c) Agency expansion will also mean that an increasing number of local agency offices will be established in new markets (eg Russia, Eastern Europe, China). Agencies may need to take a **long term perspective** on emerging markets. Initial resource requirements will be high.

Media buying and selling power continues to concentrate. On the one hand, large international media independents hold consolidated buying power and have the ability to level volume or other discounts. On the other hand there is increasing concentration in global media ownership.

 EXAM TIP

concept

Rather than thinking about advertising agencies solely from the 'outside', ie from the point of view of the client company, the CIM recommends an alternative approach: as an exercise, imagine yourself as an employee at a marketing agency that is pitching for a new contract with a company, perhaps one like Innocent Drinks.

Think about how the prospective client would judge your agency, how they would want to measure your performance, and how the relationship might be managed.

Learning objectives	Covered
1 Critically evaluate and select the most appropriate marketing communications agency for the utilisation of marketing communications capability against agreed criteria	☑ The role of marketing agencies (1.1)
	☑ Marketing service providers (1.2)
	☑ How agencies are structured (1.3)
	☑ Agency selection (1.4)
	☑ Fees and fee structures (1.5)
2 Recommend and justify an approach to managing agency relationships including reporting, monitoring and measuring performance	☑ Managing agencies (2.1)
	☑ Management and control issues (2.2)

1 Why would a company be well advised to take the advice offered by an advertising agency or other external marketing consultancy?

2 What is a 'full service' advertising agency?

3 How can an organisation ensure that it makes cost effective use of a PR agency?

4 What should the 'brief' to an advertising agency contain?

5 What are the stages of an agency selection procedure?

6 How do agencies receive the bulk of their fees?

7 Outline the importance of monitoring and feedback in managing agency relationships.

8 What is the role of the traffic/production team in a full service agency?

9 List some of the areas covered by the expertise of a PR consultancy.

10 What are the options available to advertisers seeking to manage an advertising campaign?

1 Market Research Limited will provide retailers of different kinds of products with useful information as well as the product manufacturers, most likely consumer goods given this description. Children and Youth – companies producing goods and services aimed at the youth market, who want to conduct research but may not have the resources to undertake surveys independently.

2 **Budget**

Client and agency need to be clear about what the budget covers. For example, how many new photographs need to be shot? This will have a bearing on the production costs. The budget for media will determine the choice for media selection. The agency can alter the resources according to the job.

Timetable

Important key deadlines must be listed. The agency should draw up a timetable for presentation of design concepts, proofs, final proofs and so on.

Objectives

The primary objective may be to increase sales. This can be incorporated in the design.

Target audience

The agency needs a full description of the characteristics of the audience. This will enable them to design the campaign with the audience in mind.

Product history, features and benefits

For example, is this a complete redesign, or just a freshen up?

Be clear what the USP is. For example, you cannot have high quality, cheap products, top brands and commodity goods all in the same catalogue. With a clear picture, the agency will be able to focus on producing what is required without constantly referring back to the client.

3 Ideally, the agency should be able to assure the client of experience in both consumer market generally and the toiletries market in particular. The agency should have local offices in a number of the Middle East states in which the client does business and be used to handling local and international campaigns in those countries.

The agency must demonstrate knowledge concerning cultural, legal, and media difficulties which may be encountered and be able to propose solutions for overcoming these problems. Proof of successful campaign outcomes for other British based clients advertising in related markets would also be reassuring.

1   Agencies specialise in communication and media, with wide experience and specialist knowledge that a client company is unlikely to possess.

2   A full service agency takes control of the whole campaign from start to finish.

3   Ensure cost effectiveness by setting clear objectives, negotiating a fee, briefing fully and monitoring activity and expenditure.

4   See Figure 8.2.

5   Define the campaign requirements   Presentation
    Develop a list of suppliers   Analysis
    Assess their credentials   Selection of the chosen agency
    Issue the brief to a short list of candidates   Agree contract details

6   From payment of commission.

7   Monitoring ensures that objectives are being met at each stage of the relationship. Feedback is necessary to develop trust and to overcome problems as soon as they arise.

8   Plans and schedules agency workflow, monitors progress against deadlines.

9   • Media or press relations   • Government relations
    • Corporate relations   • Community relations
    • Marketing support   • Financial relations
    • Employee relations

10 Use co-operation from people in the media eg for newspaper layout
    Carry out completely in-house
    'Delegate' to an advertising agency
    Use in house staff for some of the work and specialists for the rest

Blythe, J (2009) Principles and Practice of Marketing, 2nd edition, South-Western/Cengage Learning.

Blythe, J (2008) Essentials of Marketing, 4th edition, FT Prentice Hall.

Brassington, F and Pettitt, S (2006) Principles of Marketing, 4th edition, FT Prentice Hall.

Dibb S, Simkin L, Pride WM, Ferrell OC (2005) Marketing: Concepts and Strategies, 5th edition, Houghton Mifflin.

Jobber (2009) Principles and Practice of Marketing. 6th edition, McGraw Hill Higher Education

Chapter 9

Customer service and customer care

Topic list

1 Providing a service
2 Customer care programmes
3 Service level agreements and service quality

Introduction

Quality of service is an important issue for marketers because it is one of the most significant ways in which customers differentiate between competing products and services.

An organisation can give better service through any of the seven Ps – make a better product, do a special deal on price, open for longer hours, give more information in the brochure, refurbish its store and process orders more quickly. But the main way is through the P of people.

This chapter considers the main topics implicit in customer service and customer care. Section 1 examines the issues behind definitions of 'service' and 'service quality', and what it means to the customer. Section 2 looks at customer care programmes as an aspect of service quality and differentiation, while section 3 looks in further detail at service level agreements.

Syllabus linked learning objectives

By the end of the chapter you will be able to:

Learning objectives	Syllabus link
1 Develop clear objectives relating to the provision of service to key customer accounts	4.1
2 Develop a customer service plan and customer care programme, designed to support customer service requirements, including innovative communications; relationship management and development; support; and operations/process management	4.2
3 Assess the value, importance and financial implications of providing service level agreements to customers	4.3

1 Providing a service

1.1 What is 'service'?

KEY CONCEPT

concept

Cowell (1995) says that the significance of **services** lies in 'the relative dominance of intangible attributes in the make-up of the 'service product'.

1.1.1 Determining customer service requirements

Jobber (2009) suggests the following areas where customer service requirements are likely to need special care (for example, with CRM programmes).

- Where there is an ongoing desire for the service (eg insurance)
- Where the customer controls the selection (eg hotels)
- Where the customer has alternatives (eg restaurants)

Quality can only be defined by customers, and occurs where a firm supplies products to a specification that satisfies their needs. Customer expectations serve as standards, so when the service they receive falls short of expectations, dissatisfaction occurs.

Service quality has two key dimensions.

(a) **Technical quality** of the service encounter (ie what is received by the customer). Was the meal edible? Was the train on time? Were the shelves fully stocked? Problems of this sort must be addressed by improving the processes of production and delivery.

(b) **Functional quality** of the service encounter (ie how the service is provided). This relates to the psychological interaction between the buyer and seller and is typically perceived in a very subjective way.

- **Relationships between employees**. For instance, do these relationships appear to be professional? Do they chat to each other whilst serving the customer? Does each appear to know their role in the team and the function of their colleagues? Do they know who to refer the customer to if there is a need for more specialist advice? Are they positive about their colleagues or unduly critical?

- **Appearance and personality of service personnel**. For instance, do they seem interested in the customer and the customer's needs? Are they smartly presented? Do they convey an attractive and positive image? Do they reflect the organisation or brand (eg through uniform/livery)?

- **Service-mindedness of the personnel**. For instance, do they appear to understand and identify with the needs of the customer? Do they convey competence? Do they show willingness to help?

- **Accessibility of the service to the customer**. For instance, do the service personnel explain the service in language which the customer can understand?

- **Approachability of service personnel**. For instance, do the service personnel appear alert, interested or welcoming? Or are they day-dreaming, yawning or looking at their watches?

1.1.2 Key elements in customer expectations

Element	Comment
Tangibles	The quality of the service area, products and information must be consistent with the desired image.
Reliability	Getting it right first time is very important, not only to ensure repeat business, but as a matter of ethics, if the customer is buying a future benefit (as in financial services).
Responsiveness	Staff must be willing to deal with customer queries and problems, responding flexibly to needs.
Communication	Staff should provide appropriate information to customers in language they can understand.
Credibility	The organisation should be perceived as honest, expert and trustworthy, acting in the best interests of customers.
Security	The customer needs to feel that transactions are safe, and where necessary, private and confidential.
Competence	Service staff need to develop competence in meeting the needs of the customers and using systems efficiently.
Courtesy	Customers should experience service staff who are polite, respectful and friendly.
Understanding needs	Service staff need to listen to and meet customer needs rather than try to sell products. There is a subtle but important difference.
Access	Minimising queues, having a fair queuing system and speedy service are all factors in customer satisfaction.

1.2 Identifying customer needs and behaviours

The customer is central to the marketing orientation, but so far we have not considered this important concept in detail. Customers make up one of the groups of stakeholders whose interests management should address. The stakeholder concept suggests a wider concern than the traditional marketing approach of supplying goods and services which satisfy immediate needs. The supplier-customer relationship extends beyond the basic transaction. The customer needs to remain satisfied with his purchase and positive about his supplier long after the transaction has taken place. If his satisfaction is muted or grudging, future purchases may be reluctant or non-existent and he may advise others of his discontent. Customer tolerance in the UK is fairly high, but should not be taken for granted.

Not all customers are the same. Some appear for a single cash transaction and are never seen again. Others make frequent, regular purchases in large volumes, using credit facilities and building up a major relationship. Yet another type of customer purchases infrequently but in transactions of high value, as for instance in property markets. This variation will exist to a greater or lesser extent in all industries, though each will have a smaller typical range of behaviour. However, even within a single business, customers will vary significantly in the frequency and volume of their purchases, their reasons for buying, their sensitivity to price changes, their reaction to promotion and their overall attitude to the supplier and the product. Segmentation of the customer base can have a major impact on profitability, perhaps by simply tailoring promotion to suit the most attractive group of customers.

Many businesses sell to intermediaries rather than to the end consumer. Some sell to both categories; they have to recognise that the intermediary is just as much a customer as the eventual consumer. Examples are manufacturers who maintain their own sales organisation but appoint agents in geographically remote areas and companies who combine autonomous operations with franchising. While it is reasonable to give the highest priority to the needs of the ultimate consumer and insist on some control over the activities of the intermediary, it must be recognised that he will only perform well if his own needs are addressed. For instance, a selling agent who has invested heavily in stock after being given exclusive rights in an area should be consulted before further demands are made on his cash flow by the launch of a new product.

Customer's purchase perception of services

- Customers view service as having less consistent quality.
- Service purchasers have higher risks.
- Service purchasing is less pleasant.
- When services are bought greater consideration is given to the particular salesperson.
- Perception of the service company is an important factor when deciding to buy a service.

Customer's purchase behaviour with services

- Customers may do fewer price comparisons with services.
- Customers give greater consideration to the particular seller of services.
- Customers are less likely to be influenced by advertising and more by personal recommendations.

Personal selling of services

- Customer involvement is greater.
- Customer satisfaction is influenced by the salesperson's personality and attitude.
- Salespeople may have to spend more time reducing customer uncertainty.

  ACTIVITY 1

application

All levels of staff must be involved in customer service. To achieve this end, it is vital for senior management to promote the importance of customer service. How do you think that this might be achieved?

1.3 Customer loyalty and competitive advantage

The reason why businesses and firms need a competitive orientation is that customers have a choice, and they can compare the firm's offering with what competitors are offering. Given that the marketing orientation needs to be present in all areas of the organisation, we are led to Ohmae's strategic triangle: company, competitors and customers.

Figure 9.1 Ohmae's strategic triangle

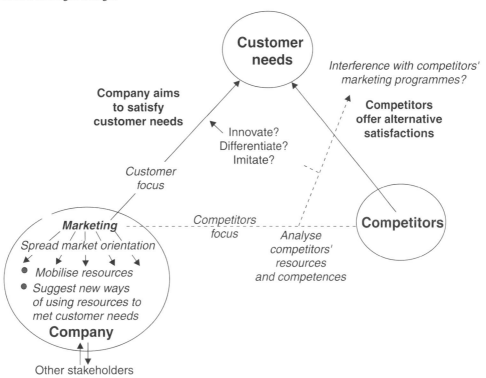

Customers are more likely to become repeat customers, loyal customers and perhaps even active advocates or recommenders of the product or service if they:

- Consistently experience satisfaction
- Are acknowledged and rewarded for their loyalty
- Perceive that they have a relationship with the supplier

Relationship marketing methods can be analysed for contributing to short- and long-term customer retention, under four broad headings.

- Service quality
- Barriers to exit
- Loyalty programmes
- Brand engagement (covered in an earlier chapter)

1.4 Service quality

 KEY CONCEPT

concept

Service quality is the totality of features and characteristics of that service which bears on its ability to meet stated or implied needs.

There are two ways that organisations can gain from improving their quality of service to customers.

- **Higher sales revenues** and **improved marketing effectiveness** may come through improved customer retention, positive word-of-mouth recommendations and the ability to increase prices.

- **Better quality improves productivity and reduces costs** because there is less rework, higher employee morale and lower employee turnover.

A high, consistent and competitive level of customer service (seen as an ongoing chain of satisfying service encounters or episodes) is a key to customer satisfaction and loyalty – and therefore to long-term relationships of mutual advantage – in many industries. It is also one of the main ways in which an organisation can add customer value.

There are many dimensions in service delivery, before and after the service encounter itself.

- The creation of a **corporate culture** which expresses and models customer-focused values, and reinforces those values through its selection, appraisal and reward systems, and the messages it sends employees at every level.

- The creation of **service-supporting internal relationships** and internal marketing: the recruitment of skilled customer-facing people; the supply of appropriate training; the empowerment of staff to take decisions that will satisfy and retain customers; and the reward and recognition of staff who deliver outstanding service.

- Gathering, analysing, communicating and acting on **customer feedback**. Feedback and adjustment (addressing customer concerns and complaints) are crucial in minimising dissatisfaction and demonstrating commitment to customer value. Constructive handling of problems and complaints (sometimes called 'service recovery') may lead to restored satisfaction – and even strengthened relationship, because of the supplier's demonstrated commitment.

- Establishing a **partnership approach** to relationships with customers, suppliers and intermediaries (distributors, retail outlets, call centres), in order to support high levels of service at all links in the value-delivery chain.

- Ensuring **promise fulfilment** (Jobber, 2009): making realistic promises (to manage customer expectations); enabling staff and service systems to deliver on promises made; and keeping promises during service encounters.

- Offering **support services** (eg warranties, servicing, user training and help-lines) to facilitate customers in using the product safely and satisfyingly, and support them through changes and difficulties.

- Reinforcing customer loyalty with **incentives and rewards**, to show that the organisation values its 'valued customers'.

- Establishing **customer-friendly systems**. It is no good expecting staff to give great service to customers if the systems, procedures, technology and information flows do not support their efforts.

1.5 Barriers to exit

 KEY CONCEPT   concept

Customer exit is the term used to describe a situation where a customer decides to end the relationship and switch to another brand or provider. In competitive markets, there may be many (or a few strong) alternative sources of a product/service, and this may make it comparatively easy for the customer to switch – unless the organisation can increase the costs of switching, or erect 'barriers to exit'.

Switching costs are barriers to exit from the company, from the perspective of the consumer.

Switching costs include a range of sub-costs:

Type of costs	Detail
Search costs	Time and energy spent looking for another supplier
Learning costs	Time and energy spent developing dealings with a new supplier, or learning to use a new product/brand
Emotional costs	Emotional investment in relationship with an organisation, brand or particular personnel (eg an account or contract manager)
Social costs	Loss of social networks and affiliations created by dealing with the supplier (eg membership in a user club)
Financial costs	Formal financial penalties for exiting the relationship (as when switching gym membership, telecom providers or mortgage providers) or loss of rewards built up over time (eg no-claims insurance, customer loyalty points or employee share option schemes)

Type of costs	Detail
Risk	Potential costs or difficulties of using an unknown supplier or brand
Inertia	The psychological difficulty of breaking long-term habits or patterns
Legal barriers	For example, a fixed-term contract with a supplier (with no early opt-out clause)

Any or all of these factors may act effectively to prevent customers from switching. However, it is worth noting the difference between them.

- Some barriers (such as emotional or social costs) are generated by **customers** themselves, as the result of genuine satisfaction and added value created by the supplier. This is arguably the most constructive and ethical approach to building exit barriers, since it involves willing participation and an exchange of value.

- Some barriers are a natural consequence of the **relationship** (eg search and learning costs, risk and inertia). The marketer can exploit this by drawing customers' attention to the costs of going elsewhere: emphasising the value of trust, familiarity and so on.

- Some barriers are deliberately applied by the supplier to '**lock customers in**' with the threats of penalties (eg legal barriers and financial penalties). This is less effective from an relationship management point of view, as the implied threat may alienate customers (especially if the product and service elements are less than satisfactory) – making it more likely that they will defect as soon as they can.

- Some barriers are deliberately applied by the supplier to **encourage retention** via incentives and opportunities to build up rewards (eg in loyalty programmes). This can be effective (as we will see below), if the rewards represent genuine value.

 MARKETING AT WORK application

Royal Society for the Protection of Birds (RSPB)

Research had shown that members who join and pay by direct debit have a much higher retention rate: 99% of members renew their membership at the end of the first year compared to only 42% for those who initially subscribe by cash or cheque. The large difference in retention rate meant that the marketing department must concentrate on trying to switch new members to direct debit after they have joined. If a member is subscribing by direct debit at the end of the first year, the Society is much more likely to build a profitable long-term relationship with them.

Promotional items for new members include bird tables, books and videos, but the gifts are always positioned to reinforce the main focus – the birds. This reflects the fact that the majority of the membership are primarily interested in birds and not the broader field of wildlife conservation.

These incentives have proved to be valuable to gain new members. The Society loses on average 10% of its membership each year, including 4% through death, and needs to recruit over 60,000 new members each year, just to cover this loss.

Cost of recruitment is a vital consideration, as it can vary greatly depending on the method of recruitment. If...expensively recruited members do not renew their membership, losses can escalate... Retention of both existing and new customers is a key priority.

www.rspb.org.uk

1.6 Loyalty programmes

The purpose of loyalty programmes, for an organisation or brand, is to establish a higher level of customer retention in profitable segments, by providing increased satisfaction and value to certain customers (Egan, 2004, p44).

Some schemes focus on securing **multiple on-going purchases**, usually with the incentive of earning points for each purchase, which can be redeemed for rewards, discounts or Fly-Buys. Reward cards memorise the redeemable points, and generate information on the holder's purchasing behaviour for the provider. Such cards lend themselves to co-branding and other forms of alliance: consortia of retail, financial services and other providers have been formed to pool resources and share information in joint loyalty schemes (eg the Nectar Loyalty Card Scheme).

Some schemes are based on receiving **added value benefits** once you reach a higher category of status/value (eg frequent flyer clubs, or 'patrons' of arts organisations).

Others use affinity marketing, by linking purchases with donations to a charity or other cause (eg building up points towards donation of books or computers to local schools). **Affinity cards**, which link a business with a charity or cause, have become a popular way for consumers to identify with a cause and donate to charity from their spending. Such schemes have been exploited for fundraising by the RSPCA, Save the Children and some commercial football clubs.

Most loyalty programmes have some kind of 'club' aspect to them, and offer a variety of **member benefits**. The Waterstones Card, for example, offers points which build towards cash discounts on further purchases; email newsletters (with book reviews, offers and competitions); a free copy of the quarterly magazine; and invitations to exclusive shopping events. (If you're curious, go to http://www.waterstones.com and click on the Waterstones Card link.)

The intention of a loyalty scheme for the organisation is that:

- A brand preference or habit will develop from repeat purchase and familiarity, which creates psychological barriers to switching.

- A sense of belonging to a community or club (even if 'virtual') will reinforce the relationship.

- The brand will be differentiated from similar competing brands and/or defended against the effect of competitors' loyalty programmes.

- The incentives and their accessories (VIP cards and so on) add economic and social benefits, which will be valued and desired by customers – creating further barriers to switching (if similar benefits are not available elsewhere).

- Customer data gathered from the scheme (details provided by the customer or point of sale data) can be used to fine-tune the marketing mix – which in turn may create a genuine bias or commitment to the brand. This data reflects actual customer behaviour and preferences, and is therefore 'much more valuable for customised product offerings than is any of the aggregate data about the 'average' customer or market segment typically used in traditional marketing practices' (Varey, 2002).

- Additional revenue can be raised through repeat purchases, cross-selling and up-selling, on the back of customer loyalty. Incentives can also be added for short-term sales promotions (eg 'double points' on selected purchases).

1.6.1 Limitations of loyalty programmes

The **profitability** of loyalty programmes has been questioned (Egan, 2004; Jobber, 2009).

- The costs of the schemes can be high, if you include technology, software, staff training, administration, communications, cards and rewards.

- Over time, the rewards may get taken for granted as part of the organisation's offering. They may even become the norm for a sector – particularly since the providers of loyalty scheme technology are promoting their products heavily to marketers : schemes may not provide competitive differentiation for long.

- The costs may therefore become another unavoidable cost of doing business – without necessarily creating a corresponding impact on sales.

- Meanwhile, in order to keep customers motivated, the organisation may get caught in a costly spiral of offering higher and higher rewards.

Egan (2004, p45) argues that all of this is, in the end, counterproductive: 'Over time, customers who receive, in effect, only bribes are likely to become promiscuous and seek the highest bribe available, as that is the only satisfaction they receive from the exchange'.

So should a firm implement, or continue, a loyalty scheme? It should certainly regularly assess whether it is gaining any of the **benefits** listed above, set against the **costs** of pursuing them. It should also assess whether focusing on one group of customers (eg frequent flyers) risks losing, through neglect, others who are potentially equally profitable. However, in markets where key competitors are operating loyalty schemes, it may simply be seen as too risky not to have one, or to discontinue one.

ACTIVITY 2

In your experience, are loyalty programmes genuine attempts to build lasting relationships with customers? Can you think ways in which they may not create genuine loyalty and relationship?

ACTIVITY 3

Assess the following loyalty programmes. What is the basis of each scheme? Does it provide meaningful incentives to repeat purchase – and in what way (if at all) might this be an expression of genuine loyalty? How vulnerable might this 'loyalty' be to competing offers? How costly do you think the scheme would be to manage? How have the organisations exploited wider stakeholder relationships in support of the scheme?

- **Tesco**: http://www.tesco.com. Click on the Tesco ClubCard link. (Note also the 'community' and 'environment' links: what messages are these giving to wider stakeholders, and how might this be tied in to customer loyalty?) Alternatively, Tesco is written up as a case study in Peck, Payne & Christopher *Relationship Marketing* (1999) at the end of Chapter 2.

- **Virgin Atlantic**: http://www.virginatlantic.com. Click on the Flying Club link.

- **Hertz Rent-a-Car**: http://www.hertz.com. Click on the #1 Club link. (Note also the menu of stakeholder audiences: partners, investors and so on. Worth exploring to see a highly networked organisation in action!)

- **Nectar Loyalty Points Card** (http://www.nectar.com). Alternatively, this is written up as a case study ('Nectar: Loyalty brings sweet rewards') in your key text: Jobber, *Principles & Practice of Marketing* (2009).

1.7 Benefits of customer acquisition and retention

1.7.1 How the organisation can gain

There are two ways that organisations can gain from improving their quality of service to customers.

- **Higher sales revenues** and improved marketing effectiveness may come through improved customer retention, positive word-of-mouth recommendations and the ability to increase prices.

- **Better quality** improves productivity and reduces costs because there is less rework, higher employee morale and lower employee turnover. Variation in customer behaviour was mentioned above. The most important aspect of this variation is whether or not the customer comes back for more. Customers should be seen as potentially providing a lifetime of purchases so that the turnover from a single individual over time might be very large indeed.

It is widely accepted that there is a non-linear relationship between customer retention and profitability in that a fairly small amount of repeat purchasing generates significant profit. This is because it is far more expensive in promotion and overhead costs to convert a non-buyer into an occasional buyer than to turn an occasional buyer into a frequent buyer. The repeat buyer does not have to be persuaded to give the product a try or be tempted by special deals; he needs less attention from sales staff and already has his credit account set up. New customers usually have to be won from competitors.

Today's highly competitive business environment means that customers are only retained if they are very satisfied with their purchasing experience. Any lesser degree of satisfaction is likely to result in the loss of the customer. Companies must be active in monitoring customer satisfaction because very few will actually complain. They will simply depart. Businesses which use intermediaries must be particularly active, since research shows that even when complaints are made, the principals hear about only a very small proportion of them.

Customer care at Smart Energy

Smart Energy is the largest operator in the UK market for domestic solar heating systems. However, Gary Payne, managing director, admits the business has faced battles, not least rooting out problems in its own sales operation ...

In 2004 ... the company gained unwelcome publicity when a BBC Watchdog campaign broadcast claims of rogue selling techniques.

The incident was down to a single salesperson who no longer works for the company, Mr Payne insists. But the fallout led to a £1m drop in sales. Mr Payne says the company used the experience to tighten its internal checks, so that every customer who agrees to meet a Smart Energy salesperson is now followed up with a separate call by a customer care team at the regional office.

'It was the only way we knew we could properly police it,' Mr Payne says.

(Jonathan Moules, *Financial Times,* 18 August 2007)

The most satisfactory way to retain customers is to offer them products which they perceive as providing superior benefits at any given price point. However, there are specific techniques which can increase customer retention. Loyalty schemes such as frequent flyer programmes, augment the product in the customer's eyes. The club concept, as used by Sainsbury and Tesco, offers small discounts on repeated purchases. The principal benefit of both these types of scheme, however, is the enhanced knowledge of the customer which they provide. Initial registration provides name, address and post code. Subsequent use of the loyalty card allows a detailed purchasing profile to be built up for individual customers. This enables highly targeted promotion and cross-selling later.

Research indicates that the single largest reason why customers abandon a supplier is poor performance by front-line staff. Any scheme for customer retention must address the need for careful selection and training of these staff. It is also a vital factor in relationship marketing.

Driving customer loyalty in a tough economic climate

In the highly competitive grocery market, strategies that drive customer loyalty are the Holy Grail for all retailers and brands.

Unfortunately, the years have shown though that the rise of the loyalty card was only able to achieve so much, and therefore the hunt is still on for a complete customer relationship management solution.

To compound this issue further, 2008 brought the new challenge of soaring food costs and a very tough and turbulent economic climate. With this hard reality retailers must ensure that all available marketing budget is spent finding the most effective method to provide value and increase customer satisfaction.

Ultimately the issue that all retailers now face is how to encourage the UK consumer to part with money; and even increase basket size, when the cost of living has already grown by a tremendous £1,000 per year per household. ... One approach which has yet to be fully embraced within the UK is... adopting an in-store customer communication strategy, underpinned by sophisticated data analysis on purchasing behaviour. This approach brings significant value as it ensures that the customer is issued with an immediate, targeted promotion designed to offer consumers savings for their loyalty. So for example, targeted consumers can be issued a voucher offering money off their next purchase ...

Not only does this activity provide brands with the opportunity to directly target the consumer but it also allows the retailers to witness an increase in frequency and basket size. Brands can benefit by driving volume without giving deep discounts and harming their price perception. Clearly a win-win for all involved.

(Dak Liyanearachchi, *Brand Republic,* 18 April 2008)

1.7.2 A cycle of loyalty and profits

Marketing literature has suggested that, rather than a trade-off, there is a positive correlation between customer satisfaction and employee satisfaction.

- Peters & Waterman (1982) argued that customer- and quality-focused values are a powerful source of **job satisfaction** for employees, giving their jobs meaning and significance beyond the mere performance of tasks. Such strong values also enable the organisation to direct and control employees' activities without resorting to close supervision and detailed rules, and this style of control is regarded as **empowering** rather than restricting by employees.

- Other writers on service marketing (such as Grönroos (2000)) have suggested that employee satisfaction and customer satisfaction are linked in a **service profit cycle or chain**.

Figure 9.2 The Service Profit Cycle (adapted from Egan, op cit, p 145)

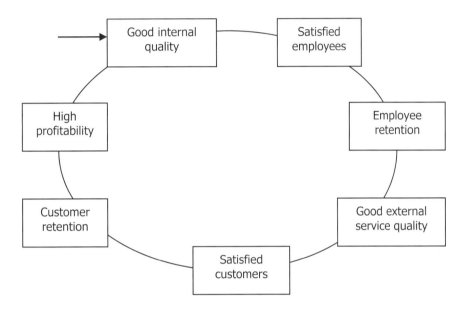

Reichheld (1996, p19) developed a **loyalty-based cycle**, based on the firm's relationships with three core stakeholders: employees, customers and investors. This model (see diagram below) shows the linkages between loyalty, value and profits.

- Superior service and value creates loyal customers.

- Revenues and market share grow as the best customers are prioritised, building repeat sales and referrals.

- Sustainable growth enables the firm to attract and retain the best employees.

- Consistent delivery of superior value to customers increases employees' loyalty by giving them pride and satisfaction in their work.

- Long-term employees get to know long-term customers, enabling further service and value enhancement, which in turn further enhances customer and employee loyalty.

- Loyal long-term employees generate superior productivity. This surplus can be used to fund superior rewards, tools and training – which further reinforce employee productivity, reward growth and loyalty.

- Increased productivity and the efficiency of dealing with loyal customers generates cost advantages over competitors – and high profits.

- High profits make it easier for the firm to attract and retain high-quality investors.

- Loyal investors stabilise the system, funding investments that increase the company's value creation potential.

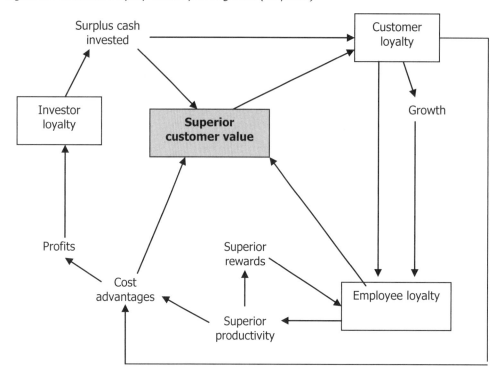

Figure 9.3 Reichheld's loyalty-based cycle of growth (simplified)

1.8 Key accounts

1.8.1 What are 'key accounts'?

Key accounts are profitable, and have potential for long-term development.

So far we have considered the retention of customers as an unquestionably desirable objective. However, for many businesses a degree of discretion will be advisable. 'Key' does not mean large. A customer's potential is very important. The definition of a key account depends on the circumstances. Key account management is about managing the future.

Customers can be assessed for desirability according to such criteria as the profitability of their accounts; the prestige they confer; the amount of non-value adding administrative work they generate; the cost of the selling effort they absorb; the rate of growth of their accounts and, for industrial customers, of the turnover of their own businesses; their willingness to adopt new products; and their credit history. Such analyses will almost certainly conform to a Pareto distribution and show, for instance, that 80% of profit comes from 20% of the customers, while a different 20% generate most of the credit control or administrative problems. Some businesses will be very aggressive about getting rid of their problem customers, but a more positive technique would be to concentrate effort on the most desirable ones.

These are the key accounts, and the company's relationship with them can be built up by appointing key account managers.

Key account management is often seen as a high-level selling task, but should in fact be a business-wide team effort about relationships and customer retention. It can be seen as a form of co-operation with the customer's supply chain management function. The key account manager's role is to integrate the efforts of the various parts of the organisation in order to deliver an enhanced service. This idea has long been used by advertising agencies and was successfully introduced into aerospace manufacturing over 40 years ago. It will be the key account manager's role to maintain communication with the customer, note any developments in his circumstances, deal with any problems arising in the relationship and develop the long-term business relationship.

1.8.2 The key account relationship

The key account relationship may progress through several stages.

(a)   At first, there may be a typical adversarial sales-purchasing relationship with emphasis on price, delivery and so on. Attempts to widen contact with the customer organisation will be seen as a threat by its purchasing staff.

(b)   Later, the sales staff may be able to foster a mutual desire to increase understanding by wider contacts. Trust may increase.

(c)   A mature partnership stage may be reached in which there are contacts at all levels and information is shared. The key account manager becomes responsible for integrating the partnership business processes and contributing to the customer's supply chain management. High 'vendor ratings', stable quality, continuous improvement and fair pricing are taken for granted.

2   Customer care programmes

2.1 Key components of a customer service plan

An organisation can use a number of methods to try to improve its quality of service and customer care.

- Development of a customer-orientated mission statement and customer care policy, with clear senior management support for quality improvement initiatives

- Customer satisfaction research, both formal (eg customer surveys, customer panels, analysis of complaints data) and informal (eg tuning in to customer feedback at the point of sale/service)

- Monitoring and control: feedback should be communicated, and standards constantly reviewed

- Customer complaints and feedback systems, with incentives to encourage customers to complain!

- Employee involvement: eg through the use of quality circles, project teams and other forms of internal communication on quality/service issues

- Customer care training and development

- Rewarding excellent service

  ACTIVITY 4  evaluation

What do you think are the most important factors in handling complaints in a way that restores stakeholder satisfaction and relationships? (You might have your own experiences of making a complaint to draw on. What made you feel good – or bad – about the way the problem was handled?)

2.2 Operations and processes

Customer handling is increasingly automated in order to increase process efficiency. Examples include web-based transactions and information provision; voice mail systems (for recording customer telephone queries); and automated call handling (ACH) and interactive voice response (IVR) systems, which allow customers to select menu options (eg for call routing, product ordering or information requests) using telephone keypad or verbal responses. You may have used such a system for telephone bill payments or taxi bookings.

The automation of customer-handling operations can have a positive impact for the customer and supplier alike.

- The organisation is available for contact 24 hours, 7 days, a week.

- Ordering can be conducted 'instantly' and at any time to suit the customer.

- Frequently asked questions (FAQs) and e-mail contacts can reduce waiting time for answers to customer queries.

- Customer information is made available to personalise the transaction and build customer relationships. This includes recognition of customer telephone numbers, for example, so that call centre staff can address customers by name and do not have to ask repeatedly for address and other details. On a fully automated level, it includes the personalisation of the customer's interface with a web page.

- Automation creates significant cost savings for the company: reducing the number of customer-service staff required, and enabling others to work from home or in (in-house or outsourced) call centres.

- Fewer 'missed' calls and better customer service supports customer attraction, retention and loyalty.

Customer Relationship Management (CRM) systems can be used to empower customers to control the purchase and service process. A well-constructed website can often provide better services than are usually received through a human-based call centre. Such a website lets customers easily access information on products and services that helps them to investigate product features and even make purchases, without help from costly sales and support staff.

Negative impacts of automation, however, include the following.

- Customers (particularly in certain age or cultural groups) may simply want to talk to a human being.
- Automation leads to the loss of customer service jobs.
- Automated call management systems can frustrate the customer by creating a lengthy 'loop' of menus.

Process issues include the following.

- The formation of **policies and codes of conduct** in regard to ethical dealings and corporate social responsibility (a key issues for many stakeholders)

- Procedures for **efficiency and standardisation** of all service provision, transactions and communications; the reduction of queuing/waiting times for services or contacts; capacity management (to match supply to demand in a timely and cost-effective way – overcoming the perishability factor in service provision)

- Efficient and ethical **information-gathering**, **processing and communication** mechanisms for customer service and stakeholder relationships. If possible, these mechanisms should be integrated to handle all stakeholder contacts, communications and transactions, for example in Customer Relationship Management or Supplier Relationship Management systems.

- Equitable and convenient **accessibility** of facilities, premises, personnel and services to all stakeholders. This may embrace CSR and diversity issues such as disabled access to premises, the use of different languages in communications (or Braille for the sight-impaired, or displays for the hearing-impaired), adjustment of premises and duties for disabled employees, and so on. However, it also includes distribution issues: processes for getting goods and services to remote or isolated areas or customers, say.

  Such provisions are particularly important in service marketing, because of the characteristic of heterogeneity or variability: the organisation needs to **standardise service provision** as far as possible, preserving minimum standards and reducing customer/stakeholder risk (or perception of risk).

3 Service level agreements and service quality

3.1 Defining service quality

Jobber (2009) comments on service quality as follows:

"... it makes sense to suggest that improving service quality will increase customer satisfaction, leading to higher sales and profits. Indeed, it has been shown that companies that are rated higher on service quality perform better in terms of market share growth and profitability. Yet, for many companies, high standards of service quality remain elusive."

Service quality can be defined as the difference between what customers expect and what they perceive themselves to be receiving. Grönroos introduced the concept of 'perceived service quality' in 1982 and extended this in the development of his widely cited model of service quality in 1984.

Figure 9.4 Grönroos (1984) Service Quality Model

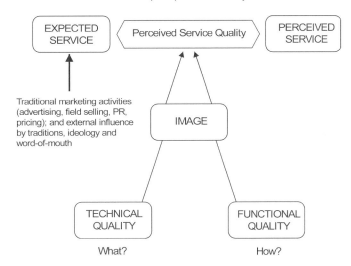

(1984) Service Quality Model

The model suggests that the quality of a given service is the outcome of an evaluation process where consumers compare what they expected to receive with what they perceive that they actually received.

Consumer expectations are influenced by marketing mix activities, external traditions, ideology and word-of-mouth communications. Grönroos also suggests previous experience with the service will influence expectations.

In terms of perceived service quality, Grönroos suggests there are two principal components of quality, technical and functional, with a third, image, acting as a mediating influence.

(a)   **Technical quality** is what the customer is left with, when the production process is finished. For example, in higher education this would be perceived as the level of attainment and understanding achieved at the end of the course. This can be much more easily measured by the consumer.

(b)   **Functional quality**, on the other hand, is more difficult to measure objectively because it involves an evaluation of how the consumer receives the technical quality in the interactions between customer and service provider and other customers. Grönroos' suggestion that service quality is dependent both on what you receive and how you receive it emphasises the importance of service interactions, contact employees and managing in the service experience.

Grönroos also suggests that both expectations and perceptions are affected by the consumer's view of the company and by its image. If a student has a positive image of a university or lecturer but then has a negative experience, for example a rather confused lecture, the student may still perceive the service to be satisfactory because he or she will find excuses for the negative experience. Correspondingly, Grönroos suggests that a negative image may increase perceived problems with service quality.

3.2 Quality gaps

Parasuraman, Zeithaml and Berry (1985) developed the most widely applied model of service quality. The researchers developed their model via interviews with fourteen executives in four service businesses and twelve customer focus groups. The executive interviews resulted in the idea of five gaps which are potential hurdles for a firm in attempting to deliver high quality service.

Figure 9.5 Parasuraman et al gap model

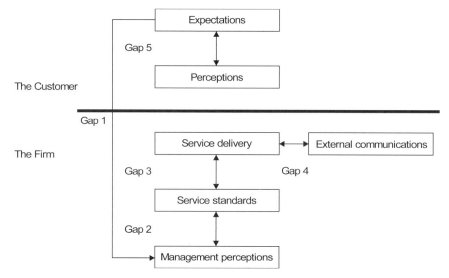

Gap 1 Consumer expectations and management perceptions gap

Essentially managers may not know what features connote high quality, what features a service must have or what levels of performance are required by customers. It becomes a 'misconception' barrier to good service.

Action

- Market research programmes
- Improvements based on customer comment and complaints
- Strategies for service recovery
- Improvements based on front line staff experience and suggestion

Gap 2 Management perceptions and service quality specification gap

Resource constraints, market conditions and/or management indifference may result in this gap, an 'inadequate resources' barrier.

Action

- New concepts of service rather than merely improving old ones
- Attention to physical evidence
- Customer focused activity goals

Gap 3 Service quality specifications and service delivery gap

Guidelines may exist but contract employees may not be willing or able to perform to the specified standards. Roles may be poorly organised, technology, supervision and team work may be unsatisfactory. This leads to an 'inadequate delivery' barrier.

Action

- Define job roles and priorities clearly
- Provide proper training
- Build teams and team working
- Empower frontline staff
- Improve technology
- Recruitment, training and reward policy improvements

Gap 4 Service delivery and external communications gap

Exaggerated promises or lack of information will affect both expectations and perceptions.

Action

- Improve communications between staff and departments
- Educate customers
- Develop service rules but do not over-promote to customers
- Marketing communications emphasise what is actually delivered

Gap 5 Expected service and perceived service gap

This gap was defined as service quality. The authors argue that gap five is influenced by the preceding four gaps so if management want to close the gap between performance and expectations it becomes imperative to design procedures for measuring service performance against expectations.

The researchers also developed a **SERVQUAL questionnaire** which purports to be a global measure of Gap 5 across all service organisations. This measures the five generic criteria that consumers use in evaluating service quality.

1. Tangibles: physical facilities, equipment, appearance of personnel
2. Reliability: ability to perform the promised service dependably and accurately
3. Responsiveness: willingness to help customers and provide prompt service
4. Assurance: knowledge and courtesy of employees and their ability to convey trust and confidence
5. Empathy: caring, individualised attention

Respondents are asked first to give their expectations of the service on a seven point scale, then to give their evaluation of the actual service on the same scale. Service quality is then calculated as the difference between perception and expectations, weighted for the importance of each item. Once a firm knows how it is performing on each of the dimensions of service quality it can use a number of methods to try to improve its quality.

(a) Development of customer-orientated mission statement and clear senior management support for quality improvement initiatives

(b) Regular customer satisfaction research including customer surveys and panels, mystery shoppers, analysis of complaints and similar industry studies for benchmarking purposes

(c) Setting and monitoring standards and communicating results

(d) Establishment of systems for customers complaints and feedback

(e) Encouragement of employee participation, ideas and initiative, often through the use of quality circles and project teams

(f) Rewarding excellent service

Customer perception of service quality can vary even when the five generic criteria are successfully managed to achieve a high standard. This is the result of the influence of four further factors.

- Product quality, where there is a physical aspect
- Price
- Situational factors such as the urgency of the customer's need
- Personal factors such as cultural and demographic influences

3.3 Service level agreements (SLAs)

 KEY CONCEPT    concept

A **service level agreement** is a formal statement of performance requirements, specifying the nature and level of service to be provided by a service supplier to a customer. It can be used as a measure of subsequent performance in meeting standards and fulfilling the agreed terms.

The purchasing of services, as opposed to materials or goods, can be complicated by the fact that they are by nature intangible and variable. It can be hard to draft specifications for service performance that adequately cover all the eventualities which may arise: it is obvious when a product fails to work properly, or is otherwise faulty, but if a photographer takes a series of photographs for a client that adhere to the terms of the brief but still do not quite capture what the client wanted, it is hard to agree where the 'fault' (if any) lies.

Everyone benefits if work can be done up-front to cover expectations regarding what (and what is not) construed as satisfactory service performance. Arrangements between organisations and their customers for the management of service levels and quality can be incorporated in a contract often referred to as the Service Level Agreement (SLA). Here is an example of an SLA for the provisional IT services.

Element	Comment
Service level	Minimum levels of service with penalties, for example: • Response time to requests for assistance/ information • System 'uptime' percentage • Deadlines for performing relevant tasks
Fees	The basis for charging should be set out in as much detail as possible.
Exit route	Arrangements for an exit route, transfer to another supplier or move back inhouse.
Time schedule	When does the contract expire? Is the timescale suitable for the organisation's needs or should it be renegotiated?
Software ownership	This covers software licensing, security and copyright (if new software is to be developed)?
Dependencies	If related services are outsourced, the level of service quality agreed should group these services together.
Employment issues	If the organisation's IT staff are to move to the third party, employer responsibilities must be specified clearly.

3.3.1 Typical service level agreements

The basic elements of an SLA are as follows.

- What services are included, and at what cost
- The standard/level of service (eg response times)
- The allocation of responsibility for particular tasks
- Procedure for monitoring and review
- Management of disputes and complaints
- How the agreement will be reviewed/revised/renewed

3.3.2 Costs of delivery

The costs of delivering service quality against a service level agreement may be looked at in a number of ways. For example, some may claim that by delivering higher quality services, costs will increase as more costly resources are likely to be required to achieve a higher standard. Others may focus on the idea that poor quality service will lead to customer dissatisfaction, which generates costs associated with complaint resolution.

There are four types of quality costs: prevention, appraisal/inspection, internal failure and external failure.

Type of cost	Definition	Examples
Prevention cost	Costs incurred prior to delivering the service – to prevent substandard services being delivered	The cost of training staff in customer service initiatives
Appraisal or inspection cost	This is a cost incurred after a service has been delivered, to ensure that the service performance meets the required quality standard	The cost of reviewing a service encounter (eg customer feedback forms)
Internal failure cost	This is a cost arising from inadequate quality, where the problem is identified before the service has been delivered	Cost of reviewing service specifications after failure or customer dissatisfaction Not charging for the service so as to pacify dissatisfied customers
External failure cost	This is a cost arising from inadequate quality, where the problem is identified after the transfer of the service from the organisation to the customer	Cost of the customer services department and its operations Loss of customer goodwill and loss of future sales

3.3.3 Benefits of SLAs

The main objective of an SLA is to quantify the minimum quality of service that will meet customer needs and provide the basis for monitoring and maintaining service levels.

- Clear identification of customer and provider, and improved trust between them
- Focusing of attention on what is required
- Identification of actual requirements, and from there, areas that may be cut to save costs
- Clearer customer awareness of what they can expect, and what it will cost them
- Basis for ongoing reviews
- Mechanism for the solving of problems and implementation of improvements
- Improved client-supplier communication

Service level agreements have been criticised, however, for over-formalising the relationship between supplier and customer, thus creating barriers to the development of a constructive relationship and genuine co-operation between them.

  EXAM TIP concept

A task might be based upon the problems of delivering high quality services. Service level agreements, service quality and service gaps models are likely to be highly relevant to the setting but, as always at this level, the emphasis in a good answer will be on using the ideas in the models to design a practical programme for the company in question, rather than on explaining the models in detail.

Learning objectives	Covered
1 Develop clear objectives relating to the provision of service to key customer accounts	☑ What is service? (1.1)
	☑ Identifying customers needs and behaviours (1.2)
	☑ Customer loyalty and competitive advantage (1.3)
	☑ Benefits of customer acquisition and retention (1.4)
	☑ Key accounts (1.5)
2 Develop a customer service plan and customer care programme, designed to support customer service requirements, including innovative communications; relationship management and development; support; and operations/process management	☑ Key components of a customer service plan (2.1)
	☑ Operations and processes (2.2)
3 Assess the value, importance and financial implications of providing service level agreements to customers	☑ Defining service quality (3.1)
	☑ Quality gaps (3.2)
	☑ Service level agreements (3.3)

1   In what two ways can firms gain by improving their quality of service to customers?

2   Explain the service profit cycle.

3   In what areas should rigorous procedures be applied to take account of the importance of people in services marketing?

4   What is 'quality' in marketing terms?

5   What is the single largest reason why customers abandon a supplier?

6   How does relationship marketing deal with failures of service?

7   What human characteristics improve the quality of client service?

8   What are some of the basic elements of a service level agreement?

9   What is 'Gap 1' in the most widely used model of service quality?

10   What are the two key features of a 'key account'?

1   **People**
Select, train and manage staff in service delivery

Care
Communicate and implement customer care values

Processes
Organise, plan and control systems and operations

Corporate competence
Understand customer expectations and convey commitment to deliver: customers don't need to know how things are done (much less how difficult they are to do…)

Physical evidence
Manage all physical factors (premises, logos etc)

Consistency
Ensure that customer contacts and experiences are alike, to establish recognition and positive associations

2   It is worth noting that commentators see many loyalty programmes as:

- More or less heavily disguised sales promotions: creating short-term customer retention (repeat transactions) – but not loyalty (emotional commitment to the organisation or brand)

- Merely tactical moves designed to defend a brand's market position in the face of competitors' offers or loyalty schemes: creating short-term disincentives to switch

- Mere reinforcing mechanisms – since they often reward customers who are already loyal, rather than creating 'new' loyalty

3   Your own research and evaluation.

4   The most important factors in efficient complaint handling, according to the general public (in a MORI survey for the UK Citizen's Charter Unit) were:

- The speed of response
- Being kept informed
- Feeling that the problem was fairly investigated
- Clearly communicated complaints procedures
- Friendliness and helpfulness of the staff handling the complaint
- Having a named contact person to deal with
- Receiving written apologies and/or explanations

1   Higher revenue and improved productivity.

2   The service profit cycle argues that good internal quality and relationships lead to employee satisfaction; which leads to employee loyalty and retention (reduced labour turnover); which leads to better external service quality; which leads to customer satisfaction; which leads to customer loyalty and retention; which improves profitability; and profits can be invested back into internal quality – renewing the cycle.

3   Selection and training; culture of service; standards of dress and behaviour; mechanisation; audit of service.

4   Quality is defined by the customer; poor quality arises from five gaps in expectations.

5   Poor performance by front-line staff.

6   A positive way of dealing with errors must be built into the customer relationship.

7   The following are all dimensions of client service quality.

   • Problem solving creativity: looking beyond the obvious and not being bound by accepted professional and technical approaches

   • Initiative: anticipating problems and opportunities and not just reacting

   • Efficiency: keeping client costs down through effective work planning and control

   • Fast response: responding to enquiries, questions, problems as quickly as possible

   • Timeliness: starting and finishing service work to agreed deadlines

   • Open-mindedness: professionals not being 'blinkered' by their technical approach

   • Sound judgement: professionals such as accountants dealing with the wider aspects o their technical specialisations

   • Functional expertise: need to bring together all the functional skills necessary from whatever sources to work on a client project

   • Industry expertise: clients expect professionals to be thoroughly familiar with their industry and recent changes in it

   • Managerial effectiveness: maintaining a focus upon the use of both the firm's and the client's resources

   • Orderly work approach: clients expect salient issues to be identified early and do not want last minute surprises before deadlines

   • Commitment: clients evaluate the calibre of the accountant and the individual attention given

   • Long-range focus: clients prefer long-term relationships rather than 'projects' or 'jobs'

   • Qualitative approach: accountants should not be seen as simple number crunchers

   • Continuity: clients do not like firms who constantly change the staff that work with them – they will evaluate staff continuity as part of an ongoing relationship

   • Personality: clients will also evaluate the friendliness, understanding and co-operation of the service provider

8   • What services are included, and at what cost
    • The standard/level of service (eg response times)
    • How the agreement will be reviewed/revised/renewed

    • Procedure for monitoring and review
    • Management of disputes and complaints
    • The allocation of responsibility for particular tasks

9   The 'consumer expectations and management perceptions' gap. Essentially managers may not know what features connote high quality, what features a service must have or what levels of performance are required by customers. It becomes a 'misconception' barrier to good service.

10 It is profitable, and it has the potential for long-term development.

Blythe, J (2009) <u>Principles and Practice of Marketing</u>, 2nd edition, South-Western/Cengage Learning.

Blythe, J (2008) <u>Essentials of Marketing</u>,4th edition, FT Prentice Hall.

Brassington, F and Pettitt, S (2006) <u>Principles of Marketing</u>, 4th edition, FT Prentice Hall.

Dibb S, Simkin L, Pride WM, Ferrell OC (2005) <u>Marketing: Concepts and Strategies</u>, 5th edition, Houghton Mifflin.

Jobber (2009) <u>Principles and Practice of Marketing</u>.6th edition, McGraw Hill Higher Education

Cowell, D. (1995), <u>Marketing of Services</u> (2nd revised edition), Butterworth-Heinemann, Oxford.

Egan, J. (2004), <u>Relationship Marketing: Exploring Relational Strategies in Marketing</u> (2nd edition), Pearson Education, Harlow.

Grönroos, C (2000), <u>Service Management and Marketing</u>, Wiley, Chichester.

Ohmae, K. (1999), <u>The Borderless World: Power and Strategy in the Interlinked Economy</u> (Rev. Ed), Harper Business, London.

Parasuraman, Zeithaml, and Berry (1985), '*A conceptual model of service quality and its implications for future research*', Journal of Marketing (fall 1985).

Peck H.L, Payne A, Christopher M & Clark M (1999), <u>Relationship Marketing: Strategy and Implementation</u>, Elsevier Butterworth-Heinemann, Oxford.

Peters, T.J. & Waterman, R.H. (1982), <u>In Search of Excellence</u>, Harper Collins, NY.

Reichheld, F.F. (1996), <u>The Loyalty Effect</u>, Harvard Business School, Boston.

Varey, R.J. (2002), <u>Marketing Communications: Principles & Practice</u>, Routledge, Abingdon, Oxon.

Chapter 10

Managing key customer relationships

Topic list

Introduction

For years the rhetoric of marketing has been that of **warfare**: targets, campaigns and offensives. The approach has been one of trying to beat the 'enemy' into submission and 'win' new customers. Many organisations now realise that there is more to be gained from **alternative strategies**.

(a) Investing in activities which seek to **retain existing customers**, based on the argument that it costs more to attract new customers

(b) Encouraging existing customers to **spend more**

Retaining customers is the basis of such relationship marketing techniques. Customers are seen not only in terms of what they are buying today, but also in terms of their **potential for future purchases**.

Although it is clear that **added services** and **quality of service** are the key to retaining customers, this still begs questions: precisely what services to add, for instance?

To be effective at **retention marketing**, the organisation has to have a good database **profiling past, present and prospective customers**, with details of the nature of the relationship; it has to know about their attitudes, their perceptions of the organisation's products and service, and their expectations. Just as importantly, the organisation must know, from systematically-acquired **customer feedback**, precisely what it is doing wrong.

This chapter examines approaches to the management of key customers (section 1) and the value of information in these relationships (section 2).

Syllabus linked learning objectives

By the end of the chapter you will be able to:

Learning objectives	Syllabus link
1 Determine the most feasible and viable approaches for managing key account customers for different organisational contexts	4.4
2 Assess the role and value to the organisation of sales/product information, including storage, retrieval and communication of information and its role in ensuring that revenue is increased or maintained for key account customers	4.5
3 Critically evaluate and assess the customer relationship for possible risks, problems and issues and prepare contingencies for dealing with those risks as they emerge	4.6

1 Approaches to key account customers

1.1 Identifying key account customers

KEY CONCEPT

concept

A **key account** is a customer in a market identified by the selling company as being of strategic importance. It often displays the following characteristics :

- It accounts for a significant proportion of sales.
- There is co-operation between channel members rather than conflict.
- There are lengthy negotiations and frequent contact.
- There are often servicing aspects, as well as delivery of physical products.

Many firms – especially in business-to-business markets – sell to a relatively small number of customers. Not all customers are as important as others, and the checklist below can help to identify the most important.

Fit between customer's needs and our capabilities, at present and potentially

Ability to serve customer compared with our major competitors, at present and potentially

'Health' of customer's industry, current and forecast

'Health' of the customer, current and forecast

Customer's growth prospects, current and forecast

What can we learn from this customer?

Can the customer help us to attract others?

Relative significance: how important is the customer compared with other customers?

What is the profitability of serving the customer?

Key customer analysis calls for six main areas of investigation into customers. A firm might wish to identify which customers offer the most profit opportunity.

Area	Detail
Key customer identity	• Name of each key customer • Location • Status in market • Products they make and sell • Size of firm (revenue, number of employees, capital employed)
Customer history	• First purchase date • Who makes the buying decision in the organisation? • What is the average order size, by product? • What is the regularity of the order, by product? • What is the trend in the size of orders? • What is the motive in purchasing? • What does the customer know about the firm's and competitors' products? • On what basis does the customer re-order? • How is the useful life of the product judged? • Were there any lost or cancelled orders? For what reason?
Relationships of customer to product	• What does the customer use the product for? • Do the products form part of the customer's own service/product?
Relationship of customer to potential market	• What is the size of the customer in relation to the total end-market? • Is the customer likely to expand, or not? Diversify or integrate?
Customer attitudes and behaviour	• What interpersonal factors exist which could affect sales by the firm and by competitors? • Does the customer also buy competitor products? • To what extent may purchases be postponed?
The financial performance of the customer	• How successful is the customer?

  ACTIVITY 1   evaluation

'Not all customers are the same'.

Do you agree with this statement? How might they differ?

1.2 The importance of people

People are an important ingredient in the management of key accounts and service relationships.

- The customer market consists of people, with different (or similar, within market segments) needs, values, attitudes and incomes.

- Suppliers, intermediaries, business contacts and competitors are people: doing business involves building relationships.

- Marketers, salespeople and customer service personnel are people. Internal marketing involves supporting people in their marketing tasks.

People play a crucial role in delivering stakeholder value, whether in service marketing or in customer service and stakeholder relationship management. The higher the level of contact involved in the delivery of a product or service, the greater the potential for added value and relationship development.

In many cases the delivery and the physical presence of the staff involved are completely inseparable. Think of counter staff in a bank, or waiting staff in a restaurant, or builders who leave your house tidier than they found it! The people involved are performing or 'producing' the service; selling the service; co-operating with the customer to promote the service, gathering information and responding to customer needs; and creating interpersonal relationships which may evolve into loyalty to the firm.

Arguably, however, all members of the organisation are involved in 'marketing': all personnel should have the skills, motivation and attitudes to do their jobs to a professional standard and with a customer value focus, and should be rewarded and valued accordingly.

Organisations need to take measures to institute a customer orientation in all sectors of activity. People issues will include the following.

• Appearance	• Professionalism
• Attitude	• Skills/competence
• Commitment (including quality/customer)	• Discretion/confidentiality
• Behaviour	• Integrity/ethics

Managers must promote values of customer service in order to create a culture of customer service. This may entail any or all of the following.

- Job design to give people the authority they need to meet customer needs

- Careful policies of recruitment and selection

- Programmes of training and development to ensure that staff have both technical competence and 'people skills'

- Standardised rules and practices, to ensure consistent basic levels of service

- Effective programmes of staff motivation and reward, creating commitment to the organisation, quality and customers

- Effective communication of quality, service and customer care values

 MARKETING AT WORK application

Complaints are among the best things that can happen to a company. They give managers:

- The chance to rectify the situation over and above customer expectations
- Low cost feedback on how products and services are perceived

Handled properly, they create 'goodwill ambassadors' for your brand. The Institute of Customer Service, the trade body, recently published research into how and why people in the UK complain and how they are dealt with. Among other findings, it confirmed the old management cliché that people tend not to complain - they simply walk away. It is the expense of replacing customers that makes handling complaints well so cost-effective.

So what is the 'right' way to handle a complaint? Almost everyone agrees on step one: listen, and understand the problem. But what then?

An eight-step process has been advocated. After saying 'thank you' comes:

- Explaining why you appreciate the complaint
- Apologising
- Promising you will do something about it straight away
- Asking for more information
- Correcting the mistake
- Checking customer satisfaction
- Finally, preventing future mistakes

Marks and Spencer, the retailer, a UK company that is almost synonymous with handling complaints effectively, also welcomes complaints. 'The information people give you when they complain is invaluable to the organisation. We run a central database where complaints are logged, from which we can feed information back to the relevant buyer and suppliers, often on the same day. Customers are looking for a quick resolution of the problem and an assurance that we will do what we can to ensure it doesn't happen again.'

Managers of big companies can also use complaints to develop one-to-one relationships with customers.

1.3 Risks

Relationships with customers may be subject to risks and problems. This is especially likely to be the case in industrial markets. Jobber (2009) points to the fact that in such markets, a contract may be agreed before the product is made. That product may also be highly technical and fraught with unforeseen problems, to the point where the contract price ends up being uneconomic due to the extra work required.

Such uncertainties (including those arising from fear over continuity of supply, or product/supplier performance) can be alleviated to an extent by gathering as much information as possible, checking with others, and buying only from familiar and reputable suppliers, and by spreading risk through multiple sourcing.

Risk reduction for customers can be achieved through free product demonstrations, the offer of products for trial at zero or low cost, product and delivery guarantees, maintenance contracts, swift complaint handling and proactive following-up.

A key to managing risk is having adequate information. The importance of information is discussed in the next section.

2 The value of information

In a **knowledge-based economy** organisations compete by obtaining **superior information**.

2.1 Descriptive, comparative, diagnostic and predictive information

Wilson (2006) distinguishes four roles for marketing information.

(a)   Descriptive information answers questions such as which products are customers buying and where are they buying them. 'What', 'where' and 'when' questions are addressed.

(b)   Comparative information looks at how one factor compares with another, for instance how good an organisation's after-sales support is when compared with its competitors. 'How' questions are used for performance measurement.

(c)   Diagnostic information is intended to explain customer behaviour: eg why are they buying less of product A? 'Why' questions are asked.

(d)   Predictive information attempts to determine the outcome of marketing actions; eg how would customers respond if Product A were made available in larger sized packs? 'What would happen?' questions cover predictive information.

  ACTIVITY 2   application

Try to find three examples each for descriptive, comparative, diagnostic and predictive information needs. You can think of your own organisation for the purpose of this activity.

2.2 How information is used

Information is a **marketing asset**. It impacts on performance in several ways.

*   It helps to increase **responsiveness** to customer demands.
*   It helps to identify **new customer opportunities** and new product/service demands.
*   It helps to anticipate competitive attacks and threats.

Overall, marketers need information to help them to make decisions.

Many business functions deal with customers, including marketing, sales, service, logistics and financial functions. Each function will have its own reasons for being interested in customer information, and may have its own way of recording what it learns and even its own customer information system. The diverse interests of different departments make it **difficult to pull together** customer knowledge in one common format and place and the problem is magnified because all have some political reason to keep control of what they know about customers.

The more information that a firm can obtain about competitors and customers, the more it should be able to adapt its product/service offerings to meet the needs of the market place through strategies such as **differentiation**. For example, mail order companies that are able to store data about customer buying habits can exploit this data by recognising patterns of buying behaviour, and offering products at likely buying times that are in line with the customer's profile.

Good information systems may alter the way business is done and may provide organisations with **new opportunities**. The term information has strong links with IT and the role of IT in helping marketers to make decision is ever growing. Marketers often face 'information overload' where they have too much information thrown at them from multiple sources. IT systems can help alleviate this by helping to store and structure the information to hand. The key point to remember however is that technology alone does not help to cut through the sheer amount of information. Marketers need to understand the decisions that have to be made, define them well and then clearly identify the information that is then required. No IT system to date has been able to do that: human intervention and planning is always required.

2.3 Managing information

The list below shows just some of the information which is needed (and usually available) to marketers to assist in decision making and developing marketing activities.

(a)   **Markets**. Who are our customers? What are they like? How are buying decisions made?

(b)   **Share of the market**. What are total sales of our product? How do our sales compare with competitors' sales?

(c)   **Products**. What do customers think of our product? What do they do with it? Are our products in a 'growth' or 'decline' stage of their life cycle? Should we extend our range?

(d)   **Price**. How do our prices compare with others: higher, average, lower? Is the market sensitive to price?

(e)   **Distribution**. Should we distribute directly, indirectly or both? What discounts are required?

(f)   **Sales force**. Do we have enough/too many salespeople? Are their territories equal to their potential? Are they contacting the right people? Should we pay commission?

(g)   **Advertising**. Do we use the right media? Do we communicate the right message? Is it effective?

(h) **Customer attitudes**. What do they think of our product/firm/service/delivery?

(i) **Competitors' activities**. Who are our competitors? Are they more or less successful businesses? Why are they more or less successful?

(j) **Environment factors**. What factors impact on marketing planning (SLE P7 factors)

Far from being short of information, the average marketer has a wealth of data at their disposal. The trick however is being able to cut through the data, process it and establish some real meaning. Wilson (2006) argued that many of the problems associated with the ability to make decisions are as a result of the inability of marketers to filter the relevant data from the explosion of information.

 MARKETING AT WORK  application

Trout (2008) highlighted the widespread issue of information overload:

'One of the pitfalls of the multibillion-dollar marketing research industry is that researchers don't get paid for simplicity. Instead, they seem to get paid by the pound. A true story may be in order.

The scene: The office of a brand manager at Procter & Gamble. The problem is what to do with one of their largest brands. I ask a simple question as to the availability of their research. I'm surprised by the answer: "Research?" We've got a computer full of it. How do you want it? In fact, we've got so much of it that we don't know what to do with it." '

You might question the value of this 'research' in terms of the information it provides. Think about the cost and resource implications of being in a situation such as this.

Technological advances have fuelled the information explosion. The internet for example has opened a wealth of opportunities not only as a way of gathering information by observing how consumers behave online, recording transactions efficiently to build more powerful databases and opening communications with customers through forums. More recently the use of Web 2.0, online survey tools, voting buttons added to sites, analysis of social networks and virtual worlds have not only enabled new data collection methods but continue to add to the banks of information available to organisations.

2.4 Storing and accessing information

In today's environment marketing managers cannot operate unless there is lots of information coming into the organisation from a wide variety of sources such as commissioned research, third-party continuous research, databases, secondary sources of all descriptions, sales figures, customer surveys, environmental scanning and so forth. This information needs to be stored so that it can be accessed and analysed whenever required.

The collection, organisation and analysis of marketing information is the responsibility of a **marketing information system** (MkIS), which in itself is part of the hierarchy of information systems that exist within an organisation. The information collected, organised and analysed by an MkIS will typically include the following.

- Details on consumers and markets
- Sales – past, current and forecast
- Production and marketing costs
- Data on the operating environment: competitors, suppliers, distributors

 KEY CONCEPT concept

A **database** is a collection of available information on past and current customers together with future prospects, structured to allow for the implementation of effective marketing strategies.

Database marketing is a customer-oriented approach to marketing, and its special power lies in the techniques it uses to harness the capabilities of computer and telecommunications technology. Building accurate and up-to-date profiles of customers enables the company to:

- Extend help to a company's target audience
- Stimulate further demand
- Stay close to them

Keeping an electronic database of customers and prospects (and of all communications and commercial contacts) helps to improve all future contacts.

We look at customer databases in more detail below.

2.4.1 Marketing information systems

 KEY CONCEPT concept

A **marketing information system** is built up from several different systems which may not be directly related to marketing. Typical components are an internal reporting system, a marketing intelligence system, a marketing research system and a decision and analytical marketing system.

Despite being designed a long while ago, Kotler's (1994) model of marketing information systems remains true to this day because it is simple and clear.

Figure 10.1 Marketing information system

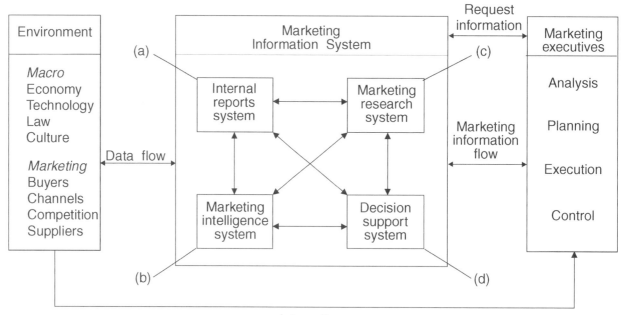

2.5 Information and revenue generation

We will later refer to information in a strategic framework. In the meantime, another way we can think about it in terms of three key areas where marketing decisions are required. Three key questions exist:

1.   How can we satisfy customer needs?
2.   How do we ensure we are competitive within the market?
3.   What external factors are likely to affect us?

To address these questions we need to gather information on customers, competitors and the marketing environment. Refer back to the table in Section 3.4 of Chapter 7 which outlines the broad issues and then focuses on some of the detail that marketers need to consider.

Blythe (2009) recognised that there is a degree of confusion about the distinction between marketing research and market research. He argues that marketing research refers to information about anything that may be of interest to marketers. Market research on the other hand refers to the investigation of customers, competitors, suppliers and market conditions in general. Chapter 7 within his text Principles and Practice of Marketing gives a very broad overview of marketing research and you may find it useful.

2.5.1 Customer databases

KEY CONCEPT

concept

Customer databases can contain a wide variety of information about the customer such as contact details, transaction history, personal details and preferences and so on. Information may come from a variety of sources besides transaction processing systems, including specialist geodemographic data and lifestyle information.

A **customer database** is 'A manual or computerised source of data relevant to marketing decision making about an organisation's customers' (Wilson 2006).

Database marketing has been defined as 'an interactive approach to marketing, which uses individually addressable marketing media and channels to extend help to a company's target audience, stimulate their demand and stay close to them by recording and keeping an electronic database memory of customer, prospect, and all communication and commercial contacts, to help them improve all future contacts and to ensure more realistic planning of all marketing'.

A marketing database can provide an organisation with much information about its customers and target groups.

Every purchase a customer makes has two functions.

*   Provision of **sales revenue**
*   Provision of **information** as to future market (revenue) opportunities

A typical customer database might include the following.

Element	Examples
Customer or company details	Account numbers, names, addresses and contact (telephone, fax, e-mail) details; basic 'mailing list' data, relationship to other customers. For business customers these fields might include sales contact, technical contact, parent company or subsidiaries, number of employees.
Professional details	Company; job title; responsibilities – especially for business-to-business marketing; industry type.
Personal details	Sex, age, number of people at the same address, spouse's name, children, interests, and any other relevant data known, such as newspapers read, journals subscribed to.

Element	Examples
Transaction history	What products/services are ordered, date, how often, how much is spent (turnover), payment methods.
Call/contact history	Sales or after sales service calls made, complaints/queries received, meetings at shows/exhibitions, mailings sent, etc.
Credit/payment history	Credit rating, amounts outstanding, aged debts.
Credit transaction details	Items currently on order, dates, prices, delivery arrangements.
Special account details	Membership number, loyalty or incentive points earned, discount awarded, (where customer loyalty or incentive schemes are used).

The **majority** of customer information will be gleaned from the orders they place and the enquiries that they make. A relatively recent development in this area is the combination of cookies or user log-ins and server logging software, which enables **tracking and recording** of a customer's progress through a **website**, perhaps revealing interests that would otherwise have gone unnoticed.

Geodemographic information relates to the characteristics of people living in different areas. Even simple post-code information can contain a lot of data about the customer.

Customer service can be used to indicate particular concerns of customers. For example, in a DIY store, if customers have to ask service staff where items are stored, the volume of complaints might indicate poor signage and labelling.

Complaints also indicate deficiencies in the product or the fact that customer expectations have been poorly communicated.

The specific information held may **vary by type of market**. For example, an industrial database will hold data on key purchasers, influencers

Databases can provide **valuable information** to marketing management.

(a) Computer databases make it easier to collect and store more **data/information**.

(b) Computer software allows the data to be **extracted** from the file and **processed** to provide whatever information management needs.

(c) In some cases businesses may have access to the databases of **external organisations**. Reuters, for example, provides an on-line information system about money market interest rates and foreign exchange rates to firms involved in money market and foreign exchange dealings, and to the treasury departments of a large number of companies.

Other benefits of database systems might include:

(a) Increased **sales and/or market share** (due to enhanced lead follow-up, cross-selling, customer contact)
(b) Increased **customer retention** (through better targeting)
(c) Better use of **resources** (targeting, less duplication of information handling)

Databases enable marketing managers to improve their **decision making**.

- Understanding customers and their preferences
- Managing customer service (help lines, complaints)
- Understanding the market (new products, channels etc)
- Understanding competitors (market share, prices)
- Managing sales operations
- Managing marketing campaigns
- Communicating with customers

A database built for marketing purposes will, like the marketing function itself, be **future orientated**. It will be possible to **exploit** the database to **drive future marketing programs**, not just glory in what has happened in the past.

2.5.2 Database applications

The range of database applications include:

- Focusing on prime prospects
- Evaluating new prospects
- Cross-selling related products
- Launching new products to potential prospects
- Identifying new distribution channels
- Building customer loyalty
- Converting occasional users to regular users
- Generating enquiries and follow-up sales
- targeting niche markets.

The most valuable information in a customer-focused organisation is knowledge of its customers. The customer database has two uses in such an organisation:

(a)   **Operational support** (for example, when a telephone banking employee checks that the password given by a caller is correct before giving out details of the account).

(b)   **Analytical uses** (the analysis by the same bank of the customers who receive a certain amount into their account each month and so may be targeted with personal loans or other offers).

2.6 Using information to develop marketing activities

 MARKETING AT WORK   application

As a quick example of a marketing management support system in action, let us visualise a company that has identified quality service as a strategic priority. To meet this goal, the system must be capable of performing a wide range of tasks, including the following.

(a)   Provide managers with real time information on how customers and staff perceive the service being given
(b)   Measure quality of both service and customer care so as to provide evidence that they do matter
(c)   Monitor how (if at all) the customer base is changing
(d)   Perhaps, provide a basis on which marketing staff bonus payments can be determined

Another way of looking at information needs in marketing management is to consider the **four key strategic questions**.

Question	Examples of information needed	Sources of information
Where are we now? Strategic, financial and marketing analysis	Current sales by product/market Market share by product/market Competitors' market shares Customer attitudes and behaviour Corporate image versus competitors' image Company strengths and weaknesses	Accounting system Customer database Market analysis/surveys Competitor intelligence Customer surveys Internal/external analyses
Where do we want to be? Strategic direction and strategy formulation	Market forecasts by segment Environmental changes Growth capabilities Opportunities and threats Competitor response New product/market potentials	Industry forecasts/surveys SLEPT analysis PIMS Competitor research Product/market research

Question	Examples of information needed	Sources of information
How might we get there? Strategic choice and evaluation	Marketing mix evaluation Buying behaviour New product development Risk evaluation Alternative strategic options	Internal/external audits Customer research Concept testing/test marketing Feasibility studies/competitor response modelling/focus groups/marketing mix research
How can we ensure arrival? Strategic implementation and control	Budgets Performance evaluation	Internal accounting, production and human resource systems Marketing information systems Marketing audit Benchmarking External (financial) auditing

2.6.1 Identifying buying trends

By tracking purchases per customer (or customer group) you may be able to identify:

(a)   **Loyal repeat customers** who cost less to retain than new customers cost to find and attract.

(b)   **'Backsliding'** or lost customers, who have reduced or ceased the frequency or volume of their purchases. These may be a useful diagnostic sample for market research into declining sales or failing customer care.

(c)   **Seasonal** or local purchase patterns (heavier consumption of soup in England in winter, for example).

(d)   **Demographic purchase patterns**. These may be quite unexpected. Lower income consumers might buy top-of-the- range products, which they value and save for. Prestige and luxury goods, which marketers promote largely to affluent white-collar consumers, are also purchased by students, secretaries and young families, who have been dubbed 'Ultra Consumers' because they transcend demographic clusters.

(e)   Purchase patterns in response to **promotional campaigns**. Increased sales volume or frequency following promotions is an important measurement of their effectiveness.

2.6.2 Identifying marketing opportunities

More detailed information (where available) on customer likes and dislikes, complaints, feedback and lifestyle values may offer useful information for:

- **Product** improvement

- **Customer care** and quality programmes

- New **product development**

- **Decision making** across the marketing mix: on prices, product specifications, distribution channels, promotional messages

Simple data fields such as 'contact type' will help to evaluate how contact is made with customers, of what types and in what numbers. Business leads may be generated most often by trade conferences and exhibitions, light users by promotional competitions and incentives, and loyal customers by personal contact through representatives.

Customers can be investigated using any data field included in the database: How many are on e-mail or the Internet? How many have spouses or children? Essentially, these parameters allow the marketer to **segment** the customer base for marketing purposes.

2.6.3 Using database information

The following is a summary of the main ways in which database information can be used.

(a) **Direct mail** used to:

   - Maintain customer contact between (or instead of) sales calls
   - Generate leads and 'warmed' prospects for sales calls
   - Promote and/or sell products and services direct to customers
   - Distribute product or service information

(b) **Transaction processing**. Databases can be linked to programmes which generate order confirmations, dispatch notes, invoices, statements and receipts.

(c) **Marketing research and planning**. The database can be used to send out market surveys, and may itself be investigated to show purchasing patterns and trends.

(d) **Contacts planning**. The database can indicate what customers need to be contacted or given incentives to maintain their level of purchase and commitment. A separate database may similarly be used to track planned and on-going contacts at conferences and trade shows and invitation lists to marketing events.

(e) **Product development and improvement**. Product purchases can be tracked through the product life cycle, and weaknesses and opportunities identified from records of customer feedback, complaints and warranty/guarantee claims.

  ACTIVITY 3

application

Think about your own organisation and try to think about the following questions for ONE aspect of your job:

(a) What information do you use on a regular basis?
(b) Where does this information come from?
(c) What do you use this information for?
(d) Who else uses the same information?

Learning objectives		Covered
1	Determine the most feasible and viable approaches for managing key account customers for different organisational contexts	☑ Identifying key account customers (1.1)
		☑ The importance of people (1.2)
2	Assess the role and value to the organisation of sales/product information, including storage, retrieval and communication of information and its role in ensuring that revenue is increased or maintained for key account customers	☑ Descriptive, comparative, diagnostic and predictive information (2.1)
		☑ How information is used (2.2)
		☑ Managing information (2.3)
		☑ Storing and accessing information (2.4)
		☑ Information and revenue generation (2.5)
		☑ Using information to develop marketing activities (2.6)
3	Critically evaluate and assess the customer relationship for possible risks, problems and issues and prepare contingencies for dealing with those risks as they emerge	☑ Risks (1.3)

1   What is a key account?

2   What are the six main areas investigated by key customer analysis?

3   '_____ play a crucial role in delivering stakeholder value'. Fill in the blank.

4   Give some ways that risk may be reduced for customers.

5   What are the four roles of marketing information, as described by Wilson?

6   'Information is a marketing _____'. Fill in the blank.

7   Give some of the information typically found in an MkIS.

8   What are typical components of an MkIS?

9   'Every purchase a customer makes has two functions'. What are they?

10 Summarise the main ways that database information is used.

1 Here are some ideas on how customers differ.

(a) Some appear for a single cash transaction and are never seen again.

(b) Others make frequent, regular purchases in large volumes, using credit facilities and building up a major relationship.

(c) Yet another type of customer purchases infrequently but in transactions of high value, as for instance in property markets.

2 Using the example of a group of dental practices, the following information needs are plausible examples:

Descriptive information	What practice advertising have patients seen in the last six months?
	Where are the nearest competitor practices to our group practices?
	When do patients tend to book appointments?
Comparative information	How similar is practice equipment compared to the nearest competitors?
	How do satisfaction levels differ between each of the group practices?
	How regularly do private patients attend for checkups compared to NHS patients?
Diagnostic information	Why do patients like to see fish in waiting rooms?
	Why do patients switch between different dentists within the group?
	Why is there not a large uptake of Saturday morning appointment times?
Predictive information	What would happen if we opened until 8pm weekdays?
	What would be the effect of a 10% price increase?
	What would be the perception of patients if we increased our service offering to include physiotherapy?

3 You will probably find that the information comes from a number of sources and that it is often quite complex pulling this all together. Think about the following example.

A marketing executive of a dental practice in the example above has been asked by the group managing director to monitor levels of patient satisfaction and to report this at monthly practice meetings. The marketing executive has collected the following information.

(a) **What information do you use on a regular basis**? Patient satisfaction information

(b) **Where does this information come from**?

(i) Patient complaints received: online, by letter, verbal complaints recorded on a complaints database, discussions with dentists, nurses, reception staff

(ii) Patient satisfaction cards returned in the comments boxes within the practices

(iii) Feedback left on the group website and individual practice microsites

(iv) Patient numbers including number of visits, returns, length of registration with the practices, number of new patients for each practice

(c) **What do you use this information for**? Satisfaction levels are monitored to ensure that we are meeting patient needs. As this information is tracked continuously, any issues that may arise within a practice are discovered quickly and the information is also useful to check whether there are any differences in the level of perceived service between practices. Any changes in practices such as redecoration, the introduction of new treatments etc can be monitored and compared with practices which have not undergone any change.

(d) **Who else uses the same information**? Nobody else uses this combination of information as it is processed and presented as a handout and slide to be used within monthly meetings by myself (the marketing executive). The final collation of the information is distributed to all staff members within the practice via the group intranet. The finance director uses the same source of information used to identify patient numbers as this data also shows sales revenue.

In this example, there are many sources of information used to collect information to address one simple question 'how satisfied are patients each month?'. It is likely that you will have some aspect of your job where you are reliant on a number of diverse sources.

1   A key account is a customer in a market identified by the selling company as being of strategic importance.

2   Key customer identity; customer history; relationship of customer to product; relationship of customer to potential market; customer attitudes and behaviour; financial performance of customer.

3   People.

4   Risk reduction for customers can be achieved through free product demonstrations, the offer of products for trial at zero or low cost, product and delivery guarantees, maintenance contracts, swift complaint handling and proactive following-up.

5
- Descriptive information
- Comparative information
- Diagnostic information
- Predictive information

6   Asset.

7
- Details on consumers and markets
- Sales – past, current and forecast
- Production and marketing costs
- Data on the operating environment: competitors, suppliers, distributors

8   Typical components are an internal reporting system, a marketing intelligence system, a marketing research system and a decision and analytical marketing system.

9
- Provision of sales revenue
- Provision of information as to future market (revenue) opportunities

10   (a)   Direct mail
      (b)   Transaction processing
      (c)   Marketing research and planning
      (d)   Contacts planning
      (e)   Product development and improvement

References

Blythe, J (2009) <u>Principles and Practice of Marketing</u>, 2nd edition, South-Western/Cengage Learning.

Blythe, J (2008) <u>Essentials of Marketing</u>,4th edition, FT Prentice Hall.

Brassington, F and Pettitt, S (2006) <u>Principles of Marketing</u>, 4th edition, FT Prentice Hall.

Dibb S, Simkin L, Pride WM, Ferrell OC (2005) <u>Marketing: Concepts and Strategies</u>, 5th edition, Houghton Mifflin.

Jobber (2009) <u>Principles and Practice of Marketing</u>.6th edition, McGraw Hill Higher Education

Kotler, P. (1994), <u>Marketing Management: Analysis, Planning, Implementation and Control</u> (8th Edition), Prentice Hall, New Jersey.

Trout, J. (2008), *'The Research Trap'* [online] available from: http://www.fores.com/opinions/2008/05/14/trout-marketingresearch-oped-cxit014trout.html.

Wilson, A. (2006), <u>Marketing Research: An Integrated Approach</u> (2nd Edition), Prentice Hall, Harlow.

Appendix

Specimen Case Study

Important notes for candidates

The examination is designed to assess your knowledge and understanding of the syllabus in the context of the chosen case study. The examiners will be making your scripts on the basis of questions put to you in the examination room. You are advised to pay particular attention to the mark allocation on the examination paper and plan your time accordingly.

Your role is outlined in the Candidate's Brief and you will be required to recommend clear courses of action.

You are advised not to waste valuable time collecting unnecessary data. The cases are based upon real-life situations and all the information you will require about the chosen organisation is contained within the case study. No useful purpose will therefore be served by contacting companies in the industry and you are strictly instructed not to do so as it may cause unnecessary confusion.

As in real life, anomalies may be found in the information provided within this Case Study. Please simply state your assumptions, where necessary, when answering questions, The Chartered Institute of Marketing is not in a position to answer queries on case data. You are tested on your overall understanding of the case and its key issues, not on minor details. There are no catch questions.

As part of your preparation for the examination, you need to carry out a detailed analysis of this Case Study. You will then need to condense your analysis into both a PESTEL and a SWOT analysis (a maximum of **FOUR** sides of A4, the font no smaller than size 11). Although no marks are awarded for the analysis you will be awarded marks for how you use them to answer the question set. The analyses must be attached, with a treasury tag, to you answer booklet at the end of the examination.

The copying of pre-prepared 'group' answers, including those written by consultants/tutors, or by any third party, is strictly forbidden and will be penalised by failure. The question will demand analysis in the examination itself and individually composed answers are required in order to pass.

Important notice

The following data has been based on real-life organisations, but details have been changed for assessment purposes and do not necessarily reflect current management practices of the industry or the views and opinions of The Chartered Institute of Marketing.

Candidates are strictly instructed **NOT** to contact individuals or organisations mentioned in the Case Study or any of the organisations mentioned in the Case Study or any other organisations in the industry. Copies of the Case Study can be downloaded from the CIM student website www.cimlearningzone.co.uk.

Professional Diploma in Marketing

Delivering customer value through marketing

Case study: The Fruit Juice Revolution

Preparation

In preparation for the examination you will need to analyse the organisation, on the basis of the case material provided. You will be given a clean copy of the Case Study on the day of the examination, but you should bring the analysis with you into the examination. You written analysis should not exceed **FOUR** A4 pages, no smaller than font size 11, and must include your CIM membership number on each page. The written analysis should be submitted with your answer book on completion of the examination.

Guidance on the preparation of the analyses

Candidates are encouraged to use a range of analytical tools and models in order to undertake a thorough investigation of the key aspects of the case. This will improves their understanding of the case and the issues faced by the organisation(s) and/or industry sectors to which it relates.

Clearly, the analysis required will vary depending on the specific case content but, as a guide, candidates should consider undertaking the following:

- SWOT analysis

- Value chain analysis

- Analysis of the external environment using PESTEL analysis

- Analysis of the competitive environment using Porter's Five Forces model

- Strategic review using Ansoff's matrix and/or Porter's generic strategies

- Stakeholder analysis

- Detailed review/analysis of each of the marketing mix elements

- Product/portfolio analysis, (eg using product life cycle analysis, Boston Consulting Group matrix, GE-McKinsey matrix).

Further information on undertaking strategic analysis and other analytical tools and methods can be found in Johnson G, Scholes K, and Whittingham R (2008), *Exploring Corporate Strategy (8th edition)* Pearson Education.

Professional Diploma in Marketing

Delivering customer value through marketing

Case study: The Fruit Juice Revolution

Candidates brief

You work as a Marketing Consultant and have a specialist interest in the fruit juice and soft drinks sector. You have been asked by the Board of Innocent Drinks to advise the company on a number of marketing related issues. In order to do this, you have been asked to review the case study profiling the company and the fruit juice sector in preparation for your meeting with the board.

Professional Diploma in Marketing

Delivering customer value through marketing

Case study: The Fruit Juice Revolution

Specimen Case Study

Introduction

The UK juice and smoothies market is fiercely competitive and has grown significantly in recent years, largely due to changes in consumer demand for healthier drinks, supported by an increase in the number of suppliers and the range of drinks available.

The healthier living campaign

'Increasing fruit and vegetable consumption is a national priority. Cancer and coronary heart disease account for 60% of all early deaths. A key feature of the UK government's prevention strategy to reduce deaths from these diseases is action to improve diet and nutrition. [...]

'Current recommendations are that everyone should eat at least five portions of a variety (of) fruit and vegetables each day, to reduce the risks of cancer and coronary heart disease and many other chronic diseases. Yet average fruit and vegetable consumption among the population in England is less than three portions a day. Consumption tends to be low among children and people on low incomes.'

The government has identified two main barriers which prevent people from consuming more fruit and vegetables. The first is access and availability, ie whether people have access to the right quality of fruit and vegetables locally, and at an affordable price. The second barrier is attitude and awareness. The Government has made considerable efforts to communicate the message to the population, because changing habits in terms of food consumption will have a significant longer-term benefit on the national cost of healthcare. However, an issue for a large number of people is that they lack the required skills and knowledge to buy and prepare the best fruit and vegetables.

In order to drive home the message and reinforce the importance of regularly consuming fruit and vegetables, the Government has introduced a 'Five a Day' programme, which, amongst other things, focuses on a national school fruit scheme (raising awareness in schools across the UK) and a national communications programme to inform the population about the importance of eating five portions of fruit and vegetables every day.

The UK market

The total UK juices and smoothies market is valued at £1.4 billion, with growth of 8.9% in 2007, following 16.7% growth in 2006. According to the TNS research, smoothies account for 9.3% of the market, with total sales of just over £130 million per annum. This was the fastest growing sector, with market growth of 37.6% year on year. The largest types of drinks, by market share, are juice drinks and those which are made from fruit concentrate. These represent 31.9% and 35.5% of the market respectively. However, annual growth in these has been low; juice drinks have remained at the same level year on year and juices made from concentrate have grown at jut 2.2%.

Again according to the TNS research, the number of people buying juice drinks and smoothies has remained stable, with shoppers tending to buy drinks less often but spending more when they do make a purchase.

Some terminology

There is much jargon used in the drinks industry and manufacturers have to exercise care to as not to mislead consumers about the content and nutritional value of drinks being marketed.

A smoothie is a drink which is produced by blending the whole fruit and a juice drink is where the juice has been extracted from the fruit. So, a smoothie contains the whole fruit including the skin. 100% pure fruit smoothies contain no other additives. Nutritionists point out that the key difference between a smoothie and a juice drink is that with a juice drink some nutrients which would be present in the skin and pulp as missing. These nutrients would be present in a smoothie as it contains the whole fruit.

A high proportion of fruit drinks are made from 'fruit concentrate'. The ' concentrate' is made by taking fruit juice and heating it through a process in order to evaporate off the water content. This reduces the coverall content volume and makes it easier to ship around the world. When it is manufactured back into drink form, water is added so that the juice returns to its original strength. Nutritionists believe that concentrated juice drinks are not as healthy as those made from pure fruit ingredients.

Freshly squeezed juice dinks are made from juice which has been locally squeezed into the bottle, ie at the point of bottling. Therefore, the fruit has not been tampered with in the same way as concentrated juices and, as a result, these juice drinks will retain their original nutritional content.

Customers

The TNS research concludes that fruit juices are consumed across all age groups, although they are becoming more important with the younger groups.

According to research undertaken by Visuality, 86% ff purchases of juices and smoothies are planned, with the remaining 14% being purchased on impulse. In the case of impulse purchases, shoppers are heavily influenced by in-store displays, advertising and promotional offers.

The Visuality research identifies a high level of brand loyalty, with 60% of respondents using the same brand of juices and smoothies each time they shopped. A quarter of respondents preferred not to buy drinks at all if their usual brand was unavailable. However, 89% of shoppers said that they would be willing to consider the supermarket's own label varieties, if available.

Innocent Drinks

The UK's best known smoothies are under the 'Innocent' brand. The business has been a major success story and now has a market leading position in the UK, with annual sales of around £130 million. Its growth has been significant, and the company has achieved considerable successes in the ten years since its launch.

In 1998 three friends embarked on an idea that was to put the word 'smoothie' on the map. Richard Reed, Adam Balon and Jon Wright met when they were students at Cambridge University and had always thought about running their own business.

Innocent Drinks began life selling from a stall at a music festival in London. Richard, Adam and Jon had developed a number of fruit smoothies recipes and spent £500 on fruit for the event. They had asked for customer feedback by returning empty drinks bottles in bins to answer the question 'Should we give up our jobs to make theses smoothies?' One bin was marked 'yes' and the other marked 'no'. By the end of the event the 'yes' bin was full. Based on this success, they all gave up their jobs so they could concentrate full-time on developing the Innocent Drinks business.

Innocent has built its reputation on recipes containing 120% pure fresh fruit. No sugar, water or any other additives, just pure fruit. From its original smoothies in 250ml bottles it has now extended its range to include 1 and 1.5 litre cartons, smoothies for kids and 'thickies' (a low-fat probiotic yoghurt with oats, fruit and honey).

The business has gone from strength to strength and has been a Sunday Times Fast Track 100 business in the last four consecutive years.

Annual sales topped £10 million in 2003 and had grown to more than £100 million by 2007. Today, more than 2 million Innocent smoothies are sold each week. The company's workforce has grown from the three founder members in 1998 to around 250 today.

Innocent's priority has been to produce drinks which taste good, using simple but 100% pure ingredients. An important aspect of its success to date has been its focus on developing new recipes and on innovation. It has maintained a programme of revitalising its range with new recipes continually being introduced.

A significant product development was the introduction of its kids smoothies in March 2005 and there are now four flavours available. A key stage in the development of the kids range was the agreement, in September 2006, by 500 schools in the UK to stock the drinks at a subsidised price, providing school children with affordable access to healthy fruit drinks.

The company now has a range of 30 different recipes, distributed via leading supermarkets (including Waitrose, Sainsbury's, Tesco, Asda, Somerfield and Morrisons), coffee shops (including Starbucks), other national retailers (including Boots) and numerous other food and drink outlets around the UK and the Republic of Ireland. In total, Innocent drinks are available from more than 12,000 retailers across the UK, Ireland, France, Denmark, Sweden, Germany, Holland and Belgium.

In 2007, Innocent took a major decision to run a trial to sell its kids smoothies in McDonalds outlets. It motives were driven by research which suggested that children, in particular, were failing to take their recommended daily intake of fruit and vegetables. So on the basis that a large number of families visit McDonalds outlets, Innocent decided to run the trial with the burger chain. As a result, Innocent received considerable negative press about their association with McDonalds, despite the fact that market research that they undertook prior to the trial indicated that 74% of people thought that it was a good idea.

It has built its reputation on healthy drinks made from natural ingredients. But the Innocent brand means much more than that. It has built an image of the 'innocent family', communicating regularly with customers, continually seeking their views and ideas for new recipes.

It has also built a reputation for having high standards of corporate social responsibility It uses only natural ingredients purchased from environmentally and socially aware organisations. Its packaging has the highest level of sustainability and it has set targets to reduce significantly its carbon footprint ('from farm to fridge').

Due to its success story, its focus on healthy food consumption and its 'quirky' brand image, Innocent has enjoyed much media attention, which has helped to build awareness and create a unique brand identity for the business as the market has become more competitive, Innocent has had to invest more money in advertising (see appendix Three).

It customer base is diverse, from children to the elderly, students to senior executives, the health conscious to those who just love the taste of a fresh fruit smoothie. Its highly visible brand has quickly established a very loyal following and at August 2007 the Innocent range of drinks enjoyed a 71% share of the UK smoothie market.

Distribution

The UK supermarket chains are the largest retailers, by market share, of juices and smoothies, with the following supplying the largest quantities: Morrisons, Tesco, Asda, Sainsbury's, Somerfield and Waitrose. In-branch promotions are key to driving sales and to persuading consumers to switch brands and try new products.

But more recently in the UK, specialist retail outlets selling their own juices and smoothies have been opening, fuelled by the message to the population to eat and dink more healthily. Two such brands are Boost Juice Bars and Crussh.

The Boost Juice Bars brand came into existence in 2000 in Australia, when mother of three Janine Allis became frustrated at the lack of healthy options for her and her children. She was inspired following a trip to the US, where juice bars (similar to coffee shops) were becoming popular.

Boost Juice Bars now have more than 200 outlets around the world including in the UK, in Manchester, Sheffield, Essex, Nottingham and Oxford. Boost sells a range of juice-based drinks and smoothies, although its range has extended into the hot drinks market, with a range of drinks and soups, such as Hotchocana, which is a creamy hot chocolate drink blended with banana. It has also introduced a section of healthy wraps (sandwich fillings wrapped in a soft flatbread) to its menu.

Crussh is another specialist retailer of its own branded drinks. It opened its first store in London in 1998 and is now the UK's biggest smoothie chain, with 23 outlets, in central London and at Bluewater shopping centre in Kent.

Recognising that smoothies and juices have more seasonal demand, Crussh also sells its own branded range of soups, porridge and coffee, as well a sandwiches, wraps and toasties (toasted sandwiches using ciabatta bread).

The challenge for all fruits juice and smoothies retailers, and manufacturers is that in the UK demand is seasonal. This together with the unpredictability of the British weather, has resulted in a trend emerging of opening fruit juice bars at indoor sites, such as shopping centres and airports. In addition, specialist retailers have moved into selling food and hot drinks to cater more for all-year-round demand.

Other players

PJ Smoothies claims to have founded the UK's smoothies market in 1994. The company began when its founder, Harry Cragoe, discovered the fruit-based drinks in California. On his return to the UK, Harry got together with Patrick Folkes and decided to produce their own smoothie drinks.

The brand was originally called Pete & Johnny's and was acquired by PepsiCo in 2005. According to IRI Infoscan, its market share has reduced to 13% (year to September 2007), largely due to the dominance of the Innocent brand in the market. However, PepsiCo has decided to reposition the brand and is determined to win back market share.

PepsiCo also owns the Tropicana (which includes Tropicana Smoothies) and Copella ranges.

Other key brands offering juice and smoothies drinks include Coca Cola, Robinsons, Ribena, Ocean Spray and several smaller organic producers. In addition, the high street retailers are attacking the market with their own brand lines, including M&S and Tesco.

And if the competition in the UK is not already intensive enough, the world's largest smoothie chain has yet to enter the market. Jamba Juice is a US-based manufacturer and retailer of its own branded range of smoothies and juices. At the end of its 2007 financial year, it had an extensive network of more than 700 stores across the US, including in excess of 500 stores that were company-owned and operated (the remainder operating as franchise units, but carrying the Jamba Juice brand and range of products).

Appendix one

The first ever Innocent report

Please download from the website below.

http://www.innocentdrinks.co.uk/AGM/innocent_annual_report_2007.pdf

Appendix two

Smoothies for the masses

PepsiCo's decision to slash the price of its PJ smoothies brand and reduce its product range may well prompt a lift in sales but critics argue that repeated revamps have confused consumers and resulted in PJ's losing its 'mojo'.

It emerged last week that PepsiCo is to reposition PJ's as a more mainstream offering by cutting its price by 30% and reducing the size of the range by half if in an effort to lure new customers to the fast-growing smoothie category.

PepsiCo claims that price is a major barrier to consumption across the sector. It wants to position PJ's as an alternative to supermarkets' own-label offerings and its 250ml smoothies will now cost 99p. This is in sharp contrast to rival Innocent, which charges between £1.79 and £1.99 for the same size bottle.

PJ's founded the smoothie market in 1994 but has seen its dominance shattered by Innocent, which has a UK market share of more than 70%. PJ's market share fell to 13% in the year to September 8, 2007 according to IRI Infoscan.

PepsiCo is backing the move with a marketing campaign from Abbott Mead Vickers.BBDO later this year. A spokesman says: 'In a recent survey, price was the biggest barrier to smoothie consumption. By removing this barrier, we hope PJ's can open the smoothie market to consumers not currently buying into the category.'

To help finance the strategy change, exotic fruits will be replaced with cheaper, more mainstream fruits such as apples and oranges. Flavours such as Rainforest Acai will be replaced by four, more traditional combinations: Orange, Mandarin & Guava, Strawberry & Banana, Apple, Kiwi & Lime and Strawberry, Apple & Rhubarb.

The move marks a change in strategy for PepsiCo, which acquired the brand in 2005. The brand was originally called Pete & Johnny's but was renamed PJ smoothies when it was relaunched with a more corporate look that replaced its original simple and quirky design. When this failed, the brand relaunched again, moving back towards its original design.

Inject fun

Derek Johnston, creative director of Landor Associates, which worked on both redesigns, says: 'the first redesign was all about appealing to the mass market. Although it helped improve sales, the brand lost a lot of its quirkiness. The strategy is now to inject more fun into the brand.'

While retail insiders have broadly backed the move to reduce prices and believe the brand is still a significant player across the category, some observers claim the latest rethink is risky and that PJ's will have a fight on its hands to wrest sales from supermarket own-label smoothies.

Claire Nutall, client director at brand agency Dragon, says: 'It will be interesting to see how much additional brand power PJ's has over own-label if it offers the same simple range for the same price. Taste is such a powerful driver in this area and retailers are pretty good at developing great tasting new flavour variants.'

Innocent, which some say imitated PJ's original quirky marketing styles, claims to be unsurprised by the move, arguing that its rival has not been performing well of late and adds that it is 'unclear what the brand now represents'.

While sales of PJ's were up almost 7% to more than £24m in the year to October 2007, sales of Innocent surged more than 60% to over £130m, according to Nielsen.

But while PepsiCo maintains it is committed to the brand, some question just how important PJ's, which was reportedly acquired for just £20m, is to its US owner, whose portfolio includes Walkers Crisps, Tropicana and Pepsi cola.

Sales of PepsiCo's market-leading pure juice brand Tropicana hit £200m in the UK in 2006, dwarfing that of PJ's and the company has another successful juice brand, Copella, in its line-up.

One former PepsiCo employee says that big corporate companies and smoothie brands are not natural bedfellows. He adds: 'For PJ's, getting a share of the voice among the company's monolithic brands has been an issue. I am not sure the smoothie market lends itself to the corporate style. Innocent's success has been down to its style, being informal and non-corporate.'

Marketing budget

While Tropicana has enjoyed vast marketing support Nielsen Media Research figures show the PJ's marketing budget was reduced from £2m in 2006 to less than £150,000 for most of 2007.

PepsiCo has successfully launched brand extensions to Tropicana, including Tropicana Go aimed at the children's market, and has a smoothie-range in the US, which observers say is likely to be launched in the UK this year. PepsiCo has tried and failed to do this before. But if PepsiCo can succeed this time another of its brands could end up further eroding PJ's sales.

The latest PJ's rethink has polarised the industry, with some calling it a last-grasp attempt to grow its market share and others hailing it as an astute move that has wrong-footed rivals.

Mark Rae, business development director at Brandhouse, says: 'Smoothies are perceived as a bit of a treat and expensive. Reducing the price could give PJ's more appeal. The challenge is to manage the price cut so there is no change in the perception of quality or health benefits.

Rae adds that reducing a brand's range may not indicate weakness, pointing to the success of the Procter & Gamble-owned Head and Shoulders brand, which saw sales grow 10% when P&G cut the number of variants of Head and Shoulders from 26 to 15.

Brand experience

Others believe the brand has 'lost its way' and think PepsiCo should better engage with consumers. Jonathan Gabay, founder of Brand Forensics, says: 'One way for PepsiCo to be distinctive is to concentrate on its Tropicana brand. However, the smoothie market is now so important it must also find something for PJ's which turns the drink into a complete brand experience.'

He suggests one way of achieving this would be to add an extra ingredient that sets it apart from competitors. PJ's could also engage better with the market on healthy issues, according to Gabay.

PepsiCo can point to the appointment of former (British Government) health secretary Alan Milburn to its recently established UK board of advisers as an effort to bolster its health and wellness credentials (MW May 10, 2007).

Such a move indicates that the company recognises the growing importance of health when marketing its products, but whether it can halt the rise of Innocent in what is still a niche market, and reinvigorate interest in its UK Smoothie brand is an entirely different proposition.

Source: *Marketing Week*, John Reynolds, 31 January 2008

Appendix three

MAIN MEDIA ADVERTISING EXPENDITURE ON FRUIT JUICES AND STILL DRINKS
YEARS ENDING 2005 AND 2006

	2005 £'000	2006 £'000
Tropicana		
Essentials drink range	452	181
Fruit juice range	105	-
Go Juice range	-	1,026
Pure Premium Orange	4,672	2,531
Pure Premium product range	186	826
Total Tropicana	**5,415**	**4,564**
Unilever – Vie Shots	1,771	3,908
Adez drinks range	-	3,666
Innocent		
Smoothies	1,083	3,003
Smoothies for kids	-	152
Total Innocent	**1,083**	**3,155**
Campbells V8 Juice	439	1,814
Coca-Cola		
Froot Refresh Minute Maid	314	-
Minute Main	2,140	1,493
Bottlers – Fruice	119	94
Total Coca-Cola	**2,573**	**1,587**
Oasis – drink	-	1,432
Hero – Fruit 2 Day drink	-	1,215
Britvic J$_2$0	1,695	1,196
Robinsons		
Fruit drinks	85	-
Fruit Shoot range	1,321	387
Fruit Spring range	-	348
High Juice range	-	395
Total Robinsons	**1,406**	**1,130**
PJ Smoothies – fruit drink	-	989
Capri-Sun – drinks range	965	836
Copella		
Apple juice	712	261
Fruit juice range	-	411
Total Copella	**712**	**672**
Ocean Spray – cranberry juice	1,481	582
Welch's – purple grape juice	-	527
Rubicon exotic fruit juice	452	444
Panda Pops – still	-	441
Sunsweet	-	396
V8 Fruit/Veg juice	-	312
RJA Foods – Pomgreat	-	280
Ribena – original blackcurrant	-	180
Knorr– Vie Shots	-	167
Ella's Kitchen	-	142
Sunny D		
Sunny D Caribbean fruit drink	77	-
Sunny D fruit drink	1,223	105
Total Sunny D	**1,300**	**104**

	2005 £'000	2006 £'000
Del Monte		
Fruit Juice range	255	-
World Fruit Drinks range	134	-
World Fruit Drinks range	88	-
Total Del Monte	**477**	**-**
Five Alive		
Berry Blast Juice	136	-
Citrus Burst	300	-
Total Five Alive		
Grove Fresh – organic fruit juice	235	-
St Clements – squeeze fruit juice	96	-
Danone – shape water drink	1,047	-
Sub-threshold brands	474	503
Total	22,056	30,242

Note: totals do not sum due to rounding

Source: Nielson Media Research

Source: 'Fruit Juices and still drinks – Media advertising expenditure on fruit juices and still drinks (£'000)', years ending 2005 and 2006, Key Note Limited 2007.

Appendix four

Smoothies that came of age

By Jenny Wiggings
Published: May 8 2007 03:00

It seems Innocent's days of influence are over.

Over the past eight years, the smoothie group – which made millions of pounds out of squashing and bottling fruit – has become one of the UK's leading soft drink brands, selling more than Oasis or Sprite.

Retail sales shot up 140 per cent last year to hit £96m, bringing Innocent into the 'Top 100' grocery brands for the first time as it expended its smoothie range from individual bottles into one-line cartons and kids' drinks.

But the group, which has built its family-friendly brand by promoting 'natural products', appears in danger of alienating some of its loyal customers. More than a few smoothie drinkers have been outraged at the group's recent decision to embark on a six-month trial selling kids' smoothies in 80 McDonald's restaurants.

'What were you thinking of – McJuice, McSmoothie or McDollar?' complained one irate drinker last week on a blog on Innocent's website. 'McSell Out', write a second. 'Another bunch of hippy capitalists sells out ...just like Body Shop. You just lost another customer', protested a third.

Adam Balon, one of the Innocent's three co-founders and its 'Chief Squeezer', says the decision to sell smoothies through the fast-food chain was not taken lightly. 'McDonald's is a magnet for huge amounts of criticism', he acknowledges.

Mr Balon argues Innocent is acting in kids' best interest. 'It's better that a kid will drink a smoothie than a fizzy cola.'

Arguments about health benefits aside, children are becoming an increasingly important part of Innocent's business. It expects to sell about £25m of kids' smoothies this year, nearly three times as much as last year, and hopes to be stocked in as many as 1,350 schools by the end of the year – up from just five schools last year.

Customers should not be surprised that Innocent wants to sell its kids' drinks through a multinational fast-food chain, given that its drinks have been on the shelves of Starbucks in the UK and Ireland for more than four years.

It is also using Starbucks as a vehicle for international expansion. Last month, it started selling smoothies in 85 German Starbucks stores.

Innocent now draws 10 per cent of its sales from abroad – from Scandinavia, Belgium, France and the Netherlands as well as Germany and Ireland – and the group is hoping international sales will reach more than 30 per cent by 2010.

The privately held company still makes all its drinks in the UK, but is setting up 'cool little funky offices' throughout Europe to help among other things to man local depots for its 'banana phones'.

The banana phone is Innocent's version of a customer care line. 'You get people just calling up, saying: "High, I'm bored" and you just start a conversation with people.' Mr Balon says: 'Sometimes they're just phoning to see whether there is a human on the end of the line. Sometimes they're like, "Tell me a joke", sometimes they're like, "Sing me a song."'

Innocent believes the banana phone is a way to keep its business 'natural' as it stops employees hiding behind 'corporate barriers'.

Innocent has tried hard to retain the feeling of a fun start-up as it expands. Last month it extended its offices in Shepherd's Bush in west London, giving it six times more space to house its 200 employees.

Mr Balon says the expansion has not changed Innocent's culture. 'It's still got grass on the floor, it's still very innocent.'

But it is clear that some customers will take further convincing that Innocent is now showing signs of becoming just another corporation. 'Innocent and McDonald's don't go together in the same sentence', one blogger complained last week. 'Let's face it, nobody will believe it's about anything but money.'

Innocent facts

- It bottles 21 different types of fruit and has 25 different drinks recipes

- Its most exotic fruit is a coconut from a small island in Indonesia accessible only by boat

- Sales of its Detox smoothie, containing bananas, pomegranates, oranges, blueberries and acai berries, are rising the fastest

- It has its own YouTube channel

- Its head office is called Fruit Towers

- It is petitioning the government to cut taxes on fruit juices from 17.5 per cent to 5 per cent

- It has nearly 70 per cent of the UK smoothie market

- It is going to stop using compostable bottles made from corn because they are difficult to recycle in the UK and will use bottles made from recycled plastic

Source: Copyright The Financial Times Limited 2008

Nestlé seeks to boost sales

By Jenny Wiggings
Published: April 6 2008 20:00

Nestlé has teamed up with Boost Juice, the chain of Australian juice bars, to attack Innocent Drinks' dominance of the smoothie market.

The two companies will this month start selling four kinds of co-branded smoothies.

'Boosted Smoothies' will go on sale in supermarkets, including Asda and Sainsbury's. Nestlé and Boost Juice will spend £5m on a marketing campaign.

Nestlé is overhauling its UK business by focusing on its core confectionery brands such as Kit Kat – which returned to profitable growth last year after losing sales and market share – and also on its 'health and wellness' products.

Total take-home sales of smoothies rose 31 per cent last year to £214m, according to the Britvic soft drinks report. Innocent, whose sales role 46 per cent to £141m, controls more than half the market.

If Nestlé's smoothies are successful in the UK it will expand sales of the drinks to other countries.

Multinational food and drink companies are increasingly trialling products in the UK because they believe British consumers are on the leading edge of trends.

PepsiCo recently started selling Pepsi Raw, made with cane sugar and extract of natural plants such as the Kola nut, in the UK to see how consumers would respond to an almost completely natural version of the soft drink.

Simon Lowden, the chief marketing officer of Pepsi International, said: 'We certainly expect it to be more broadly available than just the UK.'

This is the first time Nestlé has sold a smoothie made from fresh juices in the UK. The Swiss company spent 18 months developing the drink with Boost Juice, which has about 180 stores globally, including eight in Britain.

Source: <u>Copyright</u> The Financial Times Limited 2008

Appendix six

Not such a smooth ride for Innocent

By Jonathan Siburn
4 August 2008
Last updated: 2:14 pm BST 22 September 2008

Innocent, the ethically minded, soft and fluffy fruit juice-maker, is at war.

The independent company, which celebrates its 10th birthday next year, is finding out that growing up brings its usual share of challenges as it faces the dual threat of a consumer downturn and the efforts of a bigger rival to force it out of business.

Having introduced smoothies to the UK and watched the love affair grow spectacularly, Innocent has been forced to contend with the entrance of PepsiCo into the market, one of the food and drink industry's global giants.

'Our competitor is regarded as one of the most ferociously competitive on the planet. They have launched smoothies this year and we are their target', says Richard Reed, one of the Innocent's three founders.

'We are at the beginning of a drawn out fight. They have fired off their big gun and are waiting for the smoke to clear. We are still standing, but they have a lot more guns.'

But just as Pepsi has been taking on Innocent in its own backyard so the drinks manufacturer is preparing to sneak on to its rival's patch. The strategy is mouth-wateringly simple – Innocent is to move into the orange juice market with its product hitting the shops on Monday.

Reed, dressed in a funky floral shirt underneath an Innocent lab jacket, jokes about the move – 'Shock headline: Juice company launches orange juice' – but in future years it could be seen as a key point in the company's fortunes. Success could multiply annual sales of £100m many times over. Failure, and the impact that would have on the smoothies brand, could leave the dreams of the company's founders in tatters.

Those dreams nearly never became reality. The idea behind the business was born when Cambridge graduates Reed, Adam Balon and Jon Wright – all now in their mid-30s – set up a stall selling fresh-fruit smoothies at a music festival in the summer of 1998. They asked customers to put empty bottles in 'yes' and 'no' bins to help them decide whether they should give up their day jobs. By the end of the weekend, the three had decided to launch Innocent.

Having raised £250,000 from a US investor after a last-ditch email to friends entitled 'Do you know anyone rich?' bore fruit, the company was established. Today Innocent's smoothies are sold in 11 countries and the founders are worth an estimated £41 million each, according to The Sunday Times Rich List.

Innocent has grown hand-in-hand with its ethical image, but industry observers suggest growth and pressure from bigger rivals will make it impossible for the founders to stick to their ideals – a charge that Reed denies. 'When we started out we had a belief that if you're making something that people consume you have an absolute responsibility to make that thing natural and healthy,' he insists, pointing out that the company sources fruit from ethically aware farms, uses 100 per cent recyclable bottles and ploughs 10 per cent of its profits into charity.

'But then we were three 26-year-olds who couldn't get our phone calls returned. Now I have three people just pushing on supply chain ethics. As Innocent has got bigger we have got more innocent.'

There is a genuine religious zeal behind the strategy but Reed and colleagues are clever enough to know that ethics sell and the company's image has been key to its success.

Despite criticism about its green credentials and last year's tie-up with fast food chain McDonald's, Innocent is making a good fist at balancing size and ethics. Reed claims the company has more than a 70 per cent share of the £169m UK smoothie market but admits the company is under pressure like never before.

Pepsi's decision to launch Tropicana smoothies has shaken up the market. The drinks giant already had its PJs product – smoothies from concentrate – but the Tropicana fresh fruit version presents a more formidable challenge.

'Pepsi is out there offering supermarkets hundreds of thousands of pounds to delist our smoothie lines,' Reed claims. 'That is what they do. If you look at any market they come into, their stance is to take on the independents by running crazy promotions, take their business and then raise prices. Look at Walkers Crisps – they completely caned the competitors and became a virtual monopoly.'

According to Reed – who is swift to add that Pepsi is doing 'just what businesses do' – while the drinks giant has had some success, the battle is at an early stage.

'We have lost some listings to Tropicana but we're slowly getting them back. People will try anything new once, especially if it's half the price.'

Innocent's biggest problem is that it is not facing Pepsi on an equal footing. While Innocent offers the market's leading smoothie, Pepsi has a whole shopping trolley of leading food and drink brands.

'We're in a David and Goliath situation. If you go into the chilled fruit fridge in the supermarket, it is all owned by PepsiCo', Reed says, referring to a strategy called 'The Power of One' where Pepsi creates listings for one product by threatening to limit supply of another. 'It's a tough fight for us because Pepsi might call up the supermarkets and say: if you don't give us what we want on orange juice, we're not going to give you what you want on Walkers Crisps.'

Reed claims retailers are 'excited' about Innocent's orange juice launch – 'this is the only brand they've seen which might make inroads' – but is well aware of the challenge.

The smoothies market makes up 17 per cent of the near £1bn UK juice market and the opportunities for Innocent are huge.

'We're going in with a promise of taste, quality and ethics, while Pepsi is about cheaper prices', Reed says.

'It gives us an opportunity to dramatically widen the demographics of the brand. A litre of smoothie is £2.99, a litre of orange juice will be £1.89. People can buy into the Innocent ideals at a lower price point.'

Pepsi's threat is not the only challenge Innocent faces. Reed admits the company as already seen sales fall in the wake of the consumer downturn, though he claims Innocent is taking market share.

Reed believes Innocent is well placed to weather a downturn, though he appears to be relying on consumers focusing on smoothies' health properties rather than price. He refuses, however, to rule out price cuts. 'We would (reduce prices) if we had to', he says. 'We're looking at smaller pack sizes. We've got to find a way to make quality affordable.'

Innocent is also keeping watch on overheads – plans to hire 50 new staff this year have been scaled back to 15.

As Reed prepares for Innocent's annual music and comedy festival in London's Regent's Park today, he insists the founders are not ready to bail out and sell the company, despite the challenges.

'We genuinely do care. As long as we're proud of it excited by it and challenged by it, what the hell else are we going to do? We're trying to prove that there's profit in ethics and we haven't done that yet'.

Source: <u>The Daily Telegraph</u>.*Telegraph.co.uk*

Key concepts

Delivering customer value through marketing

Index

Notes

Notes

Notes

Notes

Notes

Review form & Free prize draw

All original review forms from the entire BPP range, completed with genuine comments, will be entered into one of two draws on 31 January 2011 and 31 July 2011. The names on the first four forms picked out on each occasion will be sent a cheque for £50.

Name: _____ **Address:** _____

_____

_____

1. How have you used this Text?
(Tick one box only)

☐ Self study (book only)

☐ On a course: college_____

☐ Other _____

3. Why did you decide to purchase this Text?
(Tick one box only)

☐ Have used companion Assessment workbook

☐ Have used BPP Texts in the past

☐ Recommendation by friend/colleague

☐ Recommendation by a lecturer at college

☐ Saw advertising in journals

☐ Saw website

☐ Other _____

2. During the past six months do you recall seeing/receiving any of the following?
(Tick as many boxes as are relevant)

☐ Our advertisement in *The Marketer*

☐ Our brochure with a letter through the post

☐ Saw website

4. Which (if any) aspects of our advertising do you find useful?
(Tick as many boxes as are relevant)

☐ Prices and publication dates of new editions

☐ Information on product content

☐ Facility to order books off-the-page

☐ None of the above

5. Have you used the companion Assessment Workbook?   Yes ☐   No ☐

6. Have you used the companion Passcards?   Yes ☐   No ☐

7. Your ratings, comments and suggestions would be appreciated on the following areas.

	Very useful	Useful	Not useful
Introductory section (How to use this text, study checklist, etc)	☐	☐	☐
Introduction	☐	☐	☐
Syllabus linked learning outcomes	☐	☐	☐
Activities and Marketing at Work examples	☐	☐	☐
Learning objective reviews	☐	☐	☐
Magic Formula references	☐	☐	☐
Content of suggested answers	☐	☐	☐
Index	☐	☐	☐
Structure and presentation	☐	☐	☐

	Excellent	Good	Adequate	Poor
Overall opinion of this Text	☐	☐	☐	☐

8. Do you intend to continue using BPP CIM Range Products?   ☐ Yes   ☐ No

9. Have you visited bpp.com/lm/cim?   ☐ Yes   ☐ No

10. If you have visited bpp.com/lm/cim, please give a score out of 10 for its overall usefulness   /10

Please note any further comments and suggestions/errors on the reverse of this page.

Please return to: Rebecca Hart, BPP Learning Media, FREEPOST, London, W12 8BR.

If you have any additional questions, feel free to email cimrange@bpp.com

Delivering Customer Value Through Marketing

Review form & Free prize draw (continued)

Please note any further comments and suggestions/errors below.

Free prize draw rules

1   Closing date for 31 January 2011 draw is 31 December 2010. Closing date for 31 July 2011 draw is 30 June 2011.

2   Restricted to entries with UK and Eire addresses only. BPP employees, their families and business associates are excluded.

3   No purchase necessary. Entry forms are available upon request from BPP Learning Media. No more than one entry per title, per person. Draw restricted to persons aged 16 and over.

4   Winners will be notified by post and receive their cheques not later than 6 weeks after the relevant draw date. List of winners will be supplied on request.

5   The decision of the promoter in all matters is final and binding. No correspondence will be entered into.

Delivering Customer Value Through Marketing